Teach Yourself
More Windows® 98
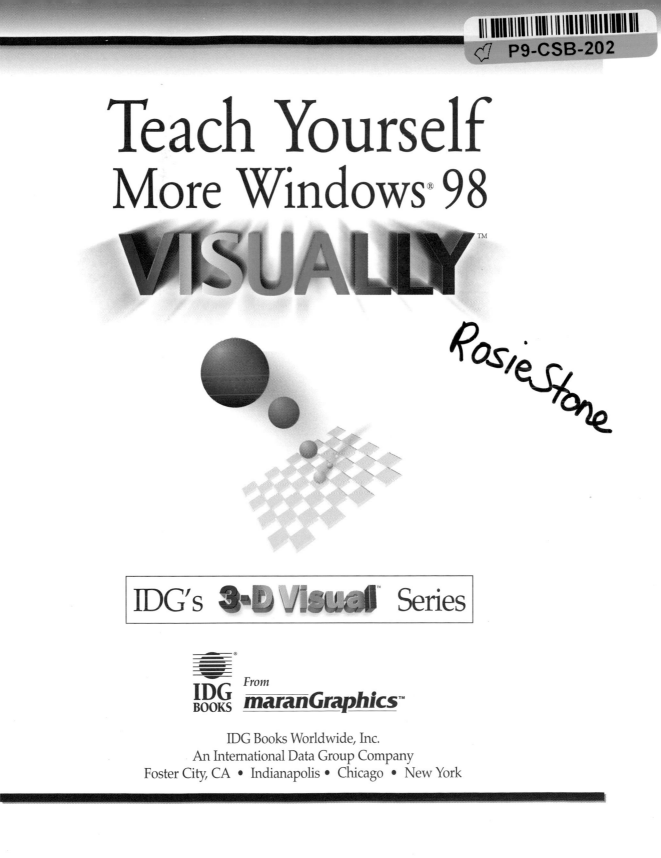

VISUALLY™

Rosie Stone

IDG's **3-D Visual**™ Series

IDG BOOKS *From* **maranGraphics**™

IDG Books Worldwide, Inc.
An International Data Group Company
Foster City, CA • Indianapolis • Chicago • New York

Teach Yourself More Windows® 98 VISUALLY™

Published by
IDG Books Worldwide, Inc.
An International Data Group Company
919 E. Hillsdale Blvd., Suite 400
Foster City, CA 94404

Library of Congress Catalog Card No.: 98-075157

ISBN: 0-7645-6044-1

Printed in the United States of America
10 9 8 7 6 5 4 3 2

Distributed in the United States by IDG Books Worldwide, Inc.

Distributed by Transworld Publishers Limited in the United Kingdom; by IDG Norge Books for Norway; by IDG Sweden Books for Sweden; by Woodslane Pty. Ltd. for Australia; by Woodslane (NZ) Ltd. for New Zealand; by Addison Wesley Longman Singapore Pte Ltd. for Singapore, Malaysia, Thailand, Indonesia and Korea; by Norma Comunicaciones S.A. for Colombia; by Intersoft for South Africa; by International Thomson Publishing for Germany, Austria and Switzerland; by Toppan Company Ltd. for Japan; by Distribuidora Cuspide for Argentina; by Livraria Cultura for Brazil; by Ediciencia S.A. for Ecuador; by Ediciones ZETA S.C.R. Ltda. for Peru; by WS Computer Publishing Corporation, Inc., for the Philippines; by Unalis Corporation for Taiwan; by Contemporanea de Ediciones for Venezuela; by Computer Book & Magazine Store for Puerto Rico; by Express Computer Distributors for the Caribbean and West Indies. Authorized Sales Agent: Anthony Rudkin Associates for the Middle East and North Africa.

For corporate orders, please call maranGraphics at 800-469-6616.

For general information on IDG Books Worldwide's books in the U.S., please call our Consumer Customer Service department at 800-762-2974.

For reseller information, including discounts and premium sales, please call our Reseller Customer Service department at 800-434-3422.

For information on where to purchase IDG Books Worldwide's books outside the U.S., please contact our International Sales department at 650-655-3200 or fax 650-655-3297.

For information on foreign language translations, please contact our Foreign & Subsidiary Rights department at 650-655-3021 or fax 650-655-3281.

For sales inquiries and special prices for bulk quantities, please contact our Sales department at 650-655-3200.

For information on using IDG Books Worldwide's books in the classroom or for ordering examination copies, please contact our Educational Sales department at 800-434-2086 or fax 317-596-5499.

For press review copies, author interviews, or other publicity information, please contact our Public Relations department at 650-655-3000 or fax 650-655-3299.

For authorization to photocopy items for corporate, personal, or educational use, please contact maranGraphics at 800-469-6616.

Trademark Acknowledgments

Permissions

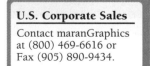

U.S. Corporate Sales	U.S. Trade Sales
Contact maranGraphics at (800) 469-6616 or Fax (905) 890-9434.	Contact IDG Books at (800) 434-3422 or (650) 655-3000.

Welcome to the world of IDG Books Worldwide.

IDG Books Worldwide, Inc., is a subsidiary of International Data Group, the world's largest publisher of computer-related information and the leading global provider of information services on information technology. IDG was founded more than 25 years ago and now employs more than 8,500 people worldwide. IDG publishes more than 270 computer publications in over 75 countries (see listing below). More than 90 million people read one or more IDG publications each month.

Launched in 1990, IDG Books Worldwide is today the #1 publisher of best-selling computer books in the United States. We are proud to have received eight awards from the Computer Press Association in recognition of editorial excellence and three from Computer Currents' First Annual Readers' Choice Awards. Our best-selling ...For Dummies® series has more than 25 million copies in print with translations in 30 languages. IDG Books Worldwide, through a joint venture with IDG's Hi-Tech Beijing, became the first U.S. publisher to publish a computer book in the People's Republic of China. In record time, IDG Books Worldwide has become the first choice for millions of readers around the world who want to learn how to better manage their businesses.

Our mission is simple: Every one of our books is designed to bring extra value and skill-building instructions to the reader. Our books are written by experts who understand and care about our readers. The knowledge base of our editorial staff comes from years of experience in publishing, education, and journalism - experience which we use to produce books for the '90s. In short, we care about books, so we attract the best people. We devote special attention to details such as audience, interior design, use of icons, and illustrations. And because we use an efficient process of authoring, editing, and desktop publishing our books electronically, we can spend more time ensuring superior content and spend less time on the technicalities of making books.

You can count on our commitment to deliver high-quality books at competitive prices on topics you want to read about. At IDG Books Worldwide, we continue in the IDG tradition of delivering quality for more than 25 years. You'll find no better book on a subject than one from IDG Books Worldwide.

John Kilcullen
CEO
IDG Books Worldwide, Inc.

Steven Berkowitz
President and Publisher
IDG Books Worldwide, Inc.

IDG Books Worldwide, Inc., is a subsidiary of International Data Group, the world's largest publisher of computer-related information and the leading global provider of information services on information technology. International Data Group publishes over 276 computer publications in over 75 countries. Ninety million people read one or more International Data Group publications each month. International Data Group's publications include: Argentina: Annuario de Informatica, Computerworld Argentina, PC World Argentina; Australia: Australian Macworld, Client/Server Journal, Computer Living, Computerworld, Computerworld 100, Digital News, IT Casebook, Network World, On-line World Australia, PC World, Publishing Essentials, Reseller, WebMaster; Austria: Computerwelt Osterreich, Networks Austria, PC Tip; Belarus: PC World Belarus; Belgium: Data News; Brazil: Annuário de Informática, Computerworld Brazil, Connections, Super Game Power, Macworld, PC Player, PC World Brazil, Publish Brazil, Reseller News; Bulgaria: Computerworld Bulgaria, Networkworld/Bulgaria, PC & MacWorld Bulgaria; Canada: CIO Canada, Client/Server World, ComputerWorld Canada, InfoCanada, Network World Canada; Chile: Computerworld Chile, PC World Chile; Colombia: Computerworld Colombia, PC World Colombia; Costa Rica: PC World Centro America; The Czech and Slovak Republics: Computerworld Czechoslovakia, Elektronika Czechoslovakia, Macworld Czech Republic, PC World Czechoslovakia; Denmark: Communications World, Computerworld Danmark, Macworld Danmark, PC Privat Danmark, PC World Danmark, PC World Danmark Supplements, TECH World; Dominican Republic: PC World Republica Dominicana; Ecuador: PC World Ecuador; Egypt: Computerworld Middle East, PC World Middle East; El Salvador: PC World Centro America; Finland: MikroPC, Tietoverkko, Tietoviikko; France: Distributique, Golden, Hebdo-Distributique, Info PC, Le Guide du Monde Informatique, Le Monde Informatique, Reseaux & Telecoms; Germany: Computer Partner, Computerwoche, Computerwoche Extra, Computerwoche Focus, I/M Information Management, Macwelt, PC Welt; Greece: GamePro, Multimedia World; Guatemala: PC World Centro America; Honduras: PC World Centro America; Hong Kong: Computerworld Hong Kong, PCWorld Hong Kong, Publish in Asia; Hungary: ABCD CD-ROM, Computerworld Szamitastechnika, PC & Mac World Hungary, PC-X Magazine; Iceland: Tolvuheimur/PC World Island; India: Information Systems Computerworld, PC World India, Publish in Asia; Indonesia: InfoKomputer PC World, Komputek Computerworld, Publish in Asia; Ireland: ComputerScope, PC Live!; Israel: People & Computers; Italy: Computerworld Italia, Computerworld Italia Special Editions, Macworld Italia, Networking Italia, PC Shopping, PC World Italia, PC World/Walt Disney; Japan: DTP World, HP Open World Japan, Macworld Japan, Nikkei Personal Computing, Open World Japan, OS/2 World Japan, SunWorld Japan, Windows World Japan; Kenya: East African Computer News; Korea: Hi-Tech Information/Computerworld, Macworld Korea, PC World Korea; Macedonia: PC World Macedonia; Malaysia: Computerworld Malaysia, PC World Malaysia, Publish in Asia; Mexico: Computerworld Mexico, Macworld, PC World Mexico; Myanmar: PC World Myanmar; Netherlands: Computer! Totaal, LAN Magazine, LanWorld Buyers Guide, Macworld, Net Magazine, Totaal! Beurskrant; New Zealand: Absolute Beginner's Guide, Computer Buyer, Computer Industry Directory, Computerworld New Zealand, MTB, Network World, PC World New Zealand; Nicaragua: PC World Centro America; Nigeria: PC World Nigeria; Norway: Computerworld Norge, Computerworld Privat (Datamagasinet), CW Rapport Norge, IDG's KURSGUIDE, Macworld Norge, Multimediaworld, PC World Ekspress, PC World Nettverk, PC World Norge, PC World's Produktguide, Windows World Spesial; Pakistan: Computerworld Pakistan, PC World Pakistan; Panama: PC World Panama; P. R. of China: China Computer Users, China Computerworld, China Infoworld, China Telecom World Weekly, Computer & Communication, Electronic Design China, Electronics Today, Electronics Weekly, Game Camp, Game Soft, Network World China, PC World China, Popular Computer Weekly, Software Weekly, Software World, Telecom World; Peru: Computerworld Peru, PC World Profesional Peru, PC World Peru; Poland: Computerworld Poland, Computerworld Special Report, Macworld, Networld, PC World Komputer; Philippines: Computerworld Philippines, PC World Philippines, Publish in Asia; Portugal: Cerebro/PC World, Computerworld/Correio Informático, Dealer World Portugal, Mac*In/PC*In, Multimedia World Portugal; Puerto Rico: PC World Puerto Rico; Romania: Computerworld Romania, PC World Romania, Telecom Romania; Russia: Computerworld Russia, Mir PK, Sety; Singapore: Computerworld Singapore, PC World Singapore, Publish in Asia; Slovenia: MONITOR; South Africa: Computing S.A., InfoWorld S.A., Network World S.A., Software World; Spain: Computerworld Espa-a, COMUNICACIONES WORLD, Dealer World, Macworld Espa-a, PC World Espa-a; Sweden: CAP&Design, Computer Sweden, Corporate Computing, MacWorld, Maxi Data, MikroDatorn, Nätverk & Kommunikation, PC/Aktiv, PC World, Windows World; Switzerland: Computerworld Schweiz, Macworld Schweiz, PCtip; Taiwan: Computerworld Taiwan, Macworld Taiwan, PC World Taiwan, Publish Taiwan, Windows World; Thailand: Thai Computerworld, Publish in Asia; Turkey: Computerworld Turkiye, MACWORLD Turkiye, PC WORLD Turkiye; Ukraine: Computerworld Kiev, Computers & Software, Multimedia World Ukraine, PC World Ukraine; United Kingdom: Acorn User, Amiga Action, Amiga Computing, Appletalk, Computing, GamePro, Macworld, Network News, Parents and Computers, PC Advisor, PC Home, PSX Pro UK, The WEB; United States: Cable in the Classroom, CD Review, CIO Magazine, Computerworld, Computerworld Client/Server Journal, Digital Video Magazine, DOS World, Federal Computer Week, GamePro, InfoWorld, I-Way, JavaWorld, Macworld, Multimedia World, Netscape World Online, Network World, PC Entertainment, PC World, Publish, SunWorld Online, SWATPro Magazine, Video Event, WebMaster; Uruguay: PC World Uruguay; Venezuela: Computerworld Venezuela, PC World Venezuela; and Vietnam: PC World Vietnam.

Every maranGraphics book represents
the extraordinary vision and commitment of a unique family:
the Maran family of Toronto, Canada.

Back Row (from left to right):   *Sherry Maran, Rob Maran, Richard Maran,
Maxine Maran, Jill Maran.*

Front Row (from left to right):   *Judy Maran, Ruth Maran.*

Richard Maran is the company founder and its inspirational leader. He developed maranGraphics' proprietary communication technology called "visual grammar." This book is built on that technology—empowering readers with the easiest and quickest way to learn about computers.

Ruth Maran is the Author and Architect—a role Richard established that now bears Ruth's distinctive touch. She creates the words and visual structure that are the basis for the books.

Judy Maran is the Project Manager. She works with Ruth, Richard and the highly talented maranGraphics illustrators, designers and editors to transform Ruth's material into its final form.

Rob Maran is the Technical and Production Specialist. He makes sure the state-of-the-art technology used to create these books always performs as it should.

Sherry Maran manages the Reception, Order Desk and any number of areas that require immediate attention and a helping hand.

Jill Maran is a jack-of-all-trades who works in the Accounting and Human Resources department.

Maxine Maran is the Business Manager and family sage. She maintains order in the business and family—and keeps everything running smoothly.

CREDITS

Author & Architect:
Ruth Maran

Project Manager:
Judy Maran

Editing & Screen Captures:
Raquel Scott
Jason M. Brown
Janice Boyer
Michelle Kirchner
James Menzies
Frances Lea
Emmet Mellow

Layout Designers:
Treena Lees
Jamie Bell

Illustrators:
Russ Marini
Jamie Bell
Peter Grecco

Illustrators & Screen Artists:
Jeff Jones
Sean Johannesen
Steven Schaerer

Indexer:
Raquel Scott

Permissions Coordinator:
Jenn Hillman

Post Production:
Robert Maran

Editorial Support:
Michael Roney

ACKNOWLEDGMENTS

Thanks to the dedicated staff of maranGraphics, including
Jamie Bell, Cathy Benn, Janice Boyer, Jason M. Brown,
Francisco Ferreira, Peter Grecco, Jenn Hillman, Sean Johannesen,
Jeff Jones, Michelle Kirchner, Wanda Lawrie, Frances Lea,
Treena Lees, Jill Maran, Judy Maran, Maxine Maran,
Robert Maran, Sherry Maran, Russ Marini, Emmet Mellow,
James Menzies, Steven Schaerer, Raquel Scott,
Roxanne Van Damme, Paul Whitehead and Kelleigh Wing.

Finally, to Richard Maran who originated the easy-to-use
graphic format of this guide. Thank you for your inspiration
and guidance.

TABLE OF CONTENTS

Chapter 1

Review of Windows Basics

Introduction to Windows 98 4

Parts of the Windows 98 Screen 5

Start Windows 6

Start a Program 8

Using Run to Start a Program.............10

Start an MS-DOS Prompt Window 12

Maximize a Window 14

Minimize a Window..........................15

Move a Window 16

Size a Window 17

Switch Between Windows 18

Close a Window 19

Show the Desktop...........................20

Shut Down Windows 21

Chapter 2

Work With Files

View Contents of Your Computer 24

Display or Hide a Toolbar 26

Close a Misbehaving Program 27

Create a New File 28

Display File Properties.......................30

Preview a File 32

Show Hidden Files 34

Add Folder to Favorites.....................36

Move or Copy Data Between
    Documents.......................................38

Copy Screen Contents 40

Put Part of a Document on the
    Desktop..42

Offline Printing.................................44

Copy a Floppy Disk 46

Chapter 3

Using Windows Accessories

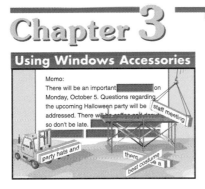

Using Notepad 52

Using Character Map 54

Using Imaging 58

Using Sound Recorder 62

Using Phone Dialer..........................66

Using Clipboard Viewer 70

TABLE OF CONTENTS

Chapter 4

Customize Windows

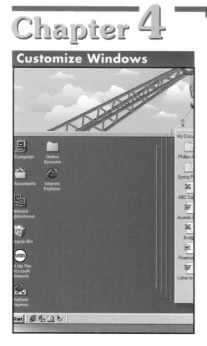

Change Desktop Icons 74

Change Visual Effects 76

Create a New Toolbar 78

Change Regional Settings 80

Change Recycle Bin Properties............82

Add Destinations to the
    Send To Menu 84

View Fonts on Your Computer 88

Add Fonts to Your Computer 90

Change Power Management Settings ..94

Using Magnifier 96

Using the Accessibility Wizard 98

Chapter 5

Customize Start Menu and Taskbar

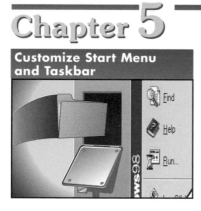

Add an Item to the Start Menu 104

Rearrange Items on the Start Menu....105

Remove an Item from the
    Start Menu 106

Add a Folder to the Start Menu 108

Add Item to Quick Launch Toolbar 112

Add a Toolbar to the Taskbar............114

Chapter 6

Work With Software and Hardware

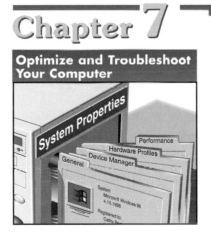

Add Windows Components..............118

Install a Program 122

Remove a Program 125

Change Keyboard Settings 126

Install a Joystick 130

Change Printer Options...................134

Change Modem Dialing Properties....138

Change Modem Properties 142

Using Multiple Monitors 144

Remove Hardware 146

Chapter 7

Optimize and Troubleshoot Your Computer

View Hardware Information..............150

View System Information 152

Create a Startup Disk 154

Start Windows in Safe Mode............158

Using Windows Update 160

Convert Your Drive to FAT32 162

Programs You Can Use With
     Windows 98 166

TABLE OF CONTENTS

Chapter 8

Back Up Files

Back Up Files..................................170

Open an Existing Backup Job 178

Restore Files..................................180

Chapter 9

Exchange E-mail

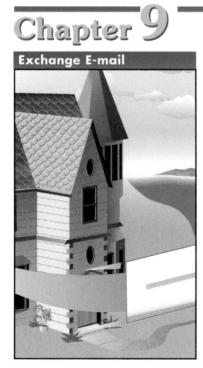

Read Messages 186

Sort Messages 188

Print Messages...............................189

Mark a Message as Unread 190

Check for New Messages
    Automatically.................................191

Compose a Message 192

Format Messages 194

Save a Draft 198

Find People on the Internet 200

Find Messages...............................202

Create a New Folder 206

Filter Messages 208

Chapter 10

Using NetMeeting

Start and Set Up NetMeeting.............214

Place a Call.....................................220

Exchange Messages 222

Using the Whiteboard 224

Share a Program 226

Chapter 11

Using Chat

Enter a Chat Room 230

Join the Conversation 234

Chapter 12

Exchange Information Between Computers

Using Briefcase 238

Using Direct Cable Connection 246

Using Dial-Up Networking.................254

Using WinPopup to Exchange
    Messages 264

Chapter 13

Watch TV on Your Computer

Start and Set Up WebTV 270

Using the Program Guide 274

Search for Programs 276

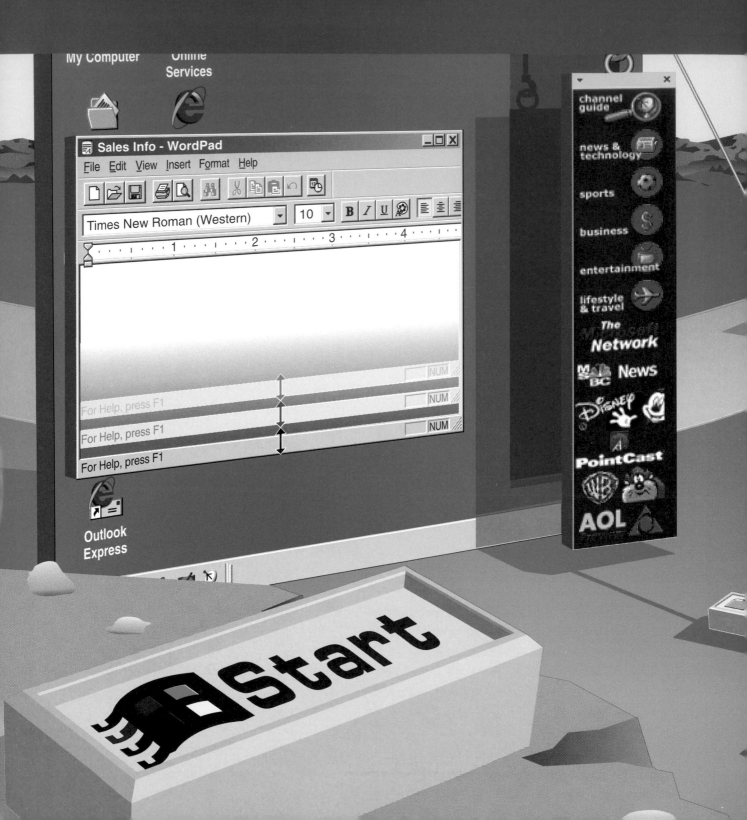

CHAPTER 1

Review of Windows Basics

In this chapter you will review the basic skills you need to work in Windows 98.

Introduction to Windows 98 4

Parts of the Windows 98 Screen 5

Start Windows 6

Start a Program 8

Using Run to Start a Program..............10

Start an MS-DOS Prompt Window 12

Maximize a Window 14

Minimize a Window..........................15

Move a Window 16

Size a Window 17

Switch Between Windows 18

Close a Window 19

Show the Desktop............................20

Shut Down Windows 21

INTRODUCTION TO WINDOWS 98

Microsoft® Windows® 98 is a program that controls the overall activity of your computer.

Windows ensures that all parts of your computer work together smoothly and efficiently.

Work With Files and Programs

Windows helps you work with the files stored on your computer. You can create new files, display file properties and preview files. Windows also includes many programs that you can use to create documents, work with scanned documents, record sounds and make telephone calls from your computer.

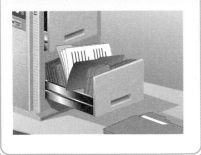

Customize and Optimize Your Computer

Windows allows you to customize and optimize your computer. You can change the desktop icons, use accessibility features and add items to the Start menu. Windows also allows you to install new programs, change printer and modem options and back up files.

Obtain Information

You can use Windows to exchange electronic mail, communicate with others over the Internet, dial in to a computer at work and watch television on your computer.

The Windows 98 screen consists of various items. The items that appear depend on the setup of your computer.

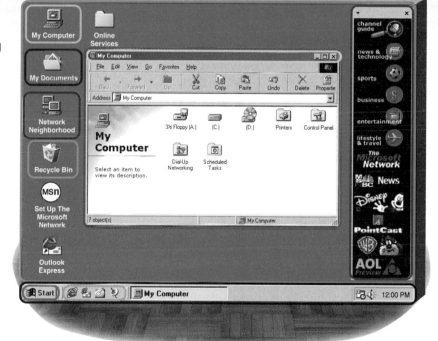

My Computer

Lets you view all the folders and files stored on your computer.

My Documents

Provides a convenient place to store your documents.

Network Neighborhood

Lets you view all the folders and files available on your network.

Recycle Bin

Stores deleted files and allows you to recover them later.

Title Bar

Displays the name of an open window.

Window

A rectangle on your screen that displays information.

Desktop

The background area of your screen.

Start Button

Gives you quick access to programs, files and Windows Help.

Quick Launch Toolbar

Gives you quick access to commonly used features, including Internet Explorer, Outlook Express, the desktop and channels.

Taskbar

Displays a button for each open window on your screen. You can use these buttons to switch between open windows.

Channel Bar

Displays specially designed Web sites you can have Windows automatically deliver to your computer.

Windows provides an easy, graphical way for you to use your computer. Windows automatically starts when you turn on your computer.

START WINDOWS

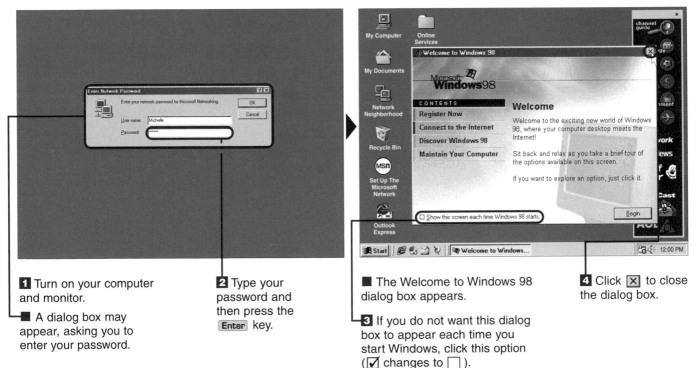

1 Turn on your computer and monitor.

■ A dialog box may appear, asking you to enter your password.

2 Type your password and then press the `Enter` key.

■ The Welcome to Windows 98 dialog box appears.

3 If you do not want this dialog box to appear each time you start Windows, click this option (☑ changes to ☐).

4 Click ☒ to close the dialog box.

?

What is the Channel Bar?

The Channel Bar displays specially designed Web sites that Windows can automatically deliver to your computer. When you first start Windows, the Channel Bar appears on your desktop. You can remove the Channel Bar if you want to free up space on your desktop.

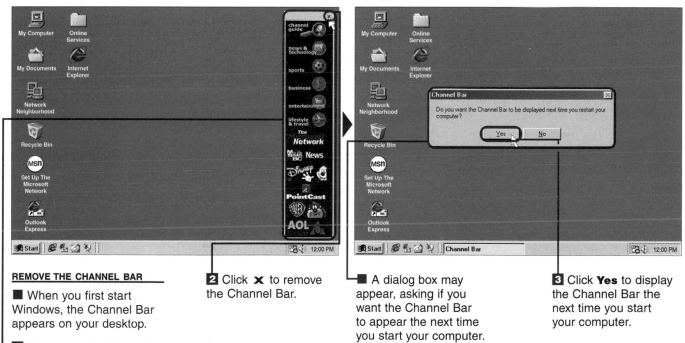

REMOVE THE CHANNEL BAR

■ When you first start Windows, the Channel Bar appears on your desktop.

1 To remove the Channel Bar, move the mouse ⌖ over the top edge of the bar.

2 Click **x** to remove the Channel Bar.

■ A dialog box may appear, asking if you want the Channel Bar to appear the next time you start your computer.

3 Click **Yes** to display the Channel Bar the next time you start your computer.

START A PROGRAM

You can use the Start
button to start your
programs.

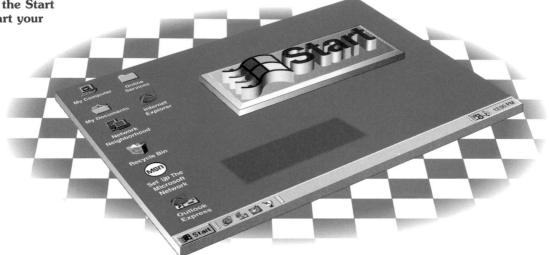

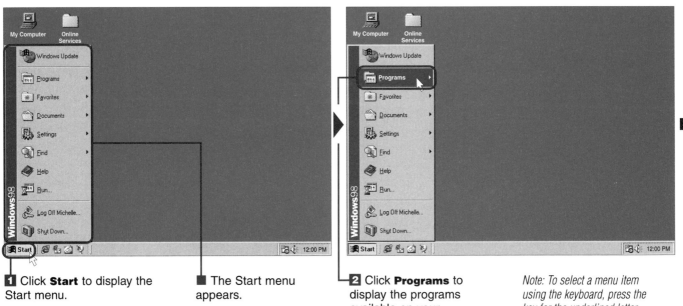

1 Click **Start** to display the
Start menu.

*Note: To display the Start menu
using the keyboard, press and
hold down the* **Ctrl** *key and
then press the* **Esc** *key.*

■ The Start menu
appears.

2 Click **Programs** to
display the programs
available on your
computer.

*Note: To select a menu item
using the keyboard, press the
key for the underlined letter
(example:* **P** *for* **P***rograms).*

8

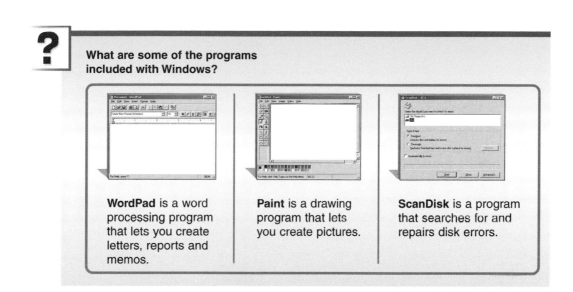

What are some of the programs included with Windows?

WordPad is a word processing program that lets you create letters, reports and memos.

Paint is a drawing program that lets you create pictures.

ScanDisk is a program that searches for and repairs disk errors.

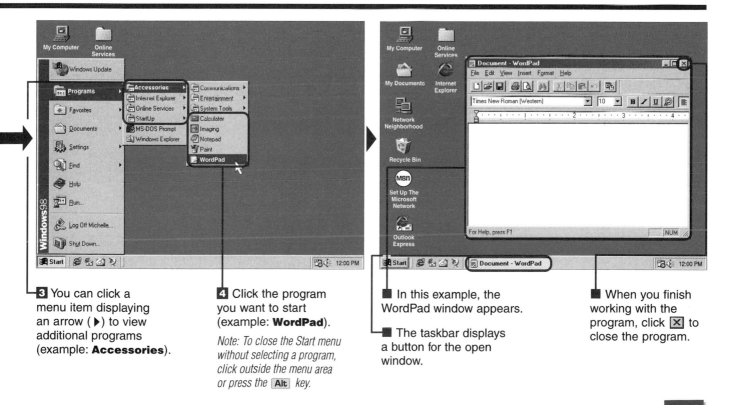

■ You can click a menu item displaying an arrow (▶) to view additional programs (example: **Accessories**).

■ Click the program you want to start (example: **WordPad**).

Note: To close the Start menu without selecting a program, click outside the menu area or press the **Alt** *key.*

■ In this example, the WordPad window appears.

■ The taskbar displays a button for the open window.

■ When you finish working with the program, click ☒ to close the program.

USING RUN TO START A PROGRAM

You can use the Run command to start a program that does not appear on the Start menu.

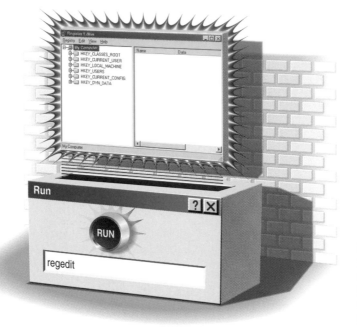

Programs that do not appear on the Start menu include some programs used to change the settings on your computer, MS-DOS programs and older Windows programs.

■■■ USING RUN TO START A PROGRAM ■■■

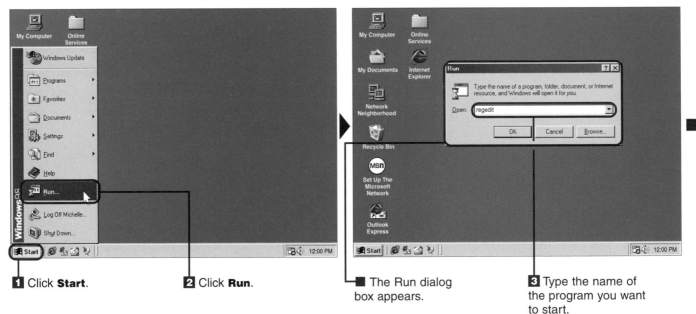

1 Click **Start**.

2 Click **Run**.

■ The Run dialog box appears.

3 Type the name of the program you want to start.

Can I use the Run command to display a Web page?

Yes. Enter the address of the Web page in the Run dialog box and Windows will display the Web page.

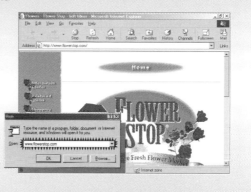

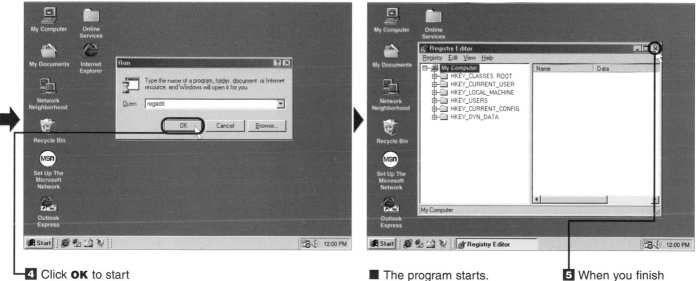

4 Click **OK** to start the program.

■ The program starts.

5 When you finish working with the program, click ☒ to close the program.

START AN MS-DOS PROMPT WINDOW

You can work with
MS-DOS programs
and commands in
Windows.

START AN MS-DOS PROMPT WINDOW

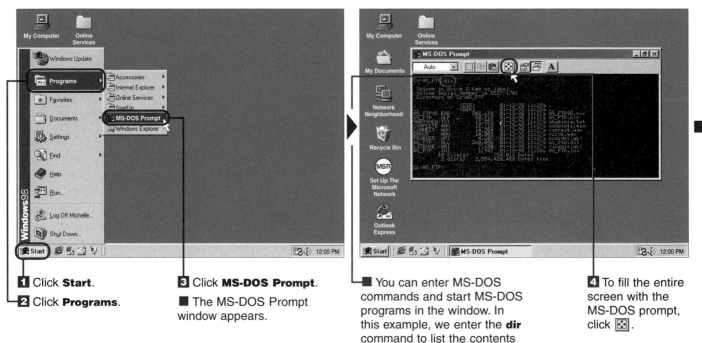

1 Click **Start**.

2 Click **Programs**.

3 Click **MS-DOS Prompt**.

■ The MS-DOS Prompt window appears.

■ You can enter MS-DOS commands and start MS-DOS programs in the window. In this example, we enter the **dir** command to list the contents of the current directory.

4 To fill the entire screen with the MS-DOS prompt, click [⊡].

?

What are some MS-DOS commands I can use?

In the MS-DOS Prompt window, type one of the commands to the right and then press the `Enter` key to run the command.

Cls	Clears the screen.
Date	Displays the current date.
Dir	Lists the contents of the current directory.
Time	Displays the current time.

```
C:\WS_FTP>dir

 Volume in drive C has no label
 Volume Serial Number is 2E37-1701
 Directory of C:\WS_FTP

.                <DIR>        01-13-98  11:28a  .
..               <DIR>        01-13-98  11:28a  ..
WS_FTP95  EXE     348,672     01-13-98  11:27a  WS_FTP95.exe
WS_FTP    HLP      80,712     01-13-98  11:27a  WS_FTP.hlp
WHATSNEW  TXT      13,821     01-13-98  11:27a  whatsnew.txt
COMPLETE  WAV      12,118     01-13-98  11:27a  complete.wav
CONNECT   WAV      14,354     01-13-98  11:27a  connect.wav
ERROR     WAV      10,008     01-13-98  11:27a  error.wav
PRORDER   WRI       4,608     01-13-98  11:27a  prorder.wri
WS_FTP    DLL     260,096     01-13-98  11:27a  ws_ftp.dll
LICENSE   WRI       7,680     01-13-98  11:27a  license.wri
WS_FTP    INI       1,947     01-13-98  11:28a  WS_FTP.ini
            10 file(s)         754,016 bytes
             2 dir(s)    2,854,420,480 bytes free

C:\WS_FTP>
```

■ The MS-DOS prompt fills the entire screen.

5 To return the MS-DOS prompt to a window, hold down the `Alt` key and then press the `Enter` key.

■ The MS-DOS prompt returns to a window.

6 When you finish using the MS-DOS Prompt window, type **exit** and then press the `Enter` key to close the window.

MAXIMIZE A WINDOW

You can enlarge a window
to fill your screen. This
lets you view more of the
window's contents.

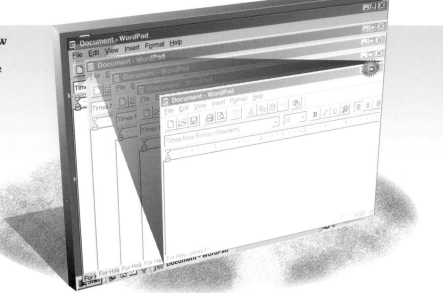

1 Click ▣ in the window
you want to maximize.

■ The window fills
your screen.

■ To return the window to
its previous size, click ▣.

14

If you are not using a
window, you can minimize
the window to remove it
from your screen. You can
redisplay the window at
any time.

MINIMIZE A WINDOW

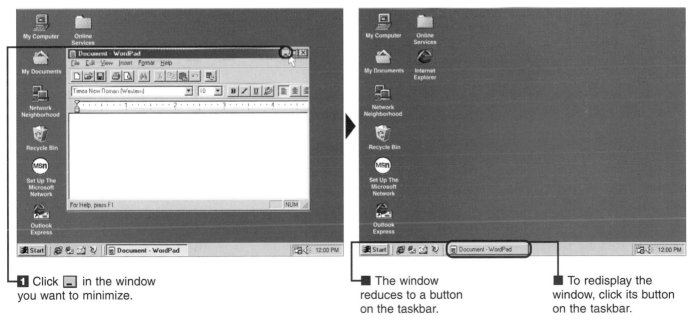

1 Click 🔲 in the window
you want to minimize.

■ The window
reduces to a button
on the taskbar.

■ To redisplay the
window, click its button
on the taskbar.

MOVE A WINDOW

If a window covers items on your screen, you can move the window to a different location.

MOVE A WINDOW

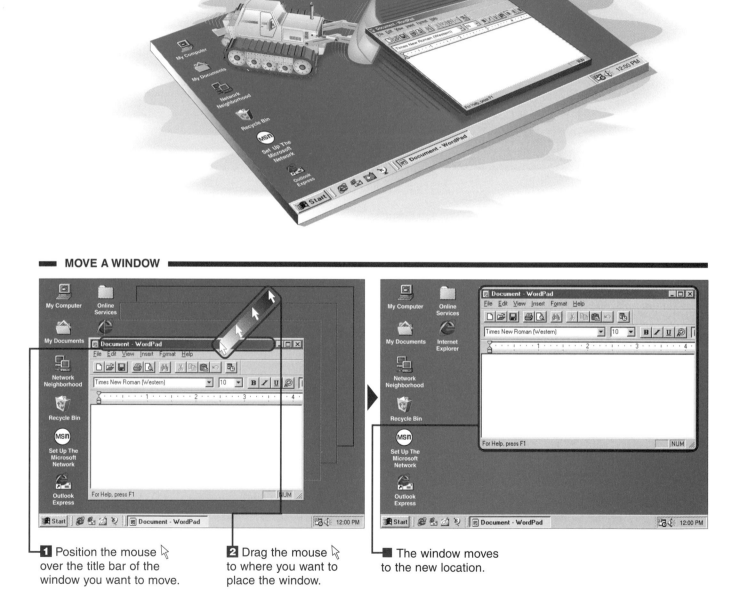

1 Position the mouse over the title bar of the window you want to move.

2 Drag the mouse to where you want to place the window.

■ The window moves to the new location.

You can change the size of a window displayed on your screen.

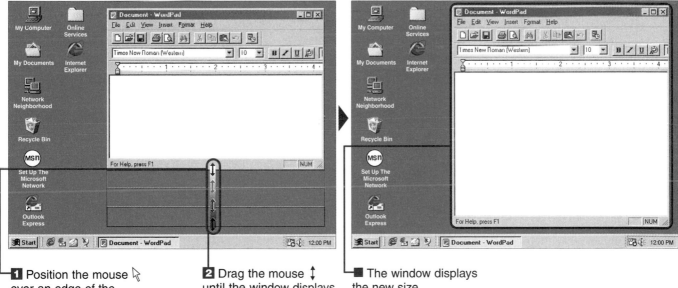

Enlarging a window lets you view more of its contents. Reducing a window lets you view items covered by the window.

SIZE A WINDOW

1 Position the mouse ⌖ over an edge of the window you want to size (⌖ changes to ↕, ↔ or ↘).

2 Drag the mouse ↕ until the window displays the size you want.

■ The window displays the new size.

SWITCH BETWEEN WINDOWS

You can have more than
one window open at a
time. You can easily
switch between all of
the open windows.

Each window is like a
separate piece of paper.
Switching between
windows is similar to
placing a different piece
of paper at the top of
the pile.

SWITCH BETWEEN WINDOWS

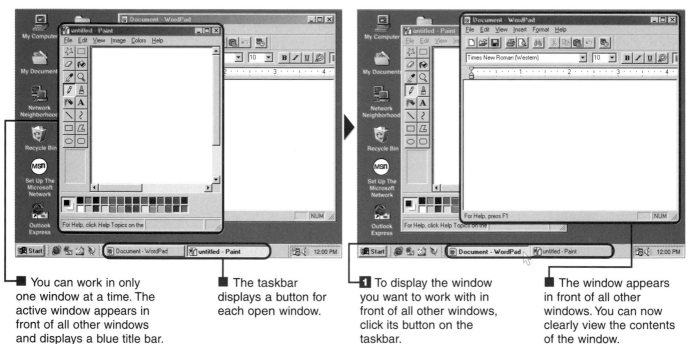

■ You can work in only
one window at a time. The
active window appears in
front of all other windows
and displays a blue title bar.

■ The taskbar
displays a button for
each open window.

1 To display the window
you want to work with in
front of all other windows,
click its button on the
taskbar.

■ The window appears
in front of all other
windows. You can now
clearly view the contents
of the window.

When you finish working
with a window, you can
close the window to
remove it from your
screen.

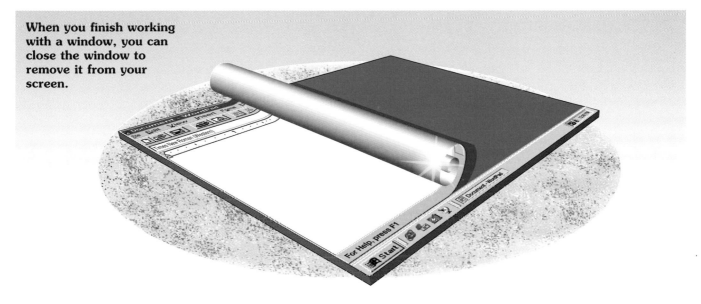

CLOSE A WINDOW

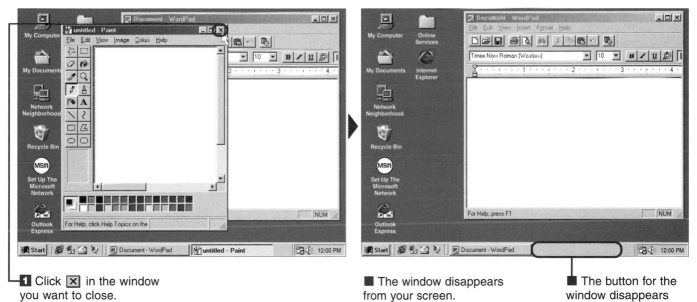

1 Click ✕ in the window
you want to close.

■ The window disappears
from your screen.

■ The button for the
window disappears
from the taskbar.

SHOW THE DESKTOP

You can instantly minimize all your open windows to remove them from your screen. This allows you to clearly view the desktop.

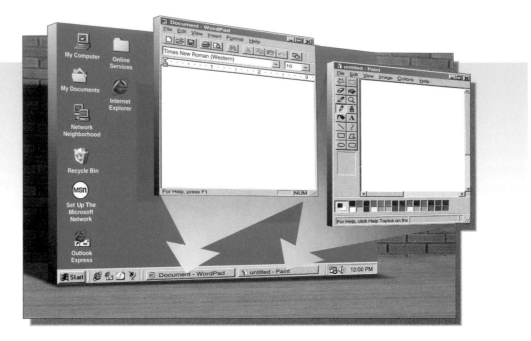

SHOW THE DESKTOP

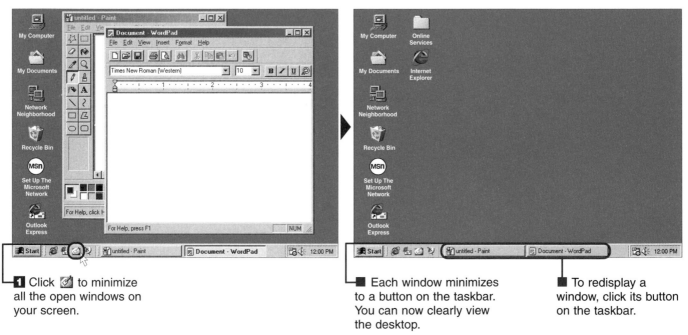

1 Click 🖌 to minimize all the open windows on your screen.

■ Each window minimizes to a button on the taskbar. You can now clearly view the desktop.

■ To redisplay a window, click its button on the taskbar.

20

When you finish using
your computer, shut
down Windows before
turning off the computer.

■ Do not turn off your
computer until this message
appears on your screen.

SHUT DOWN WINDOWS

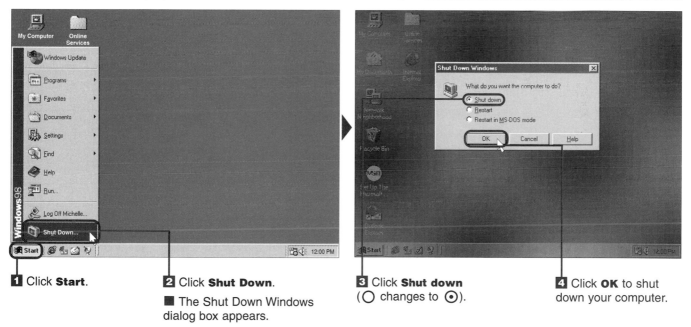

1 Click **Start**.

2 Click **Shut Down**.

■ The Shut Down Windows
dialog box appears.

3 Click **Shut down**
(○ changes to ⊙).

4 Click **OK** to shut
down your computer.

Boston Cycling Club
Newsletter - Apr. 12 to 19

Dear Member:

This year marks the Boston Cycling Club's first ever
cycle-a-thon, which takes place July 14.

The event is aimed at raising money for local charities
while raising our organization's profile in the community.

Participants are asked to solicit pledges from local businesses,
and then everyone involved will enter a five-mile bike ride.
Prizes will be awarded to those who raise the most money.

Mark Williams
President, Boston Cycling Club

CHAPTER 2

Work With Files

This chapter shows you how to perform tasks so you can work more easily with the files on your computer. You will learn how to preview a file, display hidden files and much more.

View Contents of Your Computer 24

Display or Hide a Toolbar 26

Close a Misbehaving Program 27

Create a New File 28

Display File Properties.......................30

Preview a File 32

Show Hidden Files 34

Add Folder to Favorites.....................36

Move or Copy Data
    Between Documents 38

Copy Screen Contents 40

Put Part of a Document
    on the Desktop..............................42

Offline Printing...............................44

Copy a Floppy Disk 46

General

Sales Figures

Type: Excel Worksheet

Locatio   C:\My Documents

Si   15.5KB (15.

VIEW CONTENTS OF YOUR COMPUTER

You can easily view the folders and files stored on your computer.

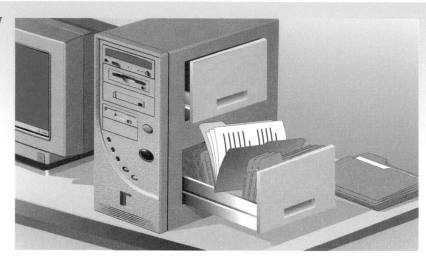

Like a filing cabinet, your computer uses folders to organize information.

◼◼ VIEW CONTENTS OF YOUR COMPUTER ◼◼◼◼◼◼◼◼

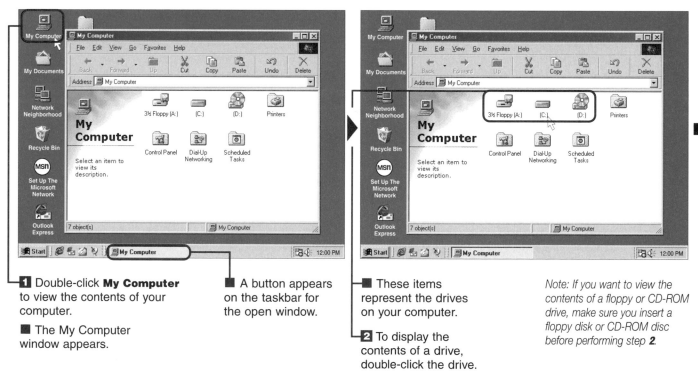

1 Double-click **My Computer** to view the contents of your computer.

◼ The My Computer window appears.

◼ A button appears on the taskbar for the open window.

◼ These items represent the drives on your computer.

2 To display the contents of a drive, double-click the drive.

Note: If you want to view the contents of a floppy or CD-ROM drive, make sure you insert a floppy disk or CD-ROM disc before performing step 2.

24

What do the symbols in a window represent?

Each item in a window displays a symbol to help you distinguish between the different types of items. Common types of items include:

Folder

Program

Paint picture

WordPad document

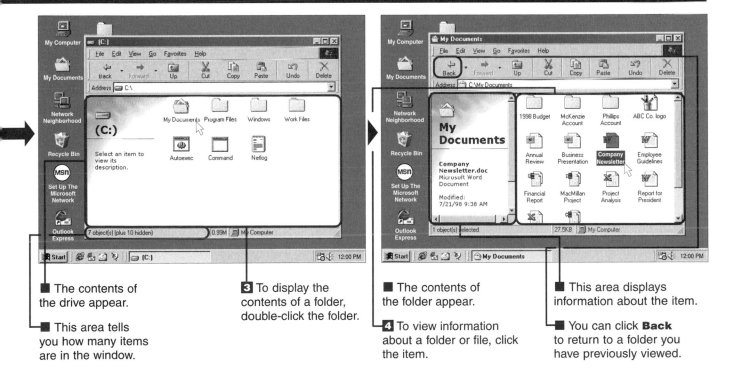

■ The contents of the drive appear.

■ This area tells you how many items are in the window.

3 To display the contents of a folder, double-click the folder.

■ The contents of the folder appear.

4 To view information about a folder or file, click the item.

■ This area displays information about the item.

■ You can click **Back** to return to a folder you have previously viewed.

DISPLAY OR HIDE A TOOLBAR

Windows offers several toolbars that you can display or hide at any time. Toolbars allow you to quickly access commonly used commands and features.

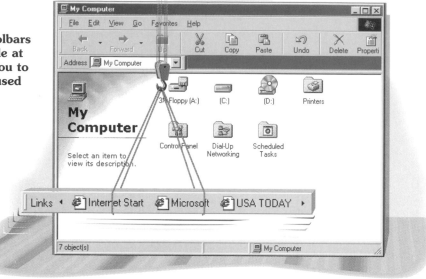

■ **DISPLAY OR HIDE A TOOLBAR** ■

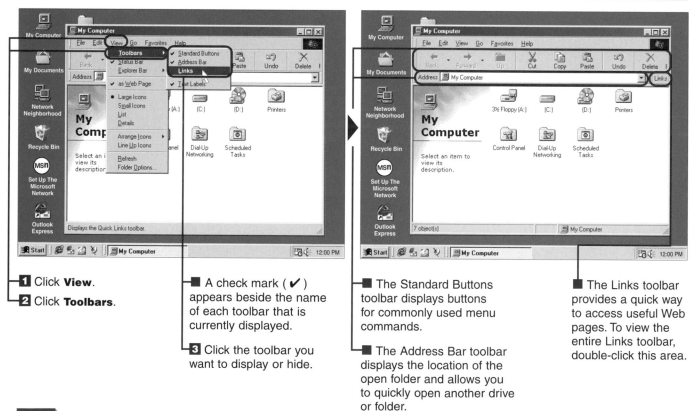

1 Click **View**.

2 Click **Toolbars**.

■ A check mark (✔) appears beside the name of each toolbar that is currently displayed.

3 Click the toolbar you want to display or hide.

■ The Standard Buttons toolbar displays buttons for commonly used menu commands.

■ The Address Bar toolbar displays the location of the open folder and allows you to quickly open another drive or folder.

■ The Links toolbar provides a quick way to access useful Web pages. To view the entire Links toolbar, double-click this area.

If a program suddenly
stops working, you can
close the program without
shutting down Windows.

■ CLOSE A MISBEHAVING PROGRAM ■

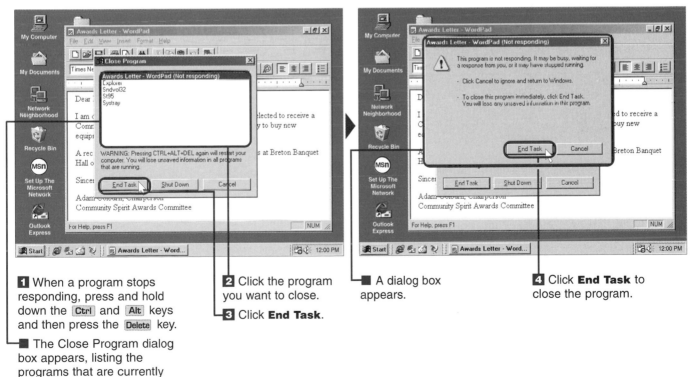

1 When a program stops
responding, press and hold
down the **Ctrl** and **Alt** keys
and then press the **Delete** key.

■ The Close Program dialog
box appears, listing the
programs that are currently
running.

2 Click the program
you want to close.

3 Click **End Task**.

■ A dialog box
appears.

4 Click **End Task** to
close the program.

CREATE A NEW FILE

You can instantly create, name and store a new file in the appropriate location without starting any programs.

You can focus on the organization of your files rather than the programs you need to accomplish your tasks.

CREATE A NEW FILE

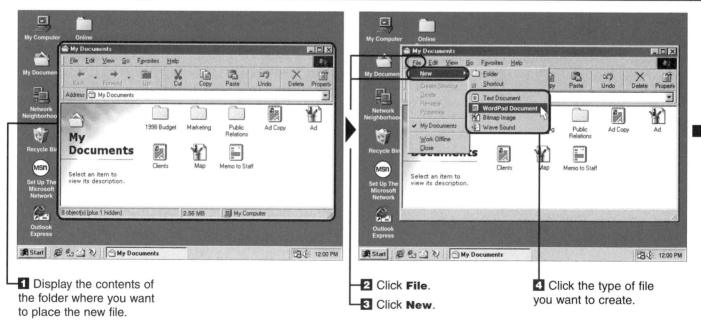

1 Display the contents of the folder where you want to place the new file.

2 Click **File**.

3 Click **New**.

4 Click the type of file you want to create.

**Can I later rename a file
I created?**

You can give a file a new
name to better describe
the contents of the file.
To rename a file, move the
mouse ⌖ over the file and
then press the left button.
Press the `F2` key, type a
new name for the file and
then press the `Enter` key.

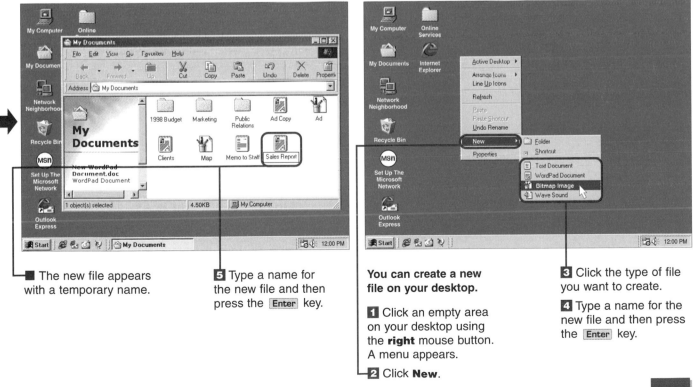

■ The new file appears
with a temporary name.

5 Type a name for
the new file and then
press the `Enter` key.

**You can create a new
file on your desktop.**

1 Click an empty area
on your desktop using
the **right** mouse button.
A menu appears.

2 Click **New**.

3 Click the type of file
you want to create.

4 Type a name for the
new file and then press
the `Enter` key.

DISPLAY FILE PROPERTIES

You can review the
properties of a file
to learn more about
the file.

Sales Figures	Units Sold	Price/Unit
Jan	573	$ 15.99
Feb	467	$ 15.99
Mar	753	$ 15.99
Apr	564	$ 15.99
May	547	$ 16.25
June	846	$ 16.25
July	784	$ 16.25
Aug	685	$ 16.25
Sept	346	$ 16.25
Oct	856	$ 16.50
Nov	354	$ 16.50
Dec	896	$ 16.50

General

Sales Figures

Type:	**Excel Worksheet**
Location:	**C:\My Documents**
Size:	**15.5KB (15,872 bytes)**
DOS name:	**SALESF~1.XLS**
Created:	**Monday, January 5, 1998**
Modified:	**Friday, January 16, 1998**

OK **Cancel**

■ DISPLAY FILE PROPERTIES ■

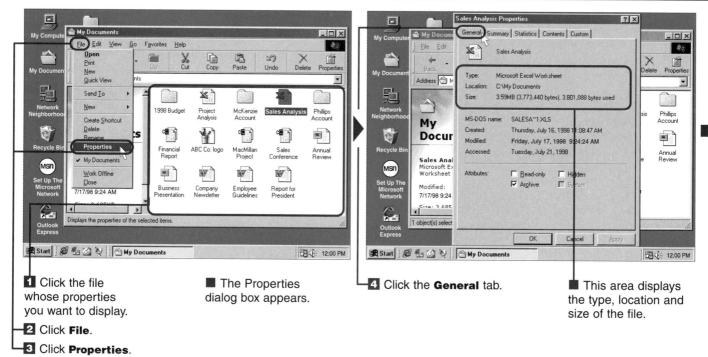

1 Click the file
whose properties
you want to display.

2 Click **File**.

3 Click **Properties**.

■ The Properties
dialog box appears.

4 Click the **General** tab.

■ This area displays
the type, location and
size of the file.

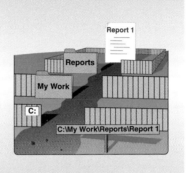

?

How can I determine the location of a file on my computer?

The Properties dialog box shows the location, or path, of a file. A path is a list of folders you must travel through to find a file on your computer. A path starts with a drive letter and is followed by folder names. Each folder name is separated by a backslash (\).

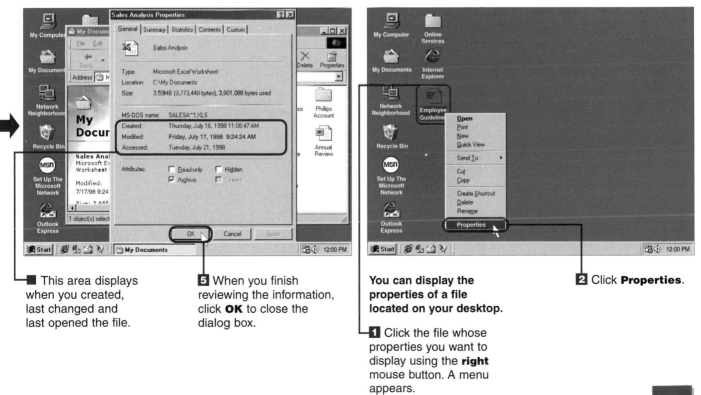

■ This area displays when you created, last changed and last opened the file.

5 When you finish reviewing the information, click **OK** to close the dialog box.

You can display the properties of a file located on your desktop.

1 Click the file whose properties you want to display using the **right** mouse button. A menu appears.

2 Click **Properties**.

PREVIEW A FILE

You can quickly view
the contents of a file
without starting the
program you used to
create the file.

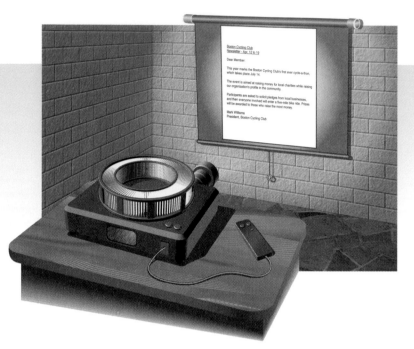

PREVIEW A FILE

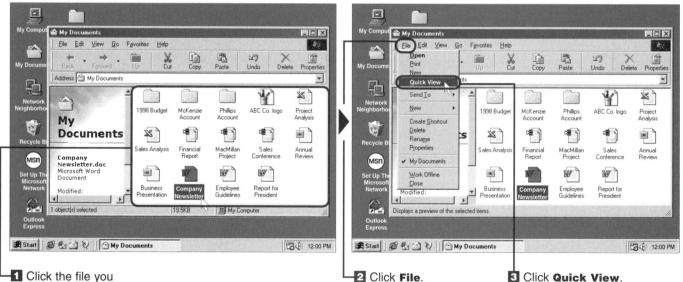

1 Click the file you
want to preview.

2 Click **File**.

3 Click **Quick View**.

?

Why is Quick View not available?

If Quick View is not available, you cannot preview the type of file you selected or you need to add the Quick View component from the Accessories category. To add Windows components, see page 118.

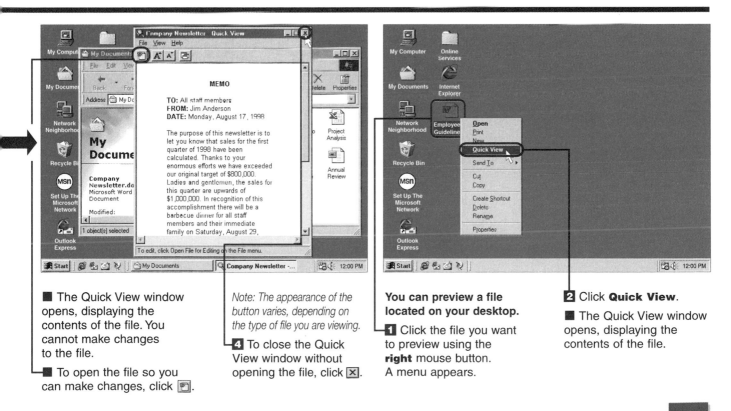

■ The Quick View window opens, displaying the contents of the file. You cannot make changes to the file.

■ To open the file so you can make changes, click 🖼.

Note: The appearance of the button varies, depending on the type of file you are viewing.

◢ To close the Quick View window without opening the file, click ☒.

You can preview a file located on your desktop.

◢ Click the file you want to preview using the **right** mouse button. A menu appears.

◢ Click **Quick View**.

■ The Quick View window opens, displaying the contents of the file.

You can have Windows
hide or display hidden
and system files.

Hidden and system
files are files that
Windows and your
programs need to
function.

SHOW HIDDEN FILES

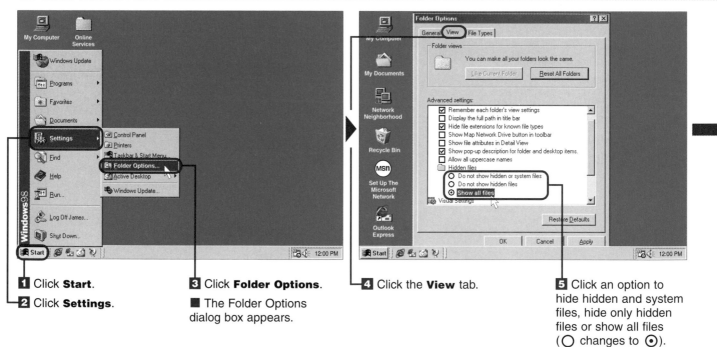

1 Click **Start**.

2 Click **Settings**.

3 Click **Folder Options**.

■ The Folder Options
dialog box appears.

4 Click the **View** tab.

5 Click an option to
hide hidden and system
files, hide only hidden
files or show all files
(○ changes to ⊙).

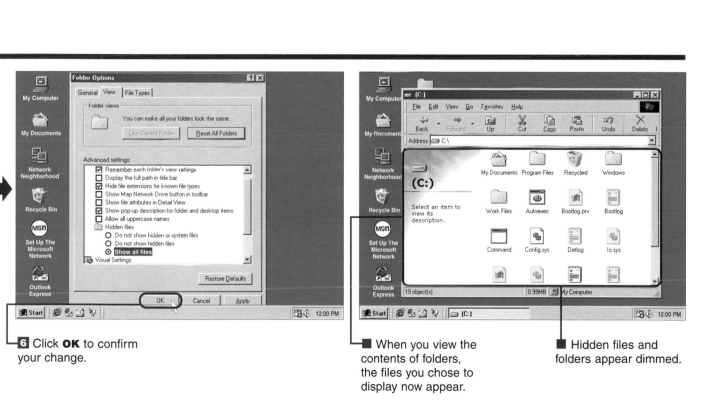

Should I choose to show hidden and system files?

If you choose to show hidden and system files, you may accidentally change or delete the files. This may cause your computer to no longer operate properly. To avoid problems, you should show hidden and system files only when necessary.

6 Click **OK** to confirm your change.

■ When you view the contents of folders, the files you chose to display now appear.

■ Hidden files and folders appear dimmed.

ADD FOLDER TO FAVORITES

You can add folders you
frequently use to the
Favorites menu. This lets
you quickly open these
folders at any time.

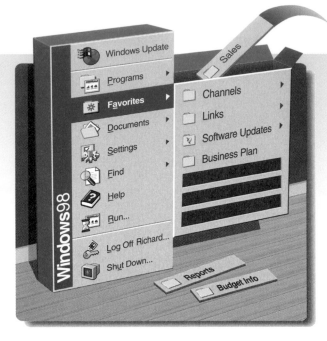

ADD FOLDER TO FAVORITES

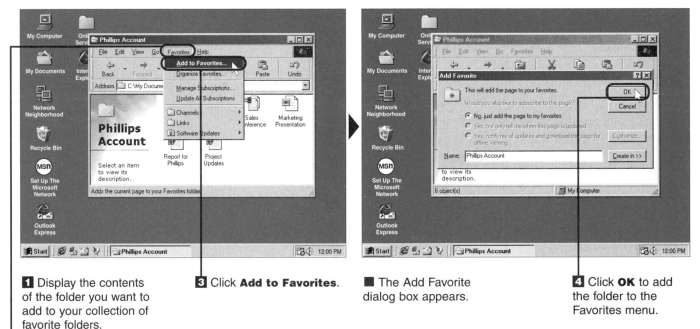

1 Display the contents
of the folder you want to
add to your collection of
favorite folders.

2 Click **Favorites**.

3 Click **Add to Favorites**.

■ The Add Favorite
dialog box appears.

4 Click **OK** to add
the folder to the
Favorites menu.

Which folders already exist on the Favorites menu?

Channels

This folder lists channels which are specially designed Web sites that Windows can automatically deliver to your computer.

Links

This folder lists useful Web pages.

Software Updates

This folder lists Web pages that allow you to update your Windows software.

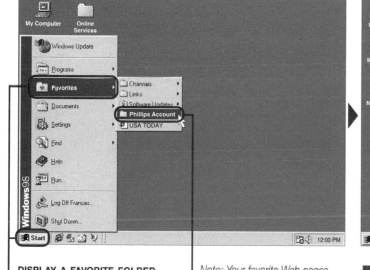

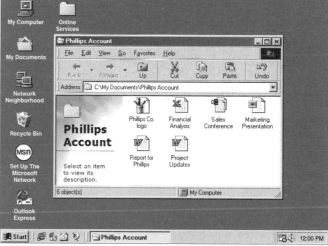

DISPLAY A FAVORITE FOLDER

1 Click **Start**.

2 Click **Favorites**. A list of your favorite folders appears.

Note: Your favorite Web pages will also appear in the list. Web pages display the 🗐 symbol.

3 Click the folder you want to open.

■ The folder you selected opens.

■ You can remove an item from the Favorites menu as you would remove an item from the Start menu. For more information, see page 106.

MOVE OR COPY DATA BETWEEN DOCUMENTS

You can move or copy data from one document to another.

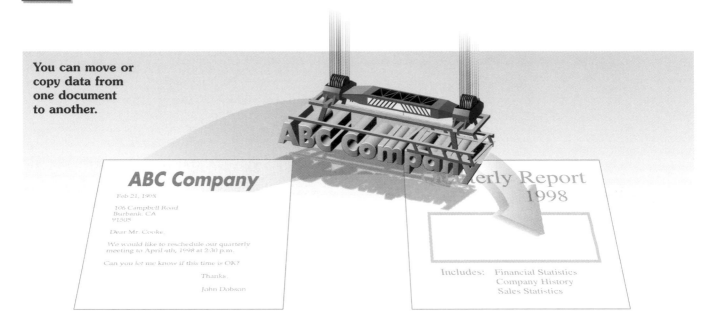

■■ MOVE OR COPY DATA BETWEEN DOCUMENTS ■■■■■■

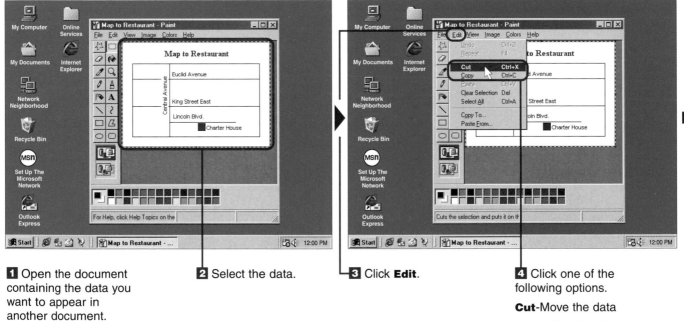

1 Open the document containing the data you want to appear in another document.

2 Select the data.

3 Click **Edit**.

4 Click one of the following options.

Cut-Move the data

Copy-Copy the data

What is the difference between moving and copying data?

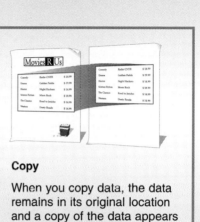

Move

When you move data, the data disappears from its original location and appears in the new location.

Copy

When you copy data, the data remains in its original location and a copy of the data appears in the new location.

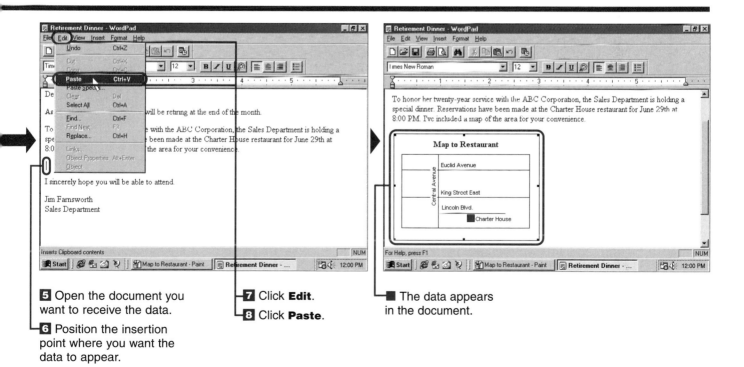

5 Open the document you want to receive the data.

6 Position the insertion point where you want the data to appear.

7 Click **Edit**.

8 Click **Paste**.

■ The data appears in the document.

You can take a picture of your entire screen. This is useful if you want to explain a computer problem or procedure and you need a visual example.

COPY SCREEN CONTENTS

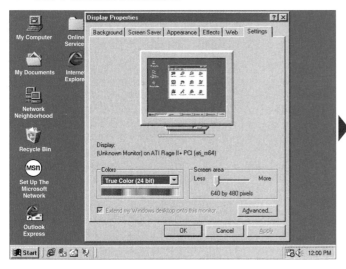

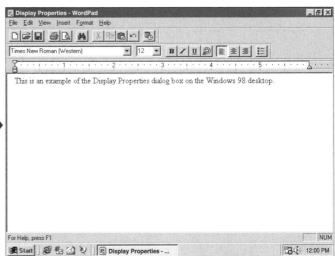

1 Press the `Print Scrn` key to copy the contents of your entire screen.

2 Open the document you want to receive a copy of the image.

? **Can I copy the contents of just the active window?**

The active window or dialog box appears in front of all other windows and usually displays a blue title bar. To copy the contents of just the active window or dialog box, press and hold down the **Alt** key as you press the **Print Scrn** key in step **1**.

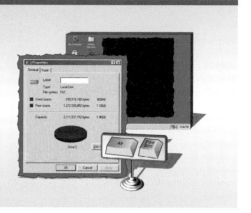

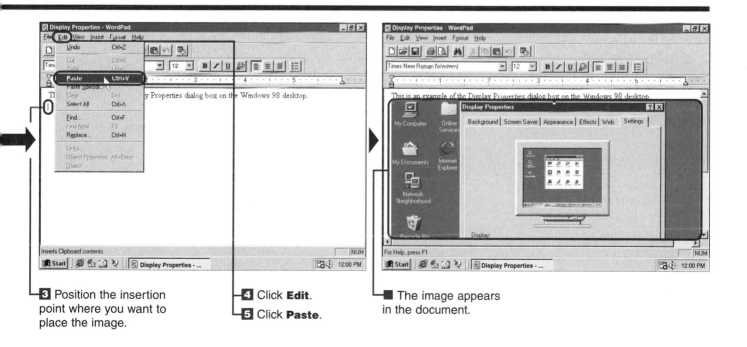

3 Position the insertion point where you want to place the image.

4 Click **Edit**.

5 Click **Paste**.

■ The image appears in the document.

PUT PART OF A DOCUMENT ON THE DESKTOP

You can place frequently used information on your desktop to give you quick access to the information.

Information you place on the desktop that contains part of a document is called a scrap.

PUT PART OF A DOCUMENT ON THE DESKTOP

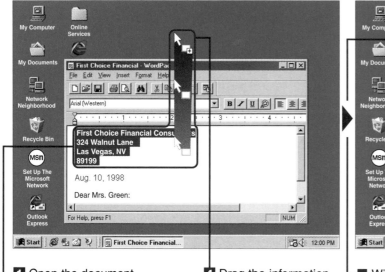

1 Open the document containing the information you want to place on the desktop.

2 Select the information.

3 Position the mouse ⬦ over the information.

4 Drag the information to a blank area on your desktop.

■ Windows creates a file called a scrap. The scrap stores the information you selected from the document.

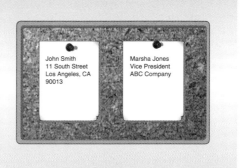

When would I use a scrap?

Scraps can save you time
when creating documents.
For example, a scrap
containing your name
and address can save
you from retyping the
information in all of your
letters.

USING SCRAPS

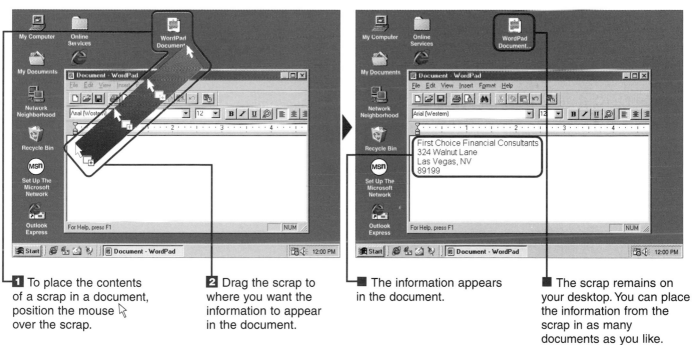

1 To place the contents
of a scrap in a document,
position the mouse
over the scrap.

2 Drag the scrap to
where you want the
information to appear
in the document.

■ The information appears
in the document.

■ The scrap remains on
your desktop. You can place
the information from the
scrap in as many
documents as you like.

If your computer is not connected to a printer, you can have Windows store documents you send to a printer until the printer is available.

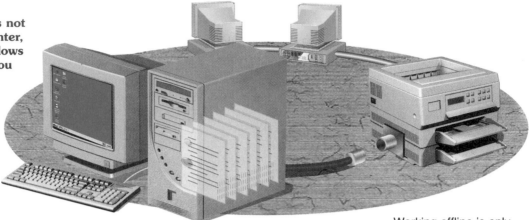

Working offline is only available for portable computers or computers using a printer on a network.

■■ **OFFLINE PRINTING** ■■

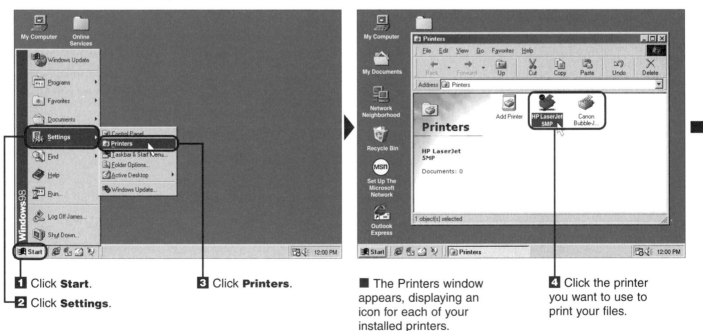

1 Click **Start**.

2 Click **Settings**.

3 Click **Printers**.

■ The Printers window appears, displaying an icon for each of your installed printers.

4 Click the printer you want to use to print your files.

When would I work offline?

You can work offline when traveling with a portable computer. You can also work offline when a printer on the network is unavailable because it needs paper, toner or maintenance. Windows will store documents you send to the printer until you are no longer working offline.

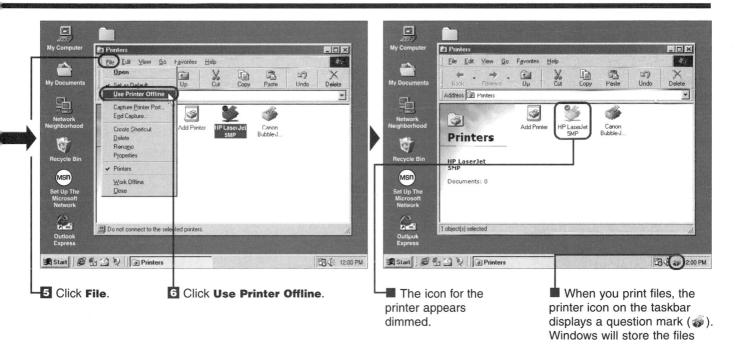

5 Click **File**.

6 Click **Use Printer Offline**.

■ The icon for the printer appears dimmed.

■ When you print files, the printer icon on the taskbar displays a question mark (🐾). Windows will store the files you send to the printer.

■ To once again work online and print the files, repeat steps **1** to **6**.

COPY A FLOPPY DISK

You can make an exact copy of a floppy disk. This is useful when you want to give a copy of a disk to a colleague or make a backup copy of important information.

COPY A FLOPPY DISK

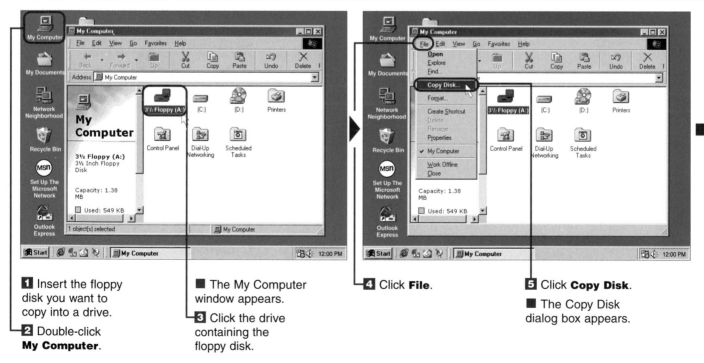

1 Insert the floppy disk you want to copy into a drive.

2 Double-click **My Computer**.

■ The My Computer window appears.

3 Click the drive containing the floppy disk.

4 Click **File**.

5 Click **Copy Disk**.

■ The Copy Disk dialog box appears.

? **When copying a floppy disk, should both disks be able to store the same amount of information?**

The original floppy disk and the disk that will receive the copy must be able to store the same amount of information.

A double-density floppy disk has one hole and can store 720 KB of information.

A high-density floppy disk has two holes and can store 1.44 MB of information.

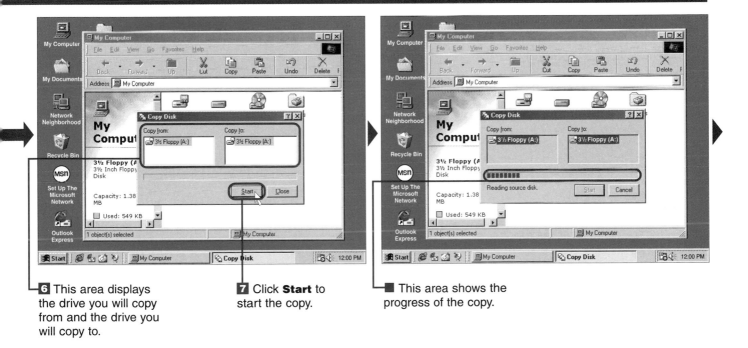

6 This area displays the drive you will copy from and the drive you will copy to.

7 Click **Start** to start the copy.

■ This area shows the progress of the copy.

CONTINUED

COPY A FLOPPY DISK

Make sure the floppy disk receiving the copy does not contain information you want to keep. Copying will remove all the information currently stored on the disk.

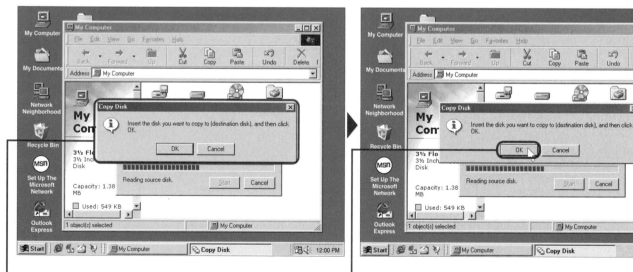

■ A dialog box appears, asking you to insert the floppy disk you want to receive the copy.

8 Remove the floppy disk from the drive and then insert the disk you want to receive the copy.

9 Click **OK** to continue.

48

How can I protect the information stored on a floppy disk?

Keep floppy disks away from magnets which can damage the information stored on the disks. Also be careful not to spill liquids, such as coffee or soda, on the disks.

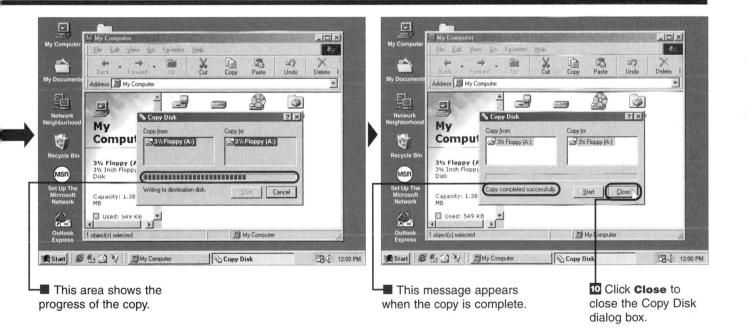

■ This area shows the progress of the copy.

■ This message appears when the copy is complete.

10 Click **Close** to close the Copy Disk dialog box.

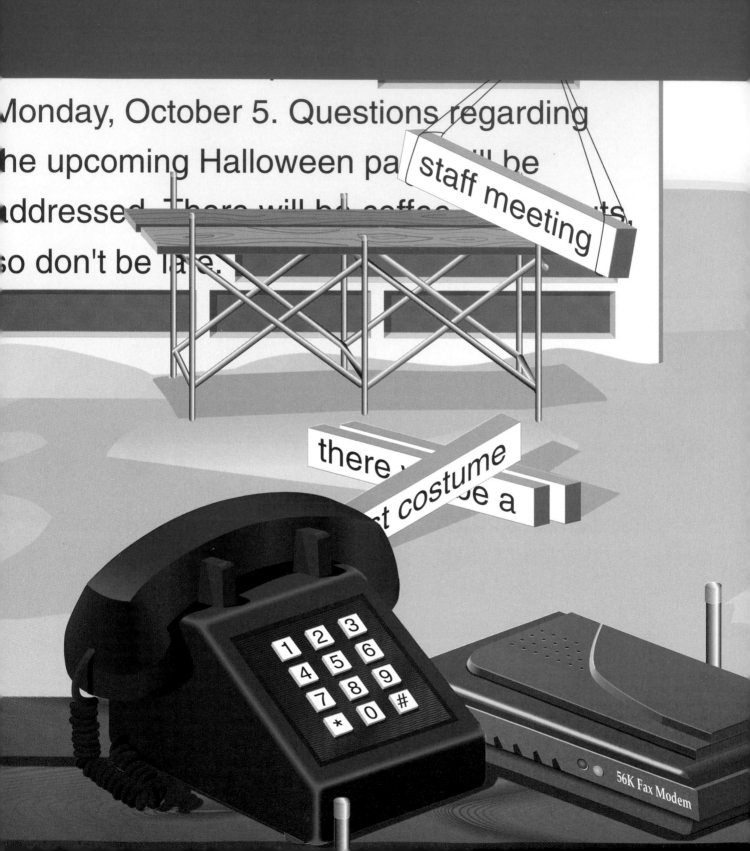

CHAPTER 3

Using Windows Accessories

You can use the accessories included with Windows 98 to perform many tasks. In this chapter you will learn to use Windows accessories to create text documents, record sounds and more.

Using Notepad 52

Using Character Map 54

Using Imaging 58

Using Sound Recorder 62

Using Phone Dialer...........................66

Using Clipboard Viewer 70

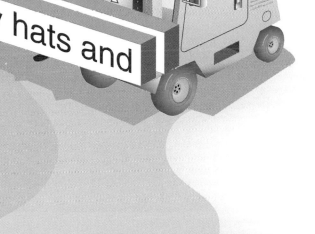

Notepad is a program that lets you create simple text documents.

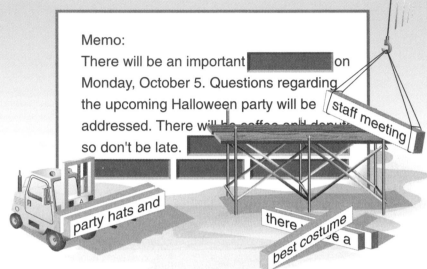

Memo:

There will be an important ▮▮▮▮▮▮ on Monday, October 5. Questions regarding the upcoming Halloween party will be addressed. There will be coffee and donuts so don't be late.

staff meeting

party hats and

there will be a

best costume

USING NOTEPAD

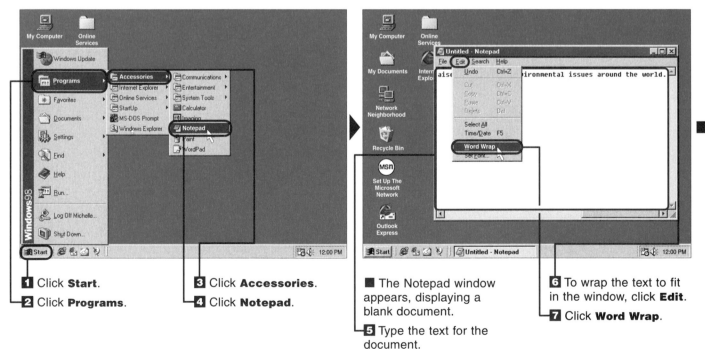

1 Click **Start**.

2 Click **Programs**.

3 Click **Accessories**.

4 Click **Notepad**.

■ The Notepad window appears, displaying a blank document.

5 Type the text for the document.

6 To wrap the text to fit in the window, click **Edit**.

7 Click **Word Wrap**.

Can I use Notepad to enter the current time and date in a document?

To enter the current time and date in your document, press the [F5] key. Notepad will automatically place the time and date at the location of the insertion point.

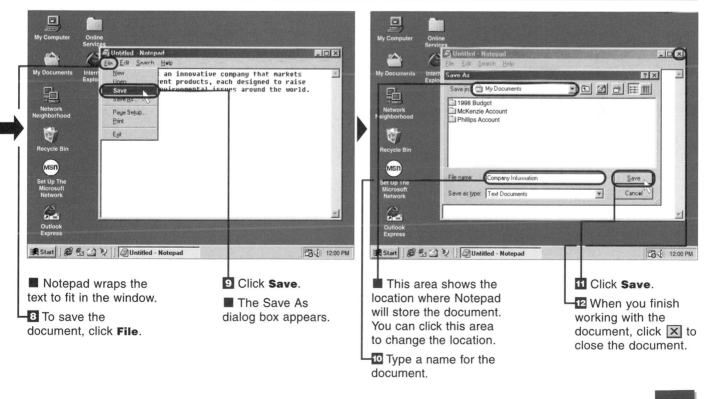

■ Notepad wraps the text to fit in the window.

8 To save the document, click **File**.

9 Click **Save**.

■ The Save As dialog box appears.

■ This area shows the location where Notepad will store the document. You can click this area to change the location.

10 Type a name for the document.

11 Click **Save**.

12 When you finish working with the document, click ⊠ to close the document.

USING CHARACTER MAP

When creating documents, you can use Character Map to include special characters that are not available on your keyboard.

If the Character Map feature is not available, you need to add the Character Map component from the System Tools category. To add Windows components, see page 118.

USING CHARACTER MAP

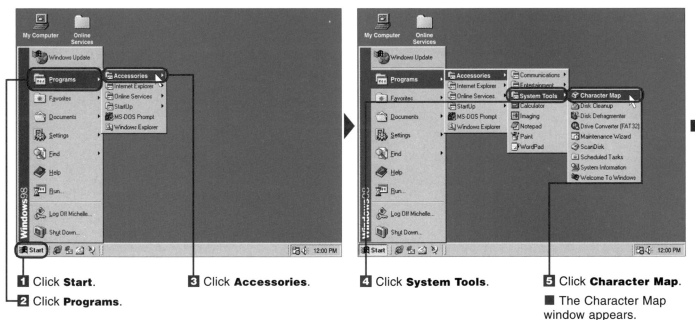

1 Click **Start**.

2 Click **Programs**.

3 Click **Accessories**.

4 Click **System Tools**.

5 Click **Character Map**.

■ The Character Map window appears.

?

What special characters are available in Character Map?

Character Map offers many special characters that you can choose from, such as ©, é, ½ and ™. Each font available in Character Map provides a different collection of special characters.

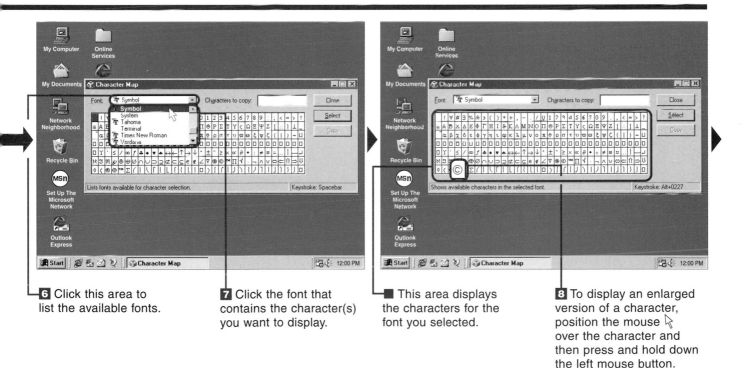

6 Click this area to list the available fonts.

7 Click the font that contains the character(s) you want to display.

■ This area displays the characters for the font you selected.

8 To display an enlarged version of a character, position the mouse ⍃ over the character and then press and hold down the left mouse button.

CONTINUED ▶

USING CHARACTER MAP

You can copy the special characters from Character Map and place them in your documents.

9 Double-click each character you want to use in a document.

■ This area displays each character you select.

10 Click **Copy** to copy the character(s) you selected.

11 Open the document you want to display the character(s).

12 Position the insertion point where you want the character(s) to appear.

How can I quickly enter special characters into my documents?

Each special character has a keystroke combination that allows you to quickly enter the character into a document. The keystroke combination for the selected character appears at the bottom right corner of the Character Map window.

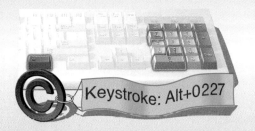

Keystroke: Alt+0227

If the keystroke combination includes numbers, you must enter the numbers using the numeric keypad on your keyboard.

13 Click **Edit**.

14 Click **Paste**.

■ The character(s) appear in the document.

■ To properly display the character(s), make sure the font matches the font you selected in Character Map in step **7**.

You can use
Imaging to work
with scanned
documents.

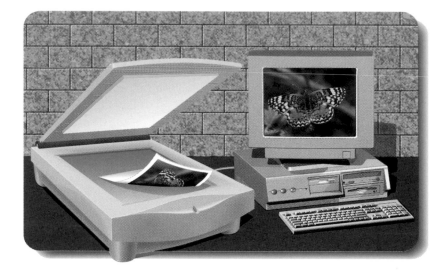

You need a scanner
to transfer paper
documents to your
computer.

■ USING IMAGING ■

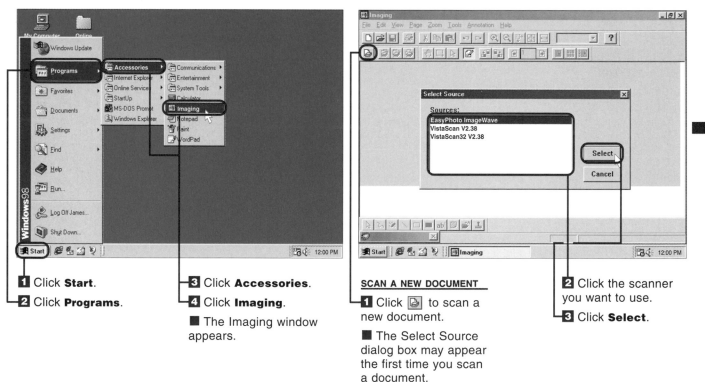

1 Click **Start**.

2 Click **Programs**.

3 Click **Accessories**.

4 Click **Imaging**.

■ The Imaging window
appears.

SCAN A NEW DOCUMENT

1 Click 🖼 to scan a
new document.

■ The Select Source
dialog box may appear
the first time you scan
a document.

2 Click the scanner
you want to use.

3 Click **Select**.

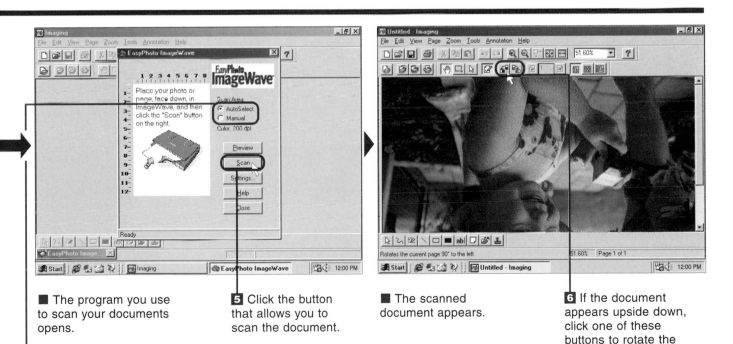

Why would I want to scan a document?

You may want to scan documents such as forms, receipts, pictures or newspaper clippings. You will be able to access the scanned documents on your computer much faster than paper documents on your desk or in your filing cabinet. You can also send scanned documents to friends and colleagues in e-mail messages.

■ The program you use to scan your documents opens.

4 Set the appropriate options for your scan. You may need to refer to the documentation that came with your scanner.

5 Click the button that allows you to scan the document.

■ The scanned document appears.

6 If the document appears upside down, click one of these buttons to rotate the document to the left (🖼️) or to the right (🖼️).

You can magnify or
reduce the size of a
document in Imaging.

CHANGE DOCUMENT SIZE

1 To magnify or reduce
the size of a document,
click one of the following
options.

Magnify

Reduce

■ The size of the
document changes.

■ You can click ⊞ to
view the entire document
on your screen.

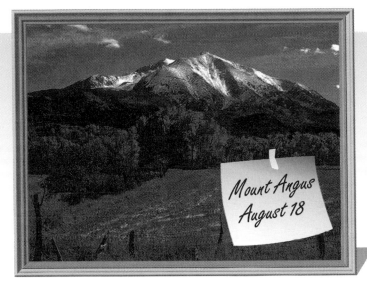

You can add a note to
an Imaging document.

Information you
add to an Imaging
document is called
an annotation.

ADD A NOTE

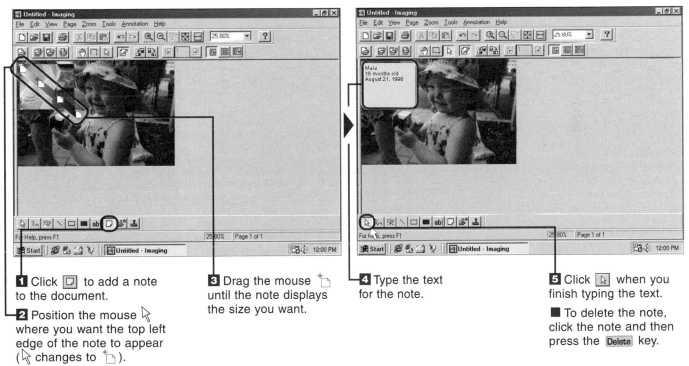

1 Click 🗋 to add a note
to the document.

2 Position the mouse ▷
where you want the top left
edge of the note to appear
(▷ changes to ⁺🗋).

3 Drag the mouse ⁺🗋
until the note displays
the size you want.

4 Type the text
for the note.

5 Click ▷ when you
finish typing the text.

■ To delete the note,
click the note and then
press the Delete key.

You can use Sound
Recorder to record
your own sounds.

You need a sound
card and speakers
to record and play
sounds.

USING SOUND RECORDER

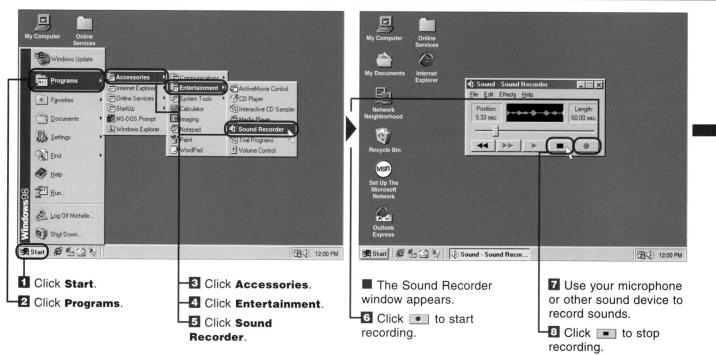

1 Click **Start**.

2 Click **Programs**.

3 Click **Accessories**.

4 Click **Entertainment**.

5 Click **Sound
Recorder**.

■ The Sound Recorder
window appears.

6 Click [•] to start
recording.

7 Use your microphone
or other sound device to
record sounds.

8 Click [■] to stop
recording.

What devices can I use to record sounds?

You can record sounds from a microphone, CD player, stereo, VCR or any other sound device connected to your computer.

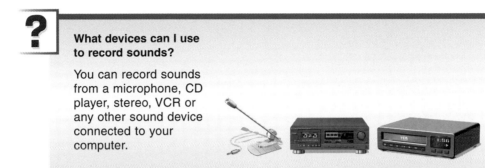

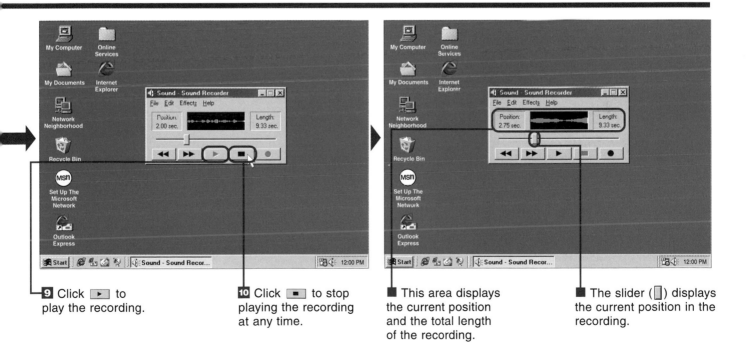

9 Click ▶ to play the recording.

10 Click ■ to stop playing the recording at any time.

■ This area displays the current position and the total length of the recording.

■ The slider (▯) displays the current position in the recording.

USING SOUND RECORDER

Sound Recorder offers several sound effects you can use to change your recording.

You can adjust the volume, adjust the speed, add an echo or play a recording in reverse.

■ USING SOUND RECORDER (CONTINUED)

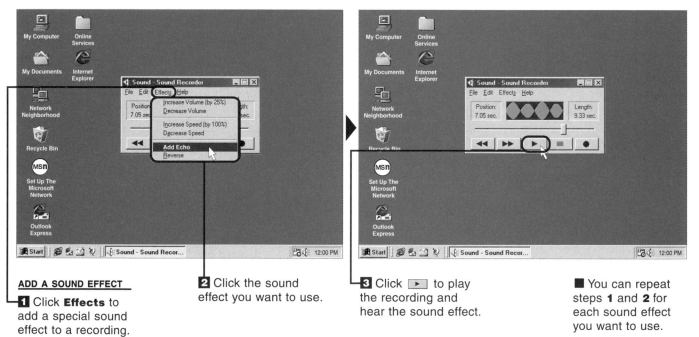

ADD A SOUND EFFECT

1 Click **Effects** to add a special sound effect to a recording.

2 Click the sound effect you want to use.

3 Click ▶ to play the recording and hear the sound effect.

■ You can repeat steps **1** and **2** for each sound effect you want to use.

?

How can I play a recording I saved?

Recordings you have saved display a specific icon () on your computer. You can double-click the icon to play the recording.

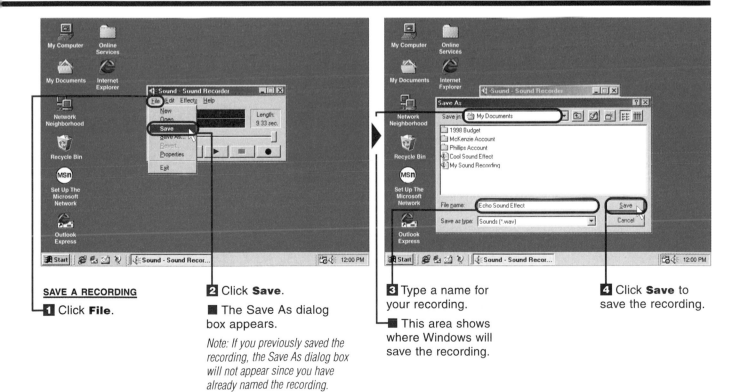

SAVE A RECORDING

1 Click **File**.

2 Click **Save**.

■ The Save As dialog box appears.

Note: If you previously saved the recording, the Save As dialog box will not appear since you have already named the recording.

3 Type a name for your recording.

■ This area shows where Windows will save the recording.

4 Click **Save** to save the recording.

USING PHONE DIALER

You can use Phone Dialer to make telephone calls from your computer.

Before you can use Phone Dialer, you need to connect a telephone to your modem.

USE PHONE DIALER

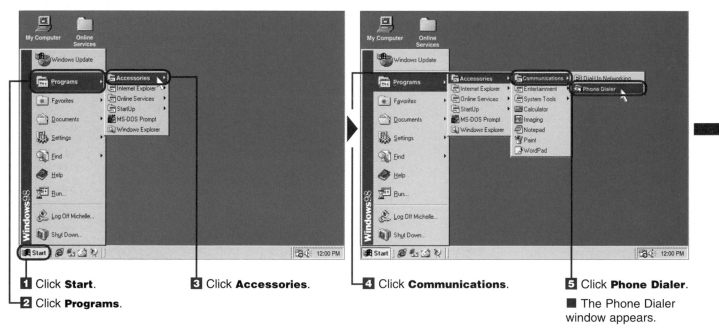

1 Click **Start**.

2 Click **Programs**.

3 Click **Accessories**.

4 Click **Communications**.

5 Click **Phone Dialer**.

■ The Phone Dialer window appears.

How do I connect a telephone to my modem?

Plug the telephone cord into the jack labeled "Phone" on your modem. If you have an internal modem, you will be able to see the edge of the modem at the back of your computer.

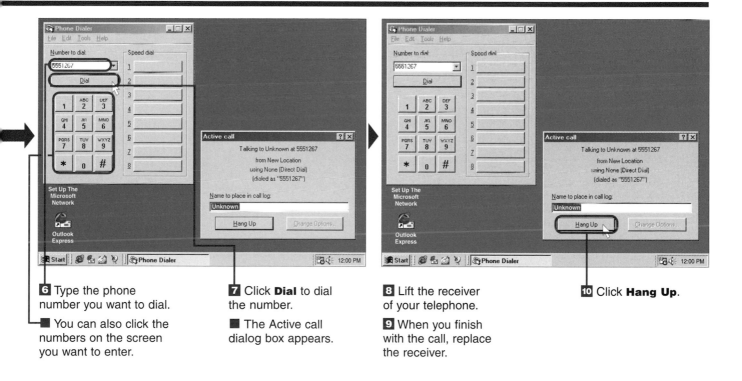

6 Type the phone number you want to dial.

■ You can also click the numbers on the screen you want to enter.

7 Click **Dial** to dial the number.

■ The Active call dialog box appears.

8 Lift the receiver of your telephone.

9 When you finish with the call, replace the receiver.

10 Click **Hang Up**.

USING PHONE DIALER

You can store phone
numbers you frequently
use on speed-dial buttons.

═══ STORE A PHONE NUMBER ═══

1 To store a phone
number, click an empty
speed-dial button.

■ The Program Speed
Dial dialog box appears.

2 Type the name
of the person whose
phone number you
want to store.

3 Click this area
and then type the
phone number.

4 Click **Save** to save the
information.

Can I use the telephone and browse the Web at the same time?

No. Although you can use the same phone line to talk on the telephone and browse the Web, you cannot perform both tasks at the same time.

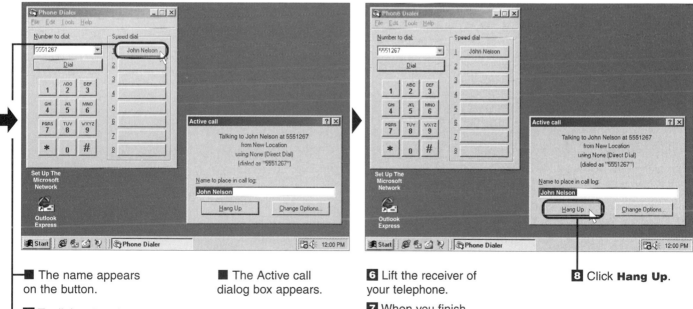

■ The name appears on the button.

5 To dial a stored phone number, click the speed-dial button for the person.

■ The Active call dialog box appears.

6 Lift the receiver of your telephone.

7 When you finish with the call, replace the receiver.

8 Click **Hang Up**.

USING CLIPBOARD VIEWER

You can use the Clipboard Viewer to view the contents of the Clipboard. The Clipboard is a temporary storage area on your computer.

USING CLIPBOARD VIEWER

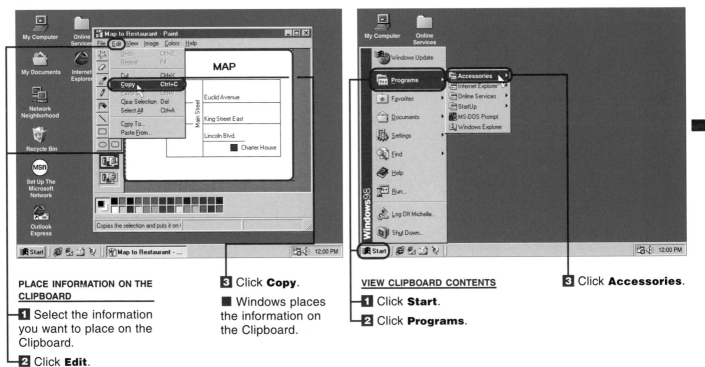

PLACE INFORMATION ON THE CLIPBOARD

1 Select the information you want to place on the Clipboard.

2 Click **Edit**.

3 Click **Copy**.

■ Windows places the information on the Clipboard.

VIEW CLIPBOARD CONTENTS

1 Click **Start**.

2 Click **Programs**.

3 Click **Accessories**.

How long does information stay on the Clipboard?

The Clipboard stores one item at a time. An item will remain on the Clipboard until you move or copy a new item or turn off your computer.

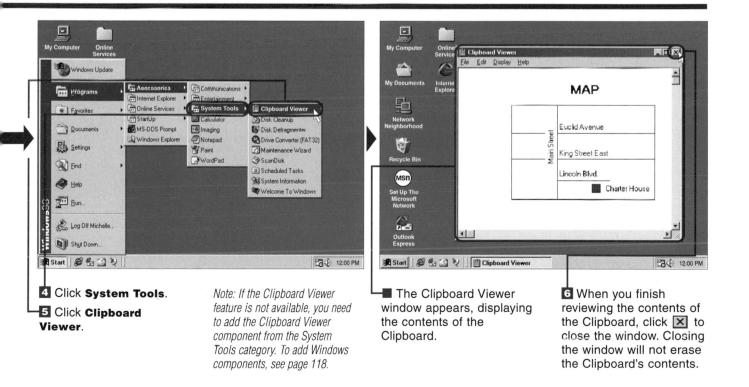

4 Click **System Tools**.

5 Click **Clipboard Viewer**.

Note: If the Clipboard Viewer feature is not available, you need to add the Clipboard Viewer component from the System Tools category. To add Windows components, see page 118.

■ The Clipboard Viewer window appears, displaying the contents of the Clipboard.

6 When you finish reviewing the contents of the Clipboard, click ☒ to close the window. Closing the window will not erase the Clipboard's contents.

CHAPTER 4

Customize Windows

You can change the appearance and behavior of Windows 98 to suit your needs. This chapter teaches you how to change desktop icons, adjust power management settings and use accessibility features.

Change Desktop Icons 74

Change Visual Effects 76

Create a New Toolbar 78

Change Regional Settings 80

Change Recycle Bin Properties...........82

Add Destinations to the
  Send To Menu 84

View Fonts on Your Computer 88

Add Fonts to Your Computer 90

Change Power Management Settings ..94

Using Magnifier 96

Using the Accessibility Wizard 98

CHANGE DESKTOP ICONS

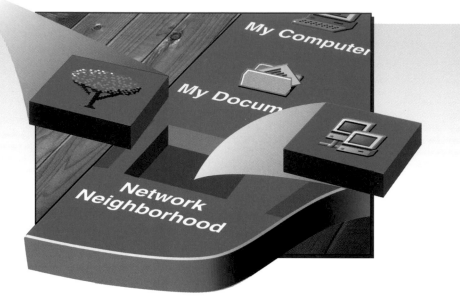

You can change the appearance of icons on your desktop to customize your computer.

CHANGE DESKTOP ICONS

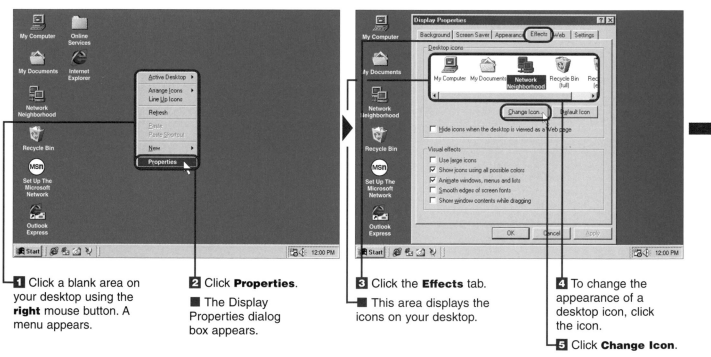

1 Click a blank area on your desktop using the **right** mouse button. A menu appears.

2 Click **Properties**.

■ The Display Properties dialog box appears.

3 Click the **Effects** tab.

■ This area displays the icons on your desktop.

4 To change the appearance of a desktop icon, click the icon.

5 Click **Change Icon**.

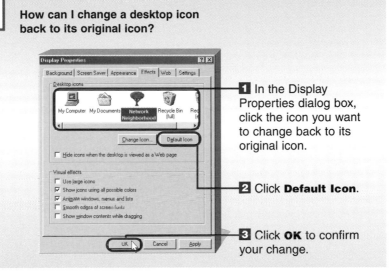

How can I change a desktop icon back to its original icon?

1 In the Display Properties dialog box, click the icon you want to change back to its original icon.

2 Click **Default Icon**.

3 Click **OK** to confirm your change.

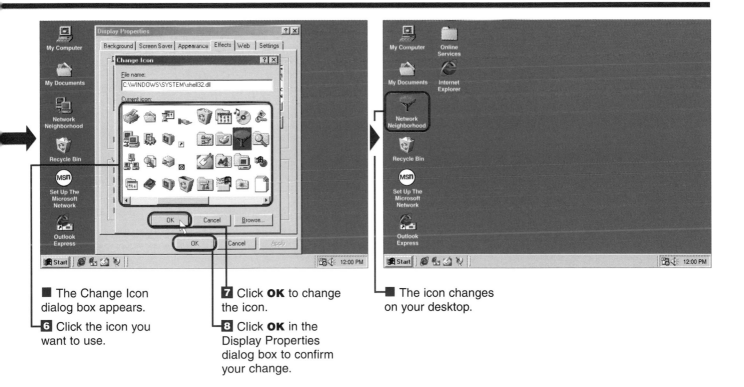

■ The Change Icon dialog box appears.

6 Click the icon you want to use.

7 Click **OK** to change the icon.

8 Click **OK** in the Display Properties dialog box to confirm your change.

■ The icon changes on your desktop.

CHANGE VISUAL EFFECTS

There are several visual effects you can select to change the way items appear on your screen.

Use large icons

Use large icons to show items on your desktop.

Show icons using all possible colors

Shows desktop items using all the colors your computer can display.

CHANGE VISUAL EFFECTS

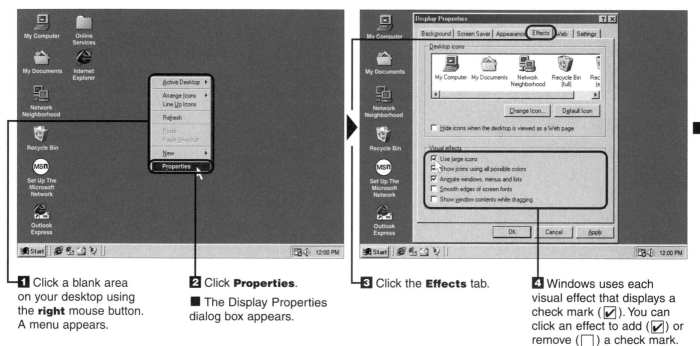

1 Click a blank area on your desktop using the **right** mouse button. A menu appears.

2 Click **Properties**.

■ The Display Properties dialog box appears.

3 Click the **Effects** tab.

4 Windows uses each visual effect that displays a check mark (☑). You can click an effect to add (☑) or remove (☐) a check mark.

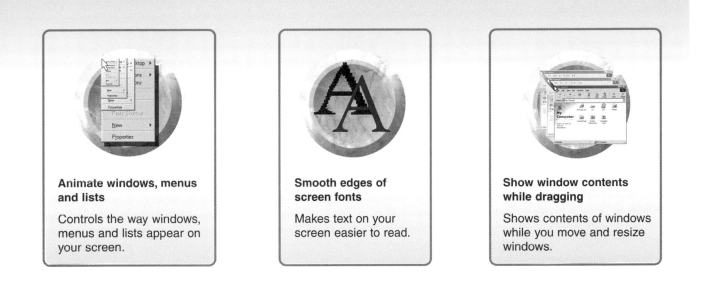

Animate windows, menus and lists

Controls the way windows, menus and lists appear on your screen.

Smooth edges of screen fonts

Makes text on your screen easier to read.

Show window contents while dragging

Shows contents of windows while you move and resize windows.

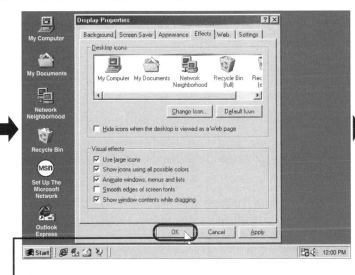

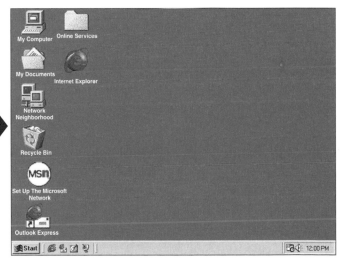

5 Click **OK** to confirm your changes.

■ Windows makes the changes to your desktop.

CREATE A NEW TOOLBAR

You can create a new toolbar
from any folder on your
computer. The new toolbar
will provide quick access
to the items in the folder.

CREATE A NEW TOOLBAR

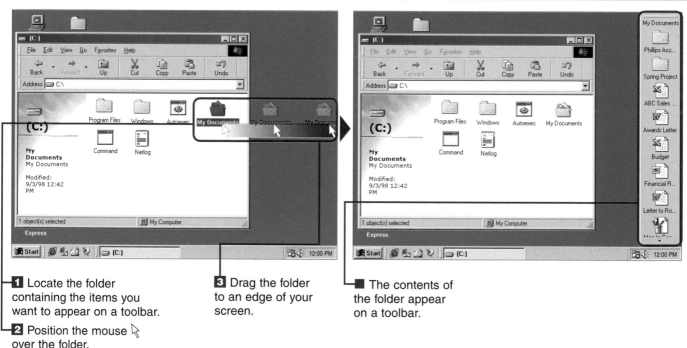

1 Locate the folder
containing the items you
want to appear on a toolbar.

2 Position the mouse
over the folder.

3 Drag the folder
to an edge of your
screen.

■ The contents of
the folder appear
on a toolbar.

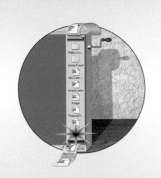

Why doesn't the toolbar display all the items in the folder?

When there are more items in a folder than will fit on the toolbar, a small black arrow (▼) appears at the edge of the toolbar. You can click this arrow to view the items that are not displayed.

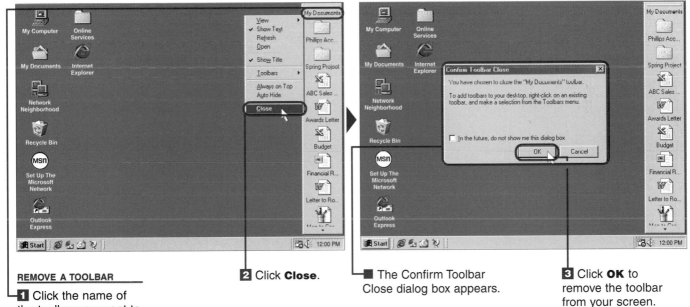

REMOVE A TOOLBAR

1 Click the name of the toolbar you want to remove using the **right** mouse button. A menu appears.

2 Click **Close**.

■ The Confirm Toolbar Close dialog box appears.

3 Click **OK** to remove the toolbar from your screen.

CHANGE REGIONAL SETTINGS

You can change the settings on your computer to correspond with your region of the world.

Changing the regional settings will affect the way numbers, currency, dates and times are displayed on your computer.

CHANGE REGIONAL SETTINGS

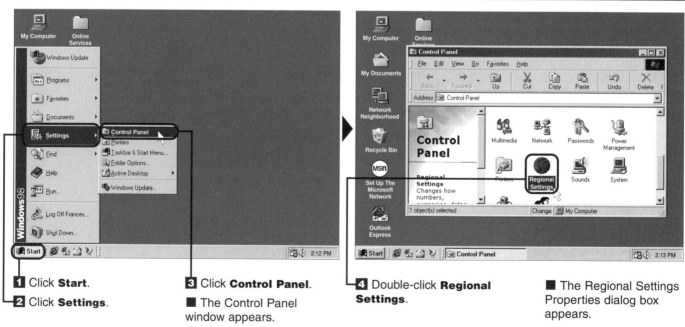

1 Click **Start**.

2 Click **Settings**.

3 Click **Control Panel**.

■ The Control Panel window appears.

4 Double-click **Regional Settings**.

■ The Regional Settings Properties dialog box appears.

How do I change the language used by Windows?

Changing the regional settings only affects the way numbers, currency, dates and times appear on your computer. To change the language shown in items such as menus and the Help feature, you must buy a copy of Windows in the language you want to use.

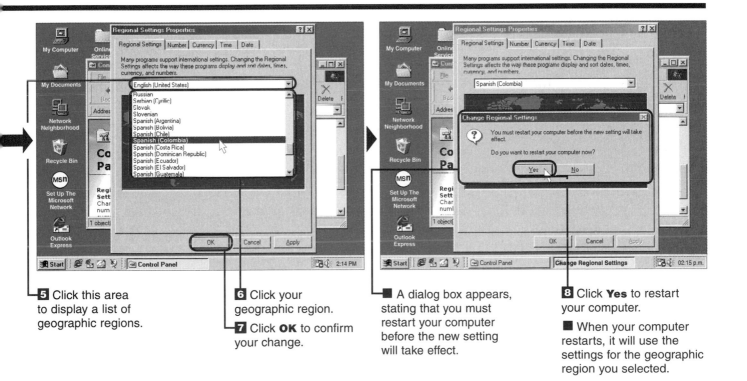

◾5 Click this area to display a list of geographic regions.

◾6 Click your geographic region.

◾7 Click **OK** to confirm your change.

◾ A dialog box appears, stating that you must restart your computer before the new setting will take effect.

◾8 Click **Yes** to restart your computer.

◾ When your computer restarts, it will use the settings for the geographic region you selected.

CHANGE RECYCLE BIN PROPERTIES

The Recycle Bin stores all the files you have deleted. You can change the way the Recycle Bin works with deleted files.

CHANGE RECYCLE BIN PROPERTIES

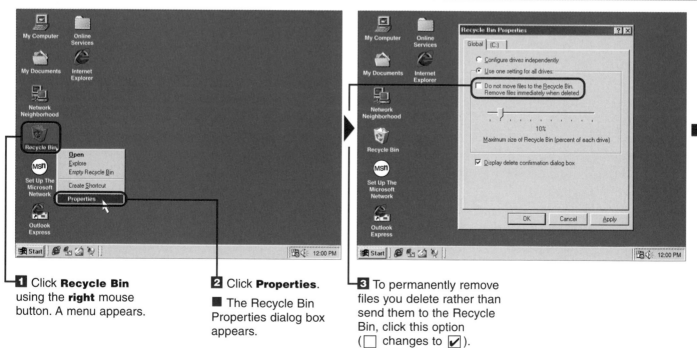

1 Click **Recycle Bin** using the **right** mouse button. A menu appears.

2 Click **Properties**.

■ The Recycle Bin Properties dialog box appears.

3 To permanently remove files you delete rather than send them to the Recycle Bin, click this option (☐ changes to ☑).

?

What Recycle Bin properties can I change?

Remove Files Immediately

You can choose to immediately delete files instead of sending the files to the Recycle Bin. This is ideal if you often delete confidential files.

Recycle Bin Size

You can change the maximum size of the Recycle Bin. This is initially set at 10% of your hard drive space.

Confirmation Message

You can choose not to display a confirmation dialog box when you delete a file. This can save you time when deleting files.

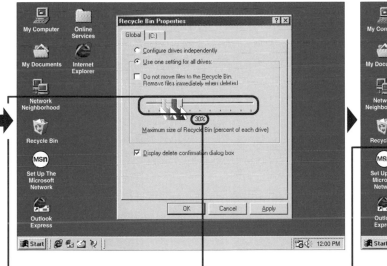

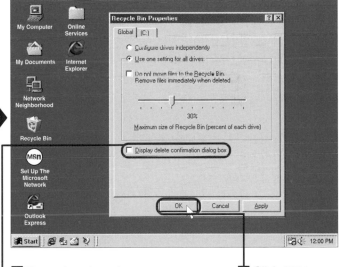

■4 To change the size of the Recycle Bin, drag the slider (▯) to a new location.

Note: This option is not available if you selected "Do not move files to the Recycle Bin" in step 3.

■ This area displays the maximum percentage of hard drive space the Recycle Bin will use to store deleted files.

■5 If you do not want a warning message to appear when you delete files, click this option (☑ changes to ☐).

Note: This option is not available if you selected "Do not move files to the Recycle Bin" in step 3.

■6 Click **OK** to confirm all of your changes.

ADD DESTINATIONS TO THE SEND TO MENU

You can use the Send To menu to quickly send files and folders to new locations. You can add new destinations to the Send To menu.

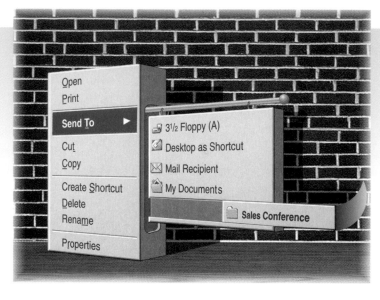

You can add items such as folders, programs and devices to the Send To menu.

ADD DESTINATIONS TO THE SEND TO MENU

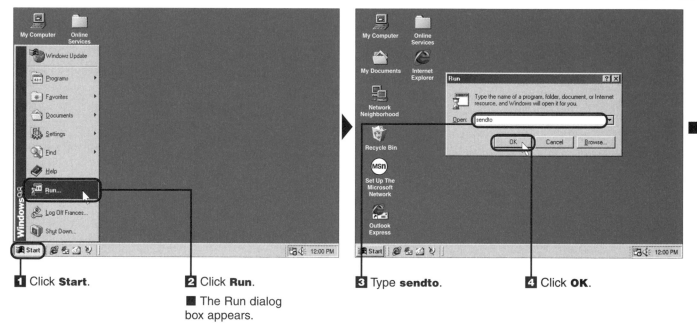

1 Click **Start**.

2 Click **Run**.

■ The Run dialog box appears.

3 Type **sendto**.

4 Click **OK**.

**What items already appear
on the Send To menu?**

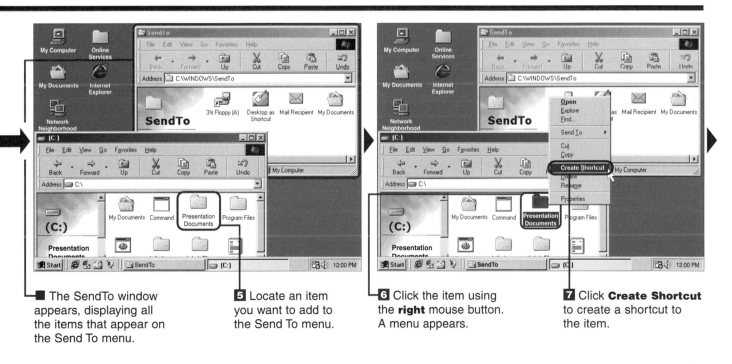

3¹/₂ Floppy (A)
Sends item to
a floppy disk.

Desktop as Shortcut
Creates a shortcut
to the item on the
desktop.

Mail Recipient
Opens a window
that allows you to
send a file in an
e-mail message.

My Documents
Sends item to the
My Documents
folder.

■ The SendTo window
appears, displaying all
the items that appear on
the Send To menu.

5 Locate an item
you want to add to
the Send To menu.

6 Click the item using
the **right** mouse button.
A menu appears.

7 Click **Create Shortcut**
to create a shortcut to
the item.

CONTINUED

Every item you add to the SendTo window will appear on the Send To menu.

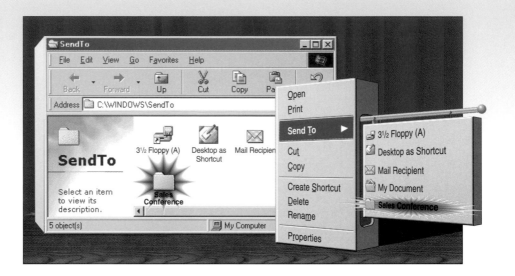

■ ADD DESTINATIONS TO THE SEND TO MENU (CONTINUED)

■ A shortcut to the item appears.

8 Position the mouse ⌖ over the shortcut.

9 Drag the shortcut to the SendTo window.

■ The shortcut appears in the SendTo window.

10 To close the SendTo window, click ☒.

? When I send a file to a folder, will Windows move or copy the file?

If the file and folder are located on the same drive, Windows moves the file.

If the file and folder are located on different drives, Windows copies the file.

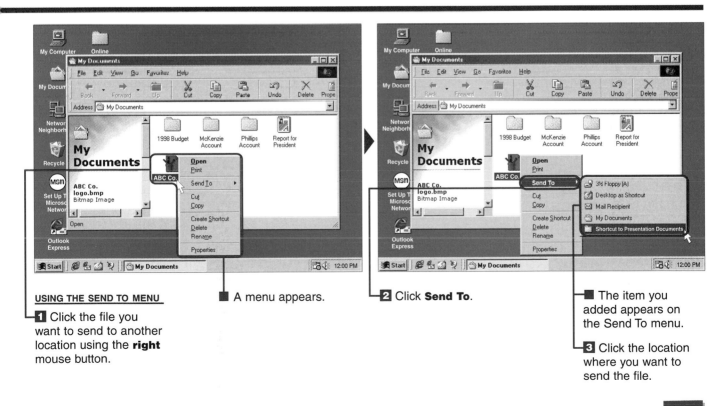

USING THE SEND TO MENU

1 Click the file you want to send to another location using the **right** mouse button.

■ A menu appears.

2 Click **Send To**.

■ The item you added appears on the Send To menu.

3 Click the location where you want to send the file.

VIEW FONTS ON YOUR COMPUTER

You can view the fonts on your computer before using the fonts in your documents.

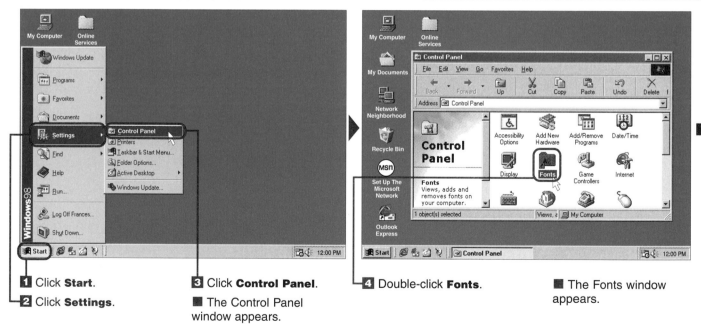

1 Click **Start**.

2 Click **Settings**.

3 Click **Control Panel**.

■ The Control Panel window appears.

4 Double-click **Fonts**.

■ The Fonts window appears.

88

? What types of fonts are available on my computer?

TrueType Fonts

Most of the fonts included with Windows are TrueType fonts. A TrueType font will print exactly as it appears on your screen.

System Fonts

Windows uses system fonts to display text in menus and dialog boxes.

Printer Fonts

Most printers include built-in fonts which are stored in the printer's memory. A printer font may not print as it appears on your screen. Printer fonts do not appear in the Fonts window.

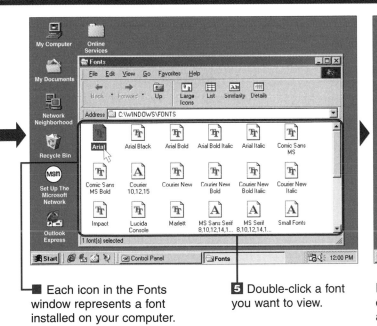

■ Each icon in the Fonts window represents a font installed on your computer.

5 Double-click a font you want to view.

■ A window appears, displaying information about the font you selected and samples of the font in various sizes.

6 When you finish reviewing the information, click **Done** to close the window.

ADD FONTS TO YOUR COMPUTER

You can add fonts to your computer to give you more choices when creating documents.

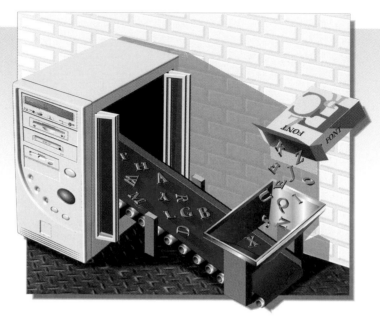

■ ADD FONTS TO YOUR COMPUTER

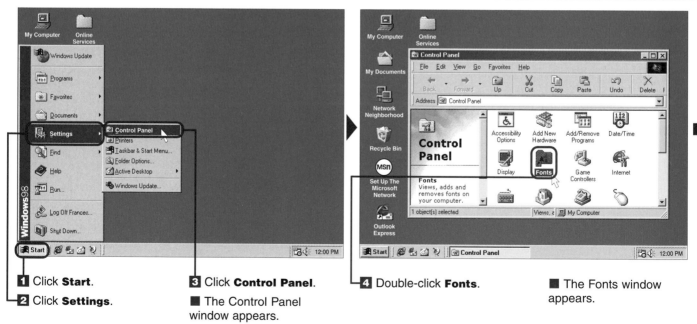

1 Click **Start**.

2 Click **Settings**.

3 Click **Control Panel**.

■ The Control Panel window appears.

4 Double-click **Fonts**.

■ The Fonts window appears.

Where can I get fonts?

You can purchase fonts wherever computer software is sold. You can also find fonts on the Internet. Fonts are available at the following Web sites:

www.fontage.com

www.fontface.com

www.tyworld.com

Some fonts on the Internet are compressed. You can use a program, such as WinZip, to decompress the fonts so you can add them to your computer. WinZip is available on the Web at www.winzip.com.

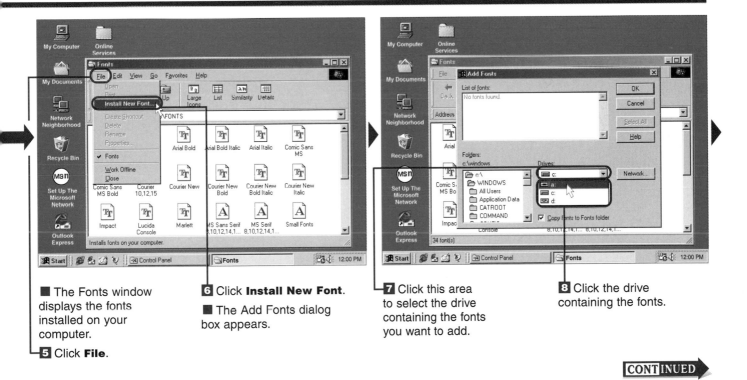

■ The Fonts window displays the fonts installed on your computer.

5 Click **File**.

6 Click **Install New Font**.

■ The Add Fonts dialog box appears.

7 Click this area to select the drive containing the fonts you want to add.

8 Click the drive containing the fonts.

CONTINUED

ADD FONTS TO YOUR COMPUTER

When you add fonts to
your computer, you will
be able to use the fonts
in all of your programs.

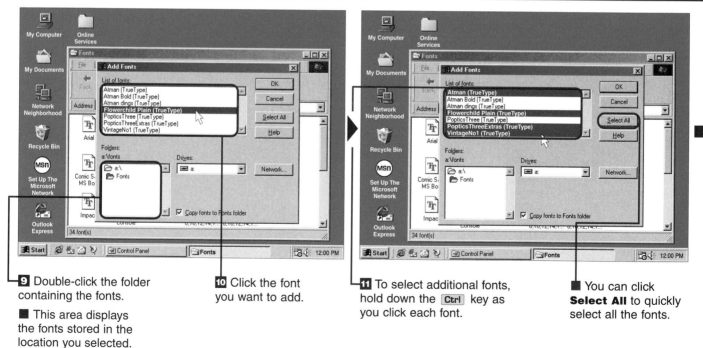

9 Double-click the folder
containing the fonts.

■ This area displays
the fonts stored in the
location you selected.

10 Click the font
you want to add.

11 To select additional fonts,
hold down the `Ctrl` key as
you click each font.

■ You can click
Select All to quickly
select all the fonts.

92

How do I delete a font I added?

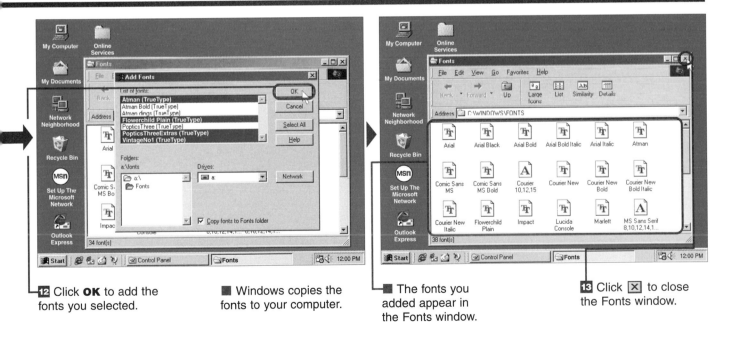

1 In the Fonts window, click the font you want to delete using the **right** mouse button. A menu appears.

2 Click **Delete**.

■ A confirmation dialog box appears. Click **Yes** to permanently delete the font.

12 Click **OK** to add the fonts you selected.

■ Windows copies the fonts to your computer.

■ The fonts you added appear in the Fonts window.

13 Click ⊠ to close the Fonts window.

CHANGE POWER MANAGEMENT SETTINGS

Windows can reduce the power used by your computer.

Power management is useful for reducing the power used by your desktop computer or increasing the battery life of a portable computer. Some computers do not support power management features.

CHANGE POWER MANAGEMENT SETTINGS

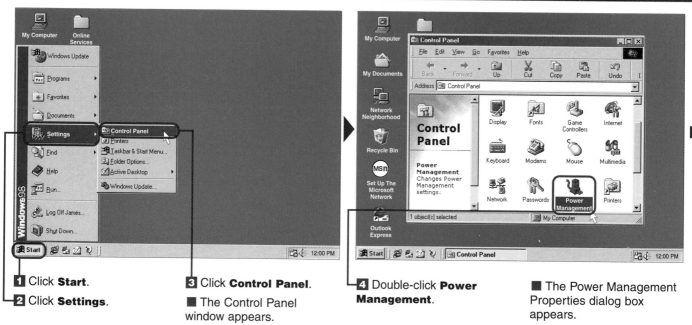

1 Click **Start**.

2 Click **Settings**.

3 Click **Control Panel**.

■ The Control Panel window appears.

4 Double-click **Power Management**.

■ The Power Management Properties dialog box appears.

?

How does Windows conserve power?

Windows can conserve power by placing your computer on standby and by turning off your monitor and hard disks when you do not use the computer for a certain period of time. You can move your mouse or press a key on your keyboard to resume working on your computer.

5 Click this area to list the available power schemes.

6 Click the power scheme that best describes the way you use your computer.

■ This area displays the amount of time your computer must be inactive before the computer goes on standby.

Note: This option may not be available.

■ This area displays the amount of time the computer must be inactive before your monitor and hard disks turn off.

7 Click **OK** to confirm your change.

USING MAGNIFIER

If you have difficulty reading the information displayed on the screen, you can use Magnifier to show an enlarged area of the screen.

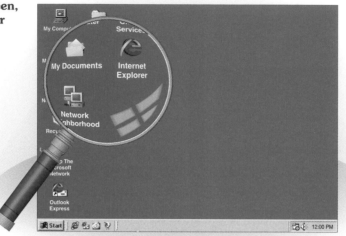

If the Accessibility menu is not available on the Start menu, you need to add the Accessibility Tools component from the Accessibility category. To add Windows components, see page 118. Adding the Accessibility Tools component will install Magnifier.

USING MAGNIFIER

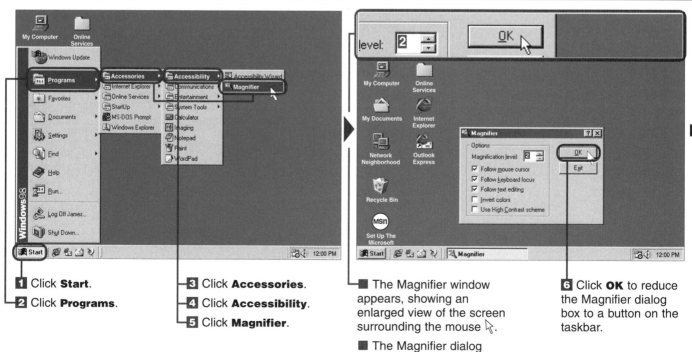

1 Click **Start**.

2 Click **Programs**.

3 Click **Accessories**.

4 Click **Accessibility**.

5 Click **Magnifier**.

■ The Magnifier window appears, showing an enlarged view of the screen surrounding the mouse.

■ The Magnifier dialog box also appears.

6 Click **OK** to reduce the Magnifier dialog box to a button on the taskbar.

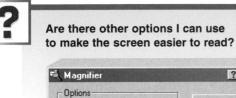

**Are there other options I can use
to make the screen easier to read?**

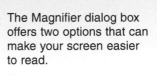

The Magnifier dialog box
offers two options that can
make your screen easier
to read.

■ Invert colors

■ High Contrast scheme

■ Click an option to turn the
option on (☑) or off (☐).

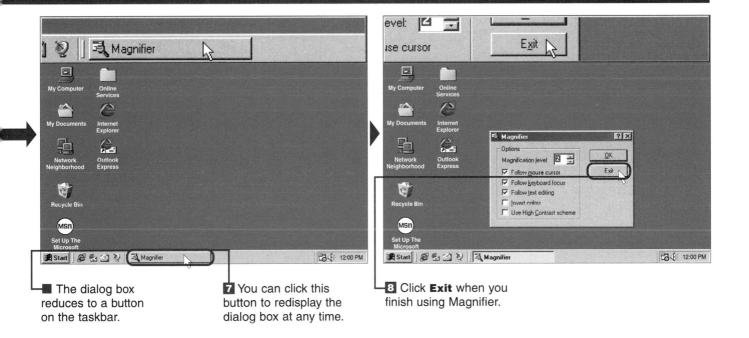

■ The dialog box
reduces to a button
on the taskbar.

7 You can click this
button to redisplay the
dialog box at any time.

8 Click **Exit** when you
finish using Magnifier.

USING THE ACCESSIBILITY WIZARD

The Accessibility Wizard can help you set up Windows to meet your vision, hearing and mobility needs.

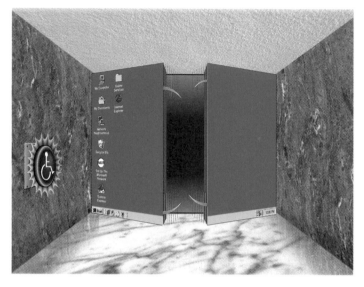

Although the accessibility options are designed for people with special needs, there are some options which may be of interest to all users.

If the Accessibility menu is not available on the Start menu, you need to add the Accessibility Tools component from the Accessibility category. To add Windows components, see page 118.

■ USING THE ACCESSIBILITY WIZARD ■

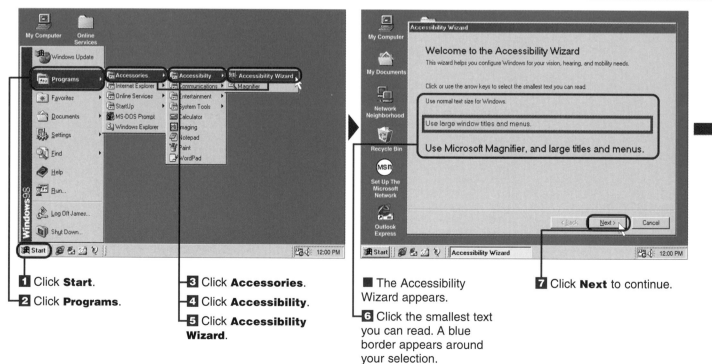

1 Click **Start**.

2 Click **Programs**.

3 Click **Accessories**.

4 Click **Accessibility**.

5 Click **Accessibility Wizard**.

■ The Accessibility Wizard appears.

6 Click the smallest text you can read. A blue border appears around your selection.

7 Click **Next** to continue.

? **What changes can the Wizard make to my computer?**

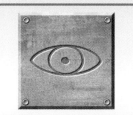

Vision

Make information easier to view by changing the size of items and the colors displayed on the screen.

Hearing

Display visual warnings when events occur and display messages for sounds.

Mobility

Make the keyboard and mouse easier to use.

8 This option changes the font size for window title bars, menus and other features. Click the option to turn the option on (☑) or off (☐).

9 This option displays an enlarged area of your screen in a separate window. Click the option to turn the option on (☑) or off (☐).

10 Click **Next** to continue.

11 Click each statement that applies to you (☐ changes to ☑).

12 Click **Next** to continue.

■ The options available in the next screens depend on the statement(s) you selected in step **11**.

CONTINUED ▶

USING THE ACCESSIBILITY WIZARD

The Accessibility Wizard helps you choose options that will benefit you the most when using Windows.

USING THE ACCESSIBILITY WIZARD (CONTINUED)

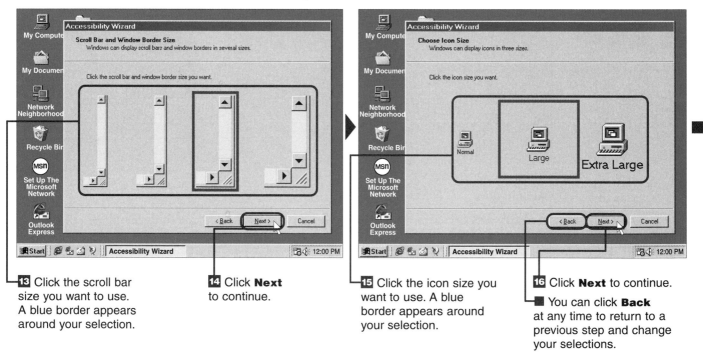

13 Click the scroll bar size you want to use. A blue border appears around your selection.

14 Click **Next** to continue.

15 Click the icon size you want to use. A blue border appears around your selection.

16 Click **Next** to continue.

■ You can click **Back** at any time to return to a previous step and change your selections.

Where can I find more information to assist users with special needs?

The Microsoft Accessibility and Disabilities Web page contains useful information to assist users with their vision, hearing and mobility needs. You can find this Web page at www.microsoft.com/enable

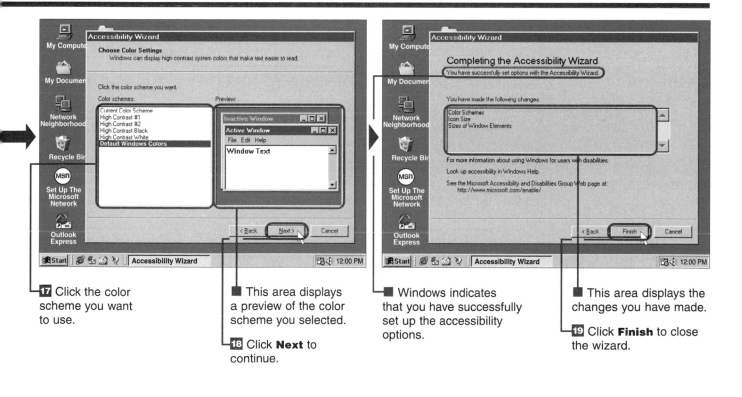

■17 Click the color scheme you want to use.

■ This area displays a preview of the color scheme you selected.

■18 Click **Next** to continue.

■ Windows indicates that you have successfully set up the accessibility options.

■ This area displays the changes you have made.

■19 Click **Finish** to close the wizard.

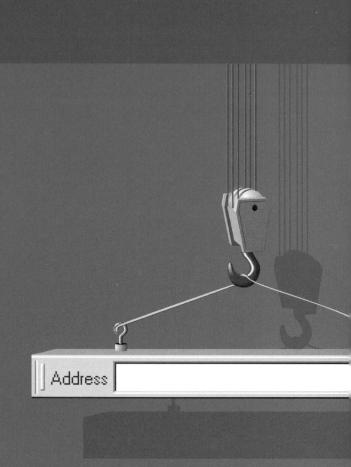

Services

My Documents

**Internet
Explorer**

**Network
Neighborhood**

Recycle Bin

MSN

**Set Up The
Microsoft
Network**

**Outlook
Express**

Start

Address

Dia

CHAPTER 5

Customize Start Menu and Taskbar

This chapter shows you how to work with items on the Start menu and change the taskbar to suit your needs.

Add an Item to the Start Menu 104

Rearrange Items on the Start Menu 105

Remove an Item from the
    Start Menu 106

Add a Folder to the Start Menu 108

Add Item to Quick Launch Toolbar 112

Add a Toolbar to the Taskbar............114

ADD AN ITEM TO THE START MENU

You can add your favorite files, folders and programs to the Start menu for quick access.

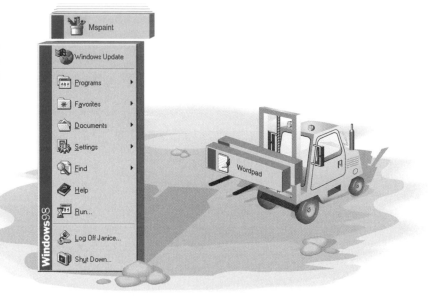

ADD AN ITEM TO THE START MENU

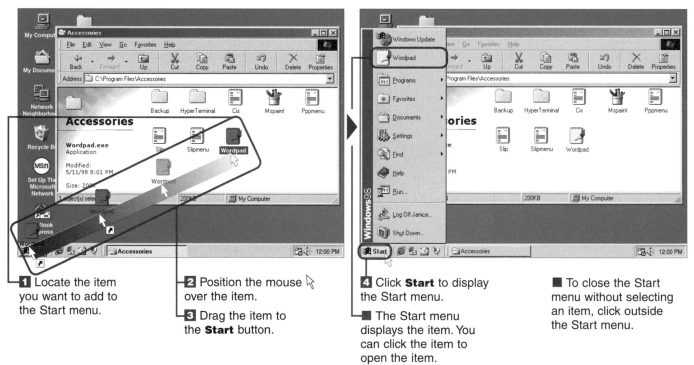

1 Locate the item you want to add to the Start menu.

2 Position the mouse over the item.

3 Drag the item to the **Start** button.

4 Click **Start** to display the Start menu.

■ The Start menu displays the item. You can click the item to open the item.

■ To close the Start menu without selecting an item, click outside the Start menu.

REARRANGE ITEMS ON THE START MENU

You can rearrange the items on the Start menu.

You cannot rearrange some items on the Start menu, such as Help or Run.

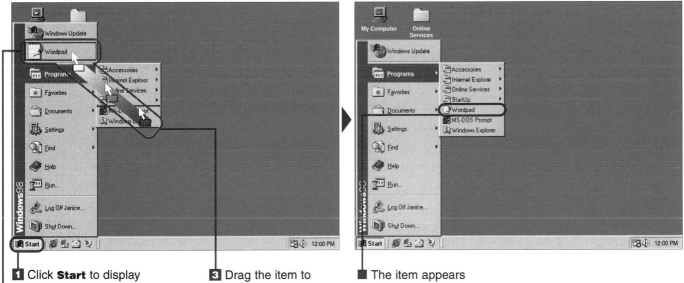

REARRANGE ITEMS ON THE START MENU

1 Click **Start** to display the Start menu.

2 Position the mouse over the item you want to move.

3 Drag the item to a new location.

Note: A black line shows you where the item will appear.

■ The item appears in the new location.

REMOVE AN ITEM FROM THE START MENU

You can remove an item you no longer want to appear on the Start menu.

You may want to remove a file or program you added to the Start menu that you no longer use.

REMOVE AN ITEM FROM THE START MENU

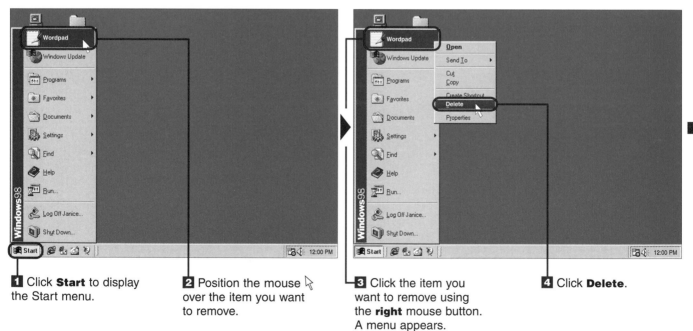

1 Click **Start** to display the Start menu.

2 Position the mouse ⬚ over the item you want to remove.

3 Click the item you want to remove using the **right** mouse button. A menu appears.

4 Click **Delete**.

Does removing an item from the Start menu delete the item from my computer?

Removing an item from the Start menu does not delete the file or program from your computer.

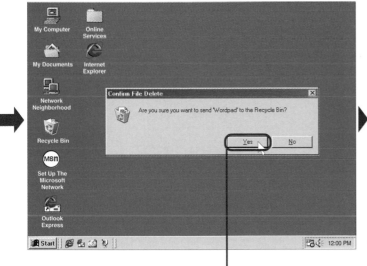

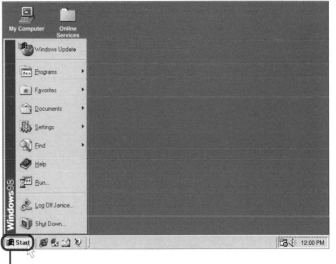

■ A dialog box appears, confirming the deletion.

5 Click **Yes** to remove the item from the Start menu.

6 To confirm that Windows removed the item, click **Start**.

■ The item no longer appears on the Start menu.

7 To close the Start menu without selecting an item, click outside the menu area.

ADD A FOLDER TO THE START MENU

You can add folders to better organize the items on the Start menu.

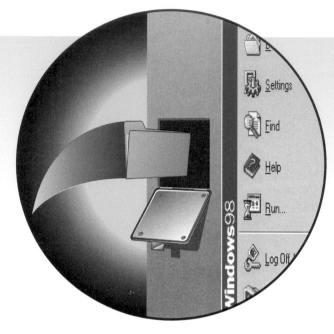

ADD A FOLDER TO THE START MENU

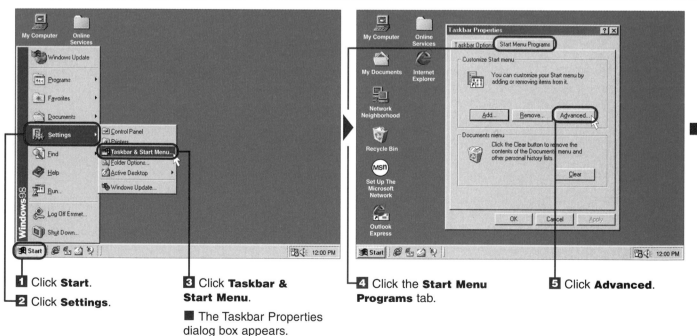

1 Click **Start**.

2 Click **Settings**.

3 Click **Taskbar & Start Menu**.

■ The Taskbar Properties dialog box appears.

4 Click the **Start Menu Programs** tab.

5 Click **Advanced**.

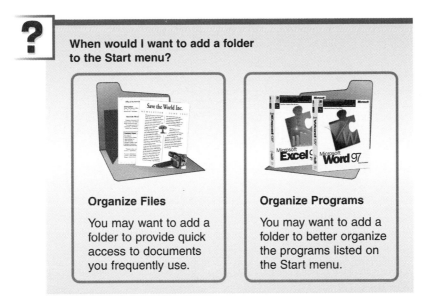

When would I want to add a folder to the Start menu?

Organize Files

You may want to add a folder to provide quick access to documents you frequently use.

Organize Programs

You may want to add a folder to better organize the programs listed on the Start menu.

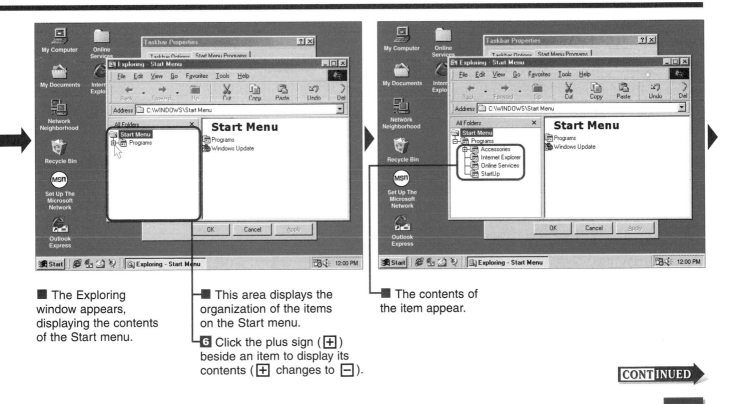

■ The Exploring window appears, displaying the contents of the Start menu.

■ This area displays the organization of the items on the Start menu.

6 Click the plus sign (⊞) beside an item to display its contents (⊞ changes to ⊟).

■ The contents of the item appear.

CONTINUED

ADD A FOLDER TO THE START MENU

After you add a folder, you can immediately see the folder on the Start menu.

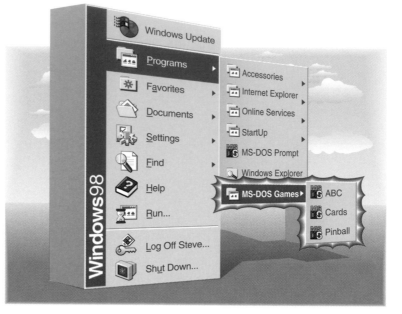

ADD A FOLDER TO THE START MENU (CONTINUED)

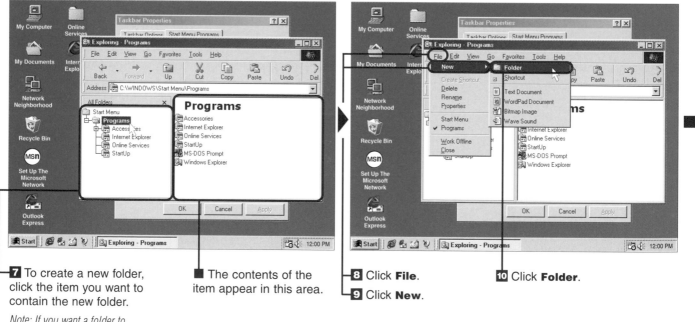

7 To create a new folder, click the item you want to contain the new folder.

*Note: If you want a folder to appear on the main Start menu, click **Start Menu**.*

■ The contents of the item appear in this area.

8 Click **File**.

9 Click **New**.

10 Click **Folder**.

110

After I add a folder to the Start menu, how do I add files and programs to the folder?

Before you can add an item to a folder, you first need to add the item to the Start menu as shown on page 104. You then need to move the item to the folder as shown on page 105.

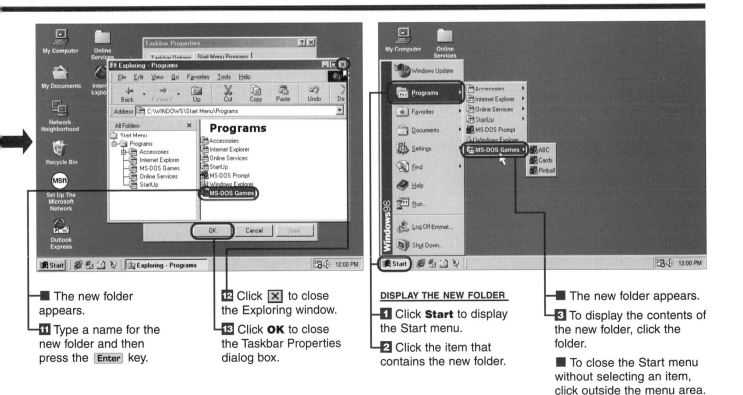

■ The new folder appears.

🗓 Type a name for the new folder and then press the Enter key.

🗓 Click ☒ to close the Exploring window.

🗓 Click **OK** to close the Taskbar Properties dialog box.

DISPLAY THE NEW FOLDER

🗓 Click **Start** to display the Start menu.

🗓 Click the item that contains the new folder.

■ The new folder appears.

🗓 To display the contents of the new folder, click the folder.

■ To close the Start menu without selecting an item, click outside the menu area.

ADD ITEM TO QUICK LAUNCH TOOLBAR

You can add a document, folder or program you frequently use to the Quick Launch toolbar.

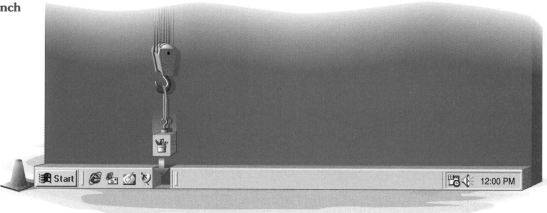

ADD ITEM TO QUICK LAUNCH TOOLBAR

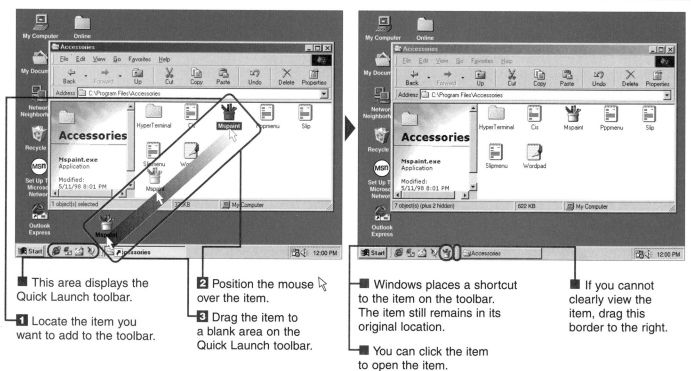

■ This area displays the Quick Launch toolbar.

1 Locate the item you want to add to the toolbar.

2 Position the mouse ⌖ over the item.

3 Drag the item to a blank area on the Quick Launch toolbar.

■ Windows places a shortcut to the item on the toolbar. The item still remains in its original location.

■ You can click the item to open the item.

■ If you cannot clearly view the item, drag this border to the right.

**Which items initially appear
on the Quick Launch toolbar?**

The Quick Launch
toolbar initially
displays 4 items.

Starts Internet
Explorer so you
can browse the
Web.

Starts Outlook
Express so you
can exchange
e-mail messages.

Minimizes all
windows so you
can clearly view
the desktop.

Allows you to
view channels
which are specially
designed Web sites
that Windows can
automatically deliver
to your computer.

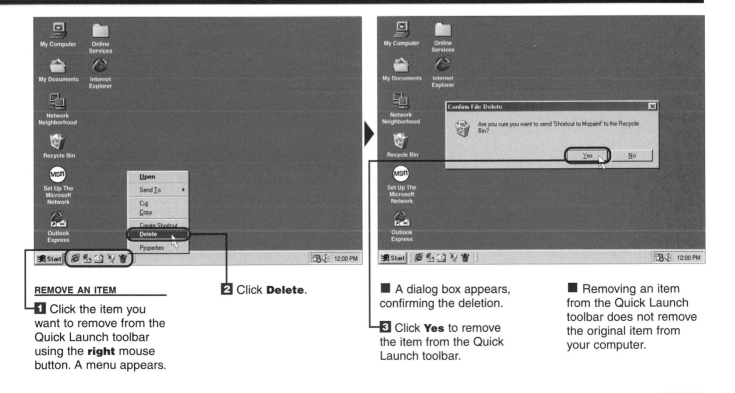

REMOVE AN ITEM

■ Click the item you
want to remove from the
Quick Launch toolbar
using the **right** mouse
button. A menu appears.

■ Click **Delete**.

■ A dialog box appears,
confirming the deletion.

■ Click **Yes** to remove
the item from the Quick
Launch toolbar.

■ Removing an item
from the Quick Launch
toolbar does not remove
the original item from
your computer.

ADD A TOOLBAR TO THE TASKBAR

Windows includes several ready-made toolbars that you can add to the taskbar. Toolbars provide instant access to commands and features.

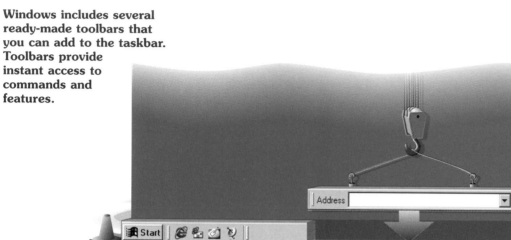

ADD A TOOLBAR TO THE TASKBAR

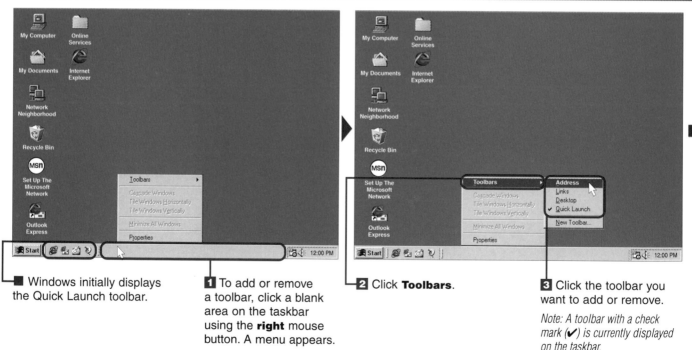

■ Windows initially displays the Quick Launch toolbar.

1 To add or remove a toolbar, click a blank area on the taskbar using the **right** mouse button. A menu appears.

2 Click **Toolbars**.

3 Click the toolbar you want to add or remove.

Note: A toolbar with a check mark (✔) is currently displayed on the taskbar.

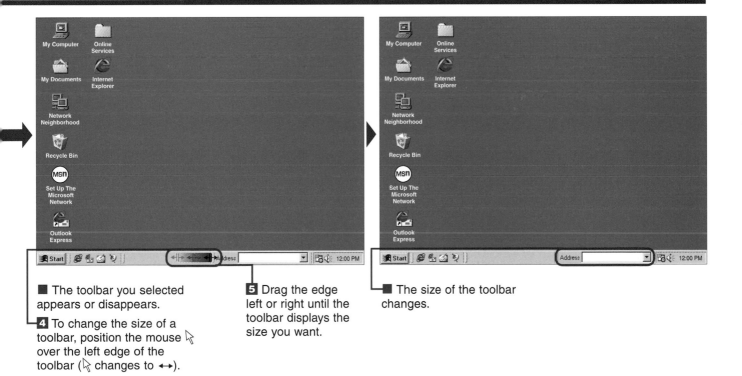

?

Which toolbars can I display on the taskbar?

Address

Provides an area where you can type a Web page address to instantly display the Web page.

Links

Provides quick access to useful Web pages.

Desktop

Provides quick access to all the items on your desktop.

Quick Launch

Provides quick access to Internet Explorer, Outlook Express, your desktop and channels.

■ The toolbar you selected appears or disappears.

4 To change the size of a toolbar, position the mouse ⬚ over the left edge of the toolbar (⬚ changes to ↔).

5 Drag the edge left or right until the toolbar displays the size you want.

■ The size of the toolbar changes.

CHAPTER 6

Work With Software and Hardware

Windows 98 includes features you can use to work with the software and hardware on your computer. In this chapter you will learn how to add Windows components, install programs and change your hardware settings.

Add Windows Components..............118

Install a Program 122

Remove a Program 125

Change Keyboard Settings 126

Install a Joystick 130

Change Printer Options...................134

Change Modem Dialing Properties....138

Change Modem Properties 142

Using Multiple Monitors 144

Remove Hardware 146

You can add Windows
components to your
computer that were
not added when
you first set up
Windows.

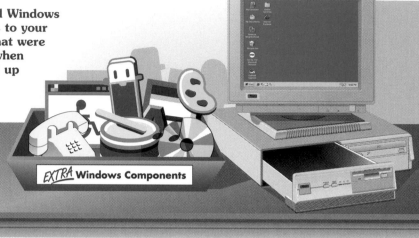

EXTRA Windows Components

When setting up Windows,
most people do not install
all the components that
come with the program.
This prevents unneeded
components from taking
up storage space on
the computer.

ADD WINDOWS COMPONENTS

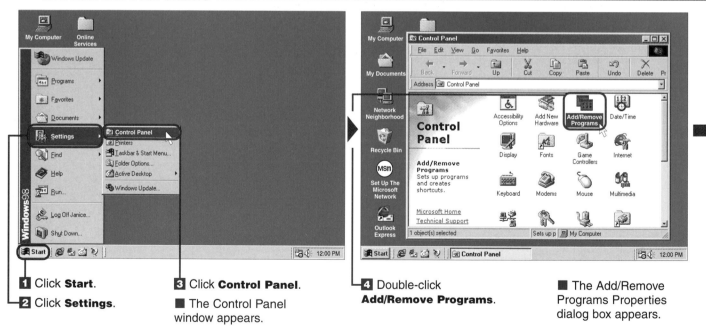

1 Click **Start**.

2 Click **Settings**.

3 Click **Control Panel**.

■ The Control Panel
window appears.

4 Double-click
Add/Remove Programs.

■ The Add/Remove
Programs Properties
dialog box appears.

? **Which Windows components can I add to my computer?**

Windows components you can add to your computer include:

Accessibility Tools

Sets up Windows to meet vision, hearing and mobility needs.

Backup

Copies important information from your computer to floppy disks or a tape drive. This will protect the information from computer failure or theft.

Web TV

Allows you to watch TV on your computer.

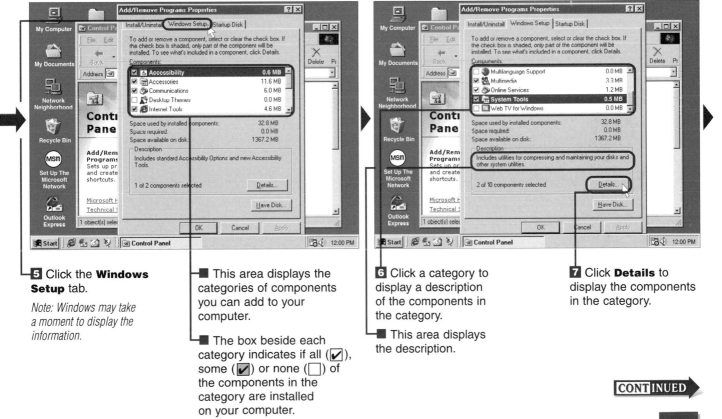

5 Click the **Windows Setup** tab.

Note: Windows may take a moment to display the information.

■ This area displays the categories of components you can add to your computer.

■ The box beside each category indicates if all (☑), some (☑) or none (☐) of the components in the category are installed on your computer.

6 Click a category to display a description of the components in the category.

■ This area displays the description.

7 Click **Details** to display the components in the category.

CONTINUED

ADD WINDOWS COMPONENTS

When adding Windows components, you will be asked to insert the CD-ROM disc you used to install Windows.

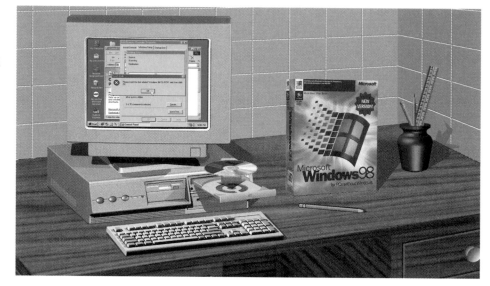

ADD WINDOWS COMPONENTS (CONTINUED)

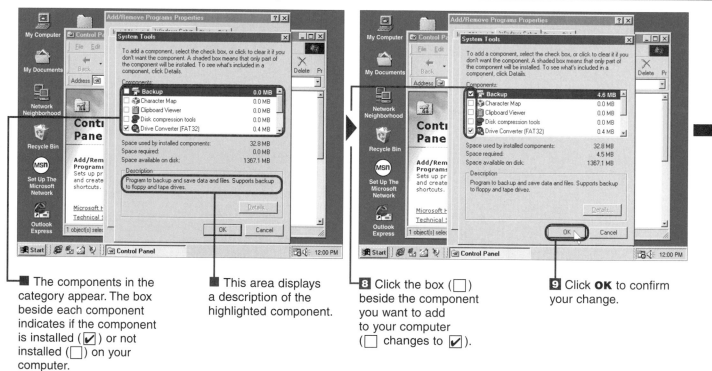

■ The components in the category appear. The box beside each component indicates if the component is installed (✔) or not installed (☐) on your computer.

■ This area displays a description of the highlighted component.

8 Click the box (☐) beside the component you want to add to your computer (☐ changes to ✔).

9 Click **OK** to confirm your change.

?

How do I remove a Windows component I do not use?

You can remove a Windows component you do not use to free up space on your computer. To remove a Windows component, perform steps **1** to **10** starting on page 118. When you select a Windows component you want to remove, ☑ changes to ☐ in step **8**.

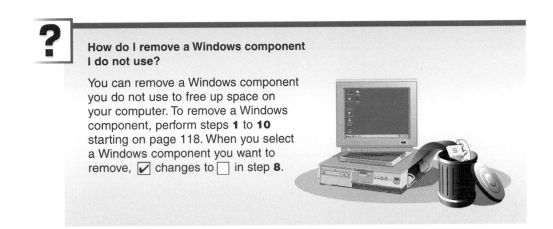

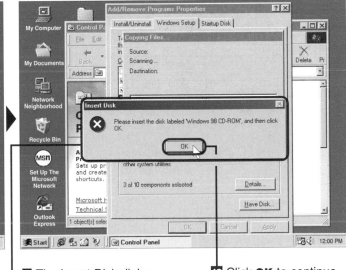

10 Click **OK** to close the Add/Remove Programs Properties dialog box.

■ The Insert Disk dialog box appears, asking you to insert the Windows 98 CD-ROM disc.

11 Insert the CD-ROM disc into the drive.

12 Click **OK** to continue.

■ Windows copies the necessary files to your computer.

Note: Windows may ask you to restart your computer.

INSTALL A PROGRAM

You can add a new program to your computer. Programs come on a CD-ROM disc or floppy disks.

After you install a program, make sure you keep the program's CD-ROM disc or floppy disks in a safe place. If your computer fails or you accidentally erase the program files, you may need to install the program again.

INSTALL A PROGRAM

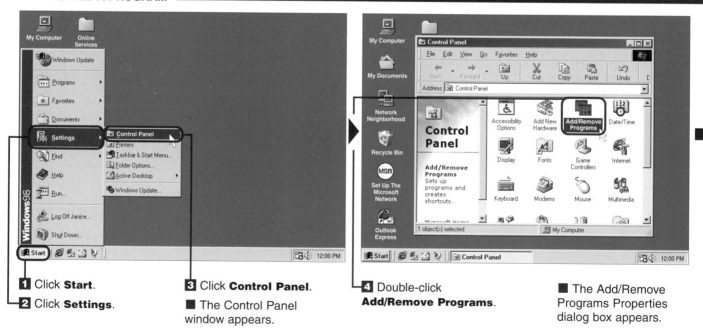

1 Click **Start**.

2 Click **Settings**.

3 Click **Control Panel**.

■ The Control Panel window appears.

4 Double-click **Add/Remove Programs**.

■ The Add/Remove Programs Properties dialog box appears.

Why did an installation program start automatically?

Most Windows programs available on a CD-ROM disc will automatically start an installation program when you insert the CD-ROM disc into the drive. Follow the instructions on your screen to install the program.

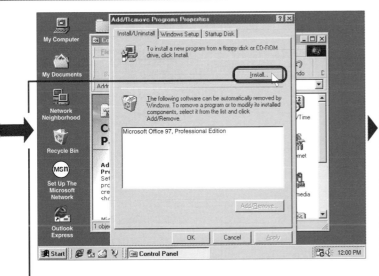

5 Click **Install** to install a new program.

■ The Install Program From Floppy Disk or CD-ROM wizard appears.

6 Insert the program's first installation floppy disk or CD-ROM disc into a drive.

7 Click **Next** to continue.

CONTINUED

123

INSTALL A PROGRAM

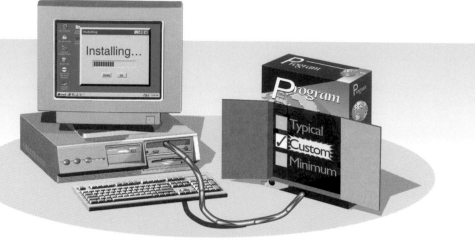

There are three common ways to install a program.

Typical

Sets up the program with the most common components.

Custom

Lets you customize the program to suit your specific needs.

Minimum

Sets up the minimum amount of the program needed. This is ideal for computers with limited disk space.

■ INSTALL A PROGRAM (CONTINUED) ■

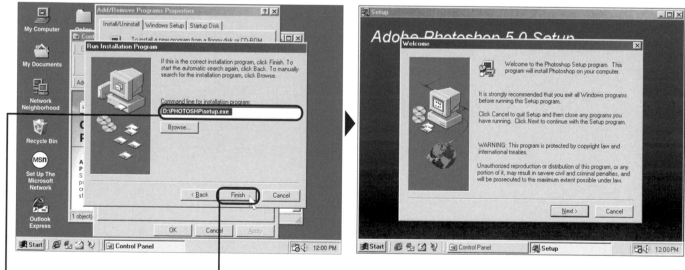

■ Windows locates the file needed to install the program.

8 Click **Finish** to install the program.

9 Follow the instructions on your screen. Every program will ask you a different set of questions.

You can remove a program from your computer that you no longer use. Removing a program will free up space on your hard drive.

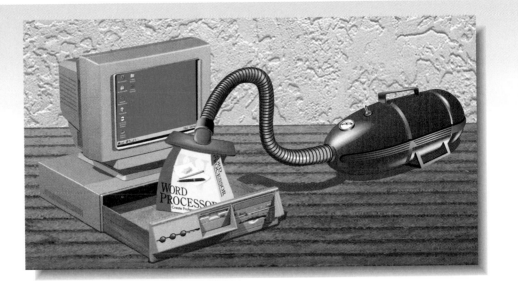

REMOVE A PROGRAM

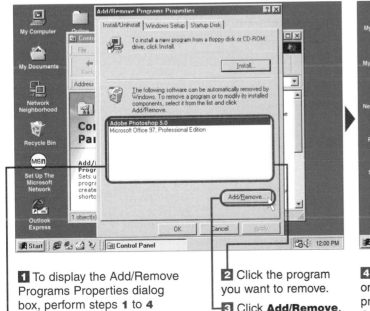

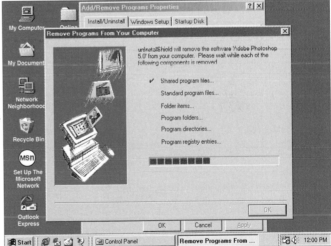

1 To display the Add/Remove Programs Properties dialog box, perform steps **1** to **4** on page 122.

■ This area lists the programs Windows can automatically remove.

2 Click the program you want to remove.

3 Click **Add/Remove**.

4 Follow the instructions on your screen. Every program will take you through different steps to remove the program.

CHANGE KEYBOARD SETTINGS

You can change the
way your keyboard
works with your
computer.

CHANGE KEYBOARD SETTINGS

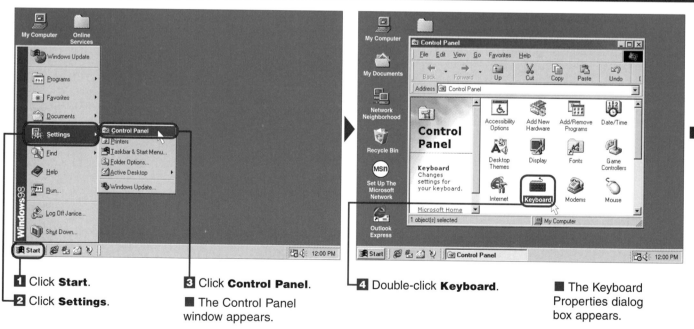

1 Click **Start**.

2 Click **Settings**.

3 Click **Control Panel**.

■ The Control Panel
window appears.

4 Double-click **Keyboard**.

■ The Keyboard
Properties dialog
box appears.

When would I change the keyboard settings?

You may want to change the keyboard settings if you often repeat characters in a document to underline, separate or emphasize text. To quickly enter repeated characters, adjust your settings to shorten the repeat delay and increase the repeat rate.

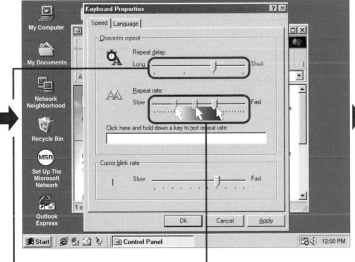

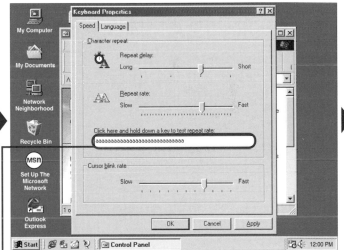

5 To change how long you must hold down a key before a character starts repeating, drag this slider (▯) to a new position.

6 To change how quickly characters repeat when you hold down a key, drag this slider (▯) to a new position.

7 To test the repeat delay or repeat rate, click this area. Then hold down a key on your keyboard.

CONTINUED

CHANGE KEYBOARD SETTINGS

You can change how quickly the cursor blinks on your screen.

The cursor indicates where the text you type will appear. Make sure the cursor blinks fast enough so it is easy to find, but slow enough so it is not distracting.

CHANGE KEYBOARD SETTINGS (CONTINUED)

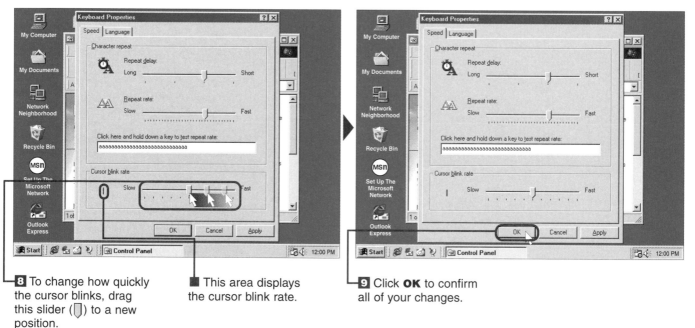

■8 To change how quickly the cursor blinks, drag this slider ( ) to a new position.

■ This area displays the cursor blink rate.

■9 Click **OK** to confirm all of your changes.

TIPS FOR USING THE KEYBOARD

Prevent Back Strain

You can avoid back strain by using a chair that provides proper back support and making sure your feet are always flat on the floor.

Prevent Wrist Strain

You can avoid wrist strain by keeping your elbows level with the keyboard and keeping your wrists straight and higher than your fingers. You can use a wrist rest to elevate your wrists and ensure they remain straight at all times.

A keyboard shelf can help keep your elbows level with the keyboard.

Prevent Neck Strain

You can avoid neck strain by placing the monitor where you can comfortably view the screen. The top edge of the monitor should be at eye level or slightly lower.

Prevent Eye Strain

You can avoid eye strain by minimizing the amount of light that reflects off the computer screen. You should also exercise the muscles in your eyes a few times an hour. To exercise your eyes, try to alternate between focusing on a distant object and focusing on a close object.

INSTALL A JOYSTICK

You can install a joystick
to control the movement
of objects in computer
games.

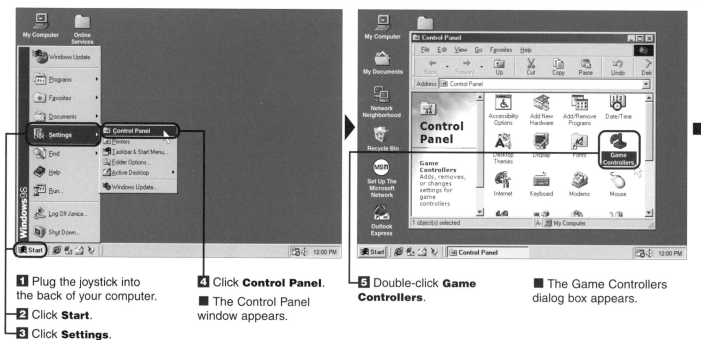

INSTALL A JOYSTICK

1 Plug the joystick into
the back of your computer.

2 Click **Start**.

3 Click **Settings**.

4 Click **Control Panel**.

■ The Control Panel
window appears.

5 Double-click **Game
Controllers**.

■ The Game Controllers
dialog box appears.

What devices can I install to control movement in my games?

Many games are designed to work with a specific type of device.

Gamepad

Joystick

Flight Yoke

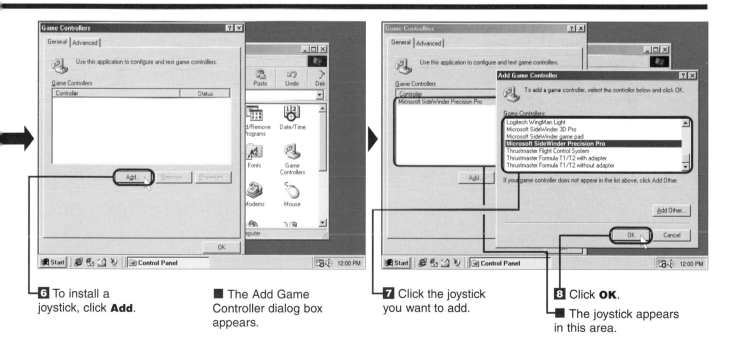

6 To install a joystick, click **Add**.

■ The Add Game Controller dialog box appears.

7 Click the joystick you want to add.

8 Click **OK**.

■ The joystick appears in this area.

INSTALL A JOYSTICK

Before using a joystick, you need to set the range of motion for the joystick.

Setting the range of motion ensures that the computer will respond correctly when you move the joystick.

■ SET JOYSTICK RANGE OF MOTION ■

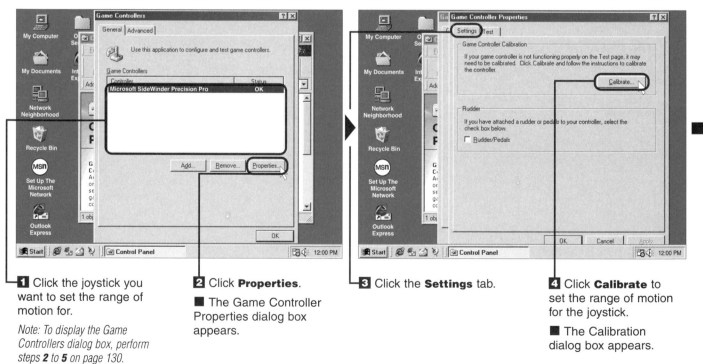

1 Click the joystick you want to set the range of motion for.

Note: To display the Game Controllers dialog box, perform steps 2 to 5 on page 130.

2 Click **Properties**.

■ The Game Controller Properties dialog box appears.

3 Click the **Settings** tab.

4 Click **Calibrate** to set the range of motion for the joystick.

■ The Calibration dialog box appears.

Where can I buy games that I can play?

You can buy games at computer stores and on the Internet. The www.shareware.com Web site offers a large collection of games and other programs.

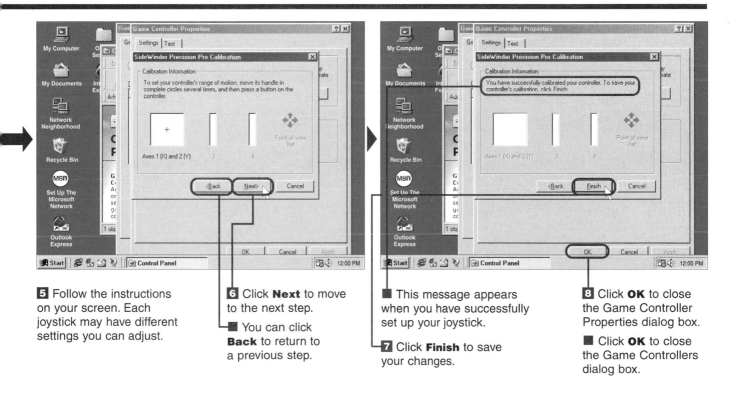

5 Follow the instructions on your screen. Each joystick may have different settings you can adjust.

6 Click **Next** to move to the next step.

■ You can click **Back** to return to a previous step.

■ This message appears when you have successfully set up your joystick.

7 Click **Finish** to save your changes.

8 Click **OK** to close the Game Controller Properties dialog box.

■ Click **OK** to close the Game Controllers dialog box.

CHANGE PRINTER OPTIONS

You can change the way your documents are printed.

The printer you are using determines the printer options you can change.

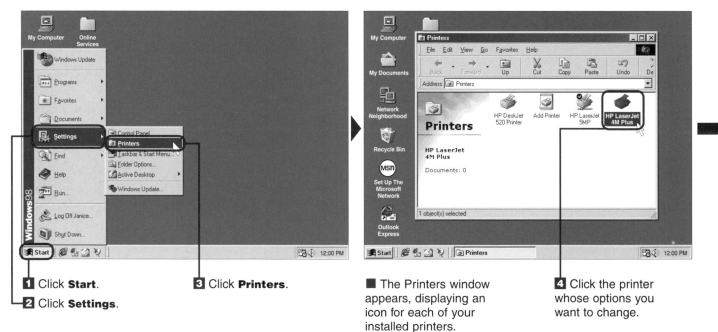

1 Click **Start**.

2 Click **Settings**.

3 Click **Printers**.

■ The Printers window appears, displaying an icon for each of your installed printers.

4 Click the printer whose options you want to change.

When would I use a separator page?

If you print many documents at once or many people use your printer, you can include a separator page between each printed document. A full separator page includes text and graphics. A simple separator page includes only text.

Full Separator Page

Simple Separator Page

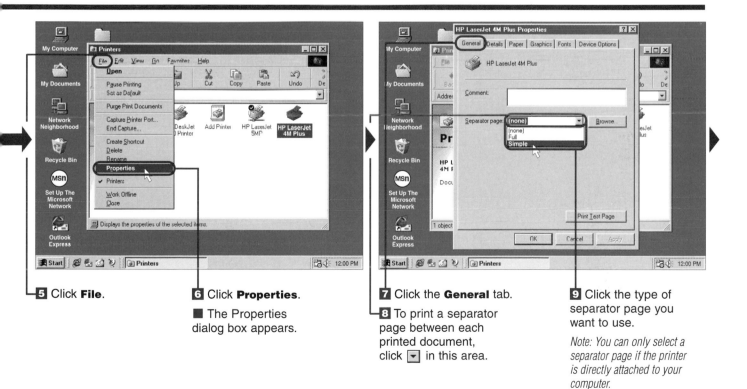

5 Click **File**.

6 Click **Properties**.

■ The Properties dialog box appears.

7 Click the **General** tab.

8 To print a separator page between each printed document, click ▼ in this area.

9 Click the type of separator page you want to use.

Note: You can only select a separator page if the printer is directly attached to your computer.

CONTINUED ▶

CHANGE PRINTER OPTIONS

Changing the printer options will affect all documents that you print.

■ **CHANGE PRINTER OPTIONS** (CONTINUED) ■

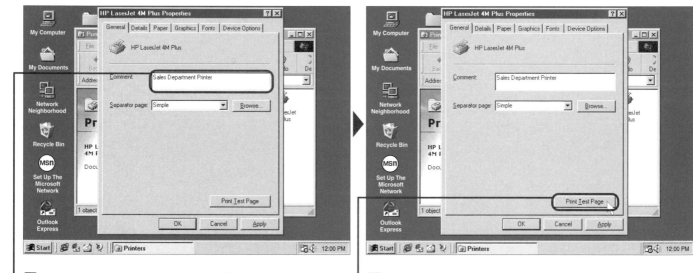

10 To add a comment about the printer, click this area and then type a comment.

Note: Other people on a network will be able to see the comment. A comment can provide useful information, such as the location or capabilities of a printer.

11 To print a test page to make sure your printer is set up correctly, click **Print Test Page**.

■ A dialog box will appear, asking if the test page printed correctly.

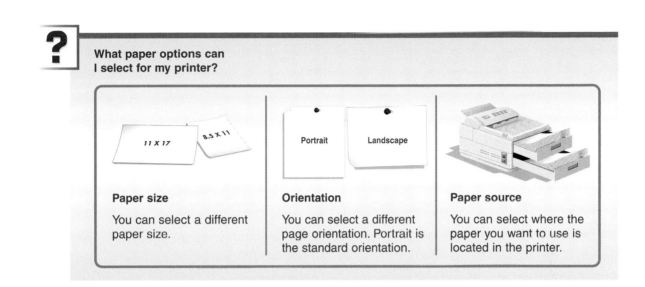

What paper options can I select for my printer?

Paper size

You can select a different paper size.

Orientation

You can select a different page orientation. Portrait is the standard orientation.

Paper source

You can select where the paper you want to use is located in the printer.

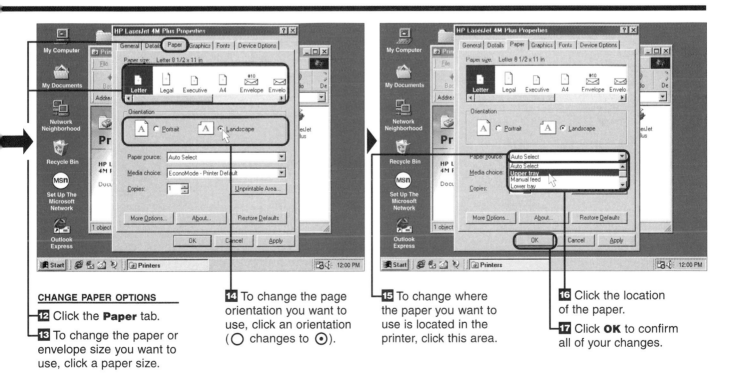

CHANGE PAPER OPTIONS

12 Click the **Paper** tab.

13 To change the paper or envelope size you want to use, click a paper size.

14 To change the page orientation you want to use, click an orientation (○ changes to ◉).

15 To change where the paper you want to use is located in the printer, click this area.

16 Click the location of the paper.

17 Click **OK** to confirm all of your changes.

CHANGE MODEM DIALING PROPERTIES

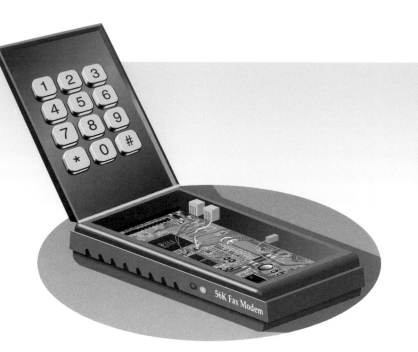

You can change the
dialing properties
for your modem to
determine how your
modem dials phone
numbers.

CHANGE MODEM DIALING PROPERTIES

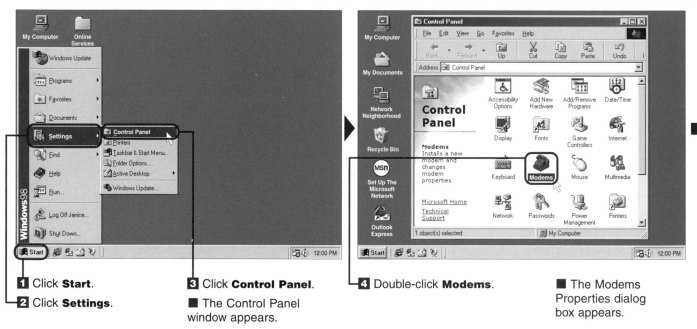

1 Click **Start**.

2 Click **Settings**.

3 Click **Control Panel**.

■ The Control Panel window appears.

4 Double-click **Modems**.

■ The Modems Properties dialog box appears.

138

What can I use my modem to access?

Internet

A modem lets you connect to the Internet so you can browse the Web.

Computer at work

When traveling or at home, a modem lets you access information stored on a computer at work. See page 254 for information on connecting to a computer at work.

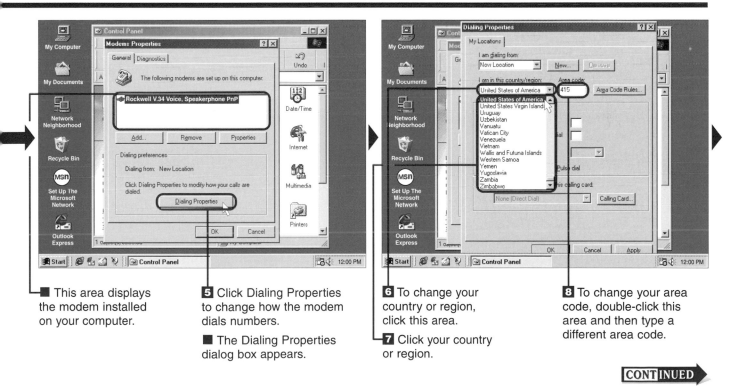

■ This area displays the modem installed on your computer.

5 Click Dialing Properties to change how the modem dials numbers.

■ The Dialing Properties dialog box appears.

6 To change your country or region, click this area.

7 Click your country or region.

8 To change your area code, double-click this area and then type a different area code.

CONTINUED

CHANGE MODEM DIALING PROPERTIES

When changing the modem dialing properties, you can specify the numbers you need to dial to make local and long-distance calls. You can also disable call waiting.

CHANGE MODEM DIALING PROPERTIES (CONTINUED)

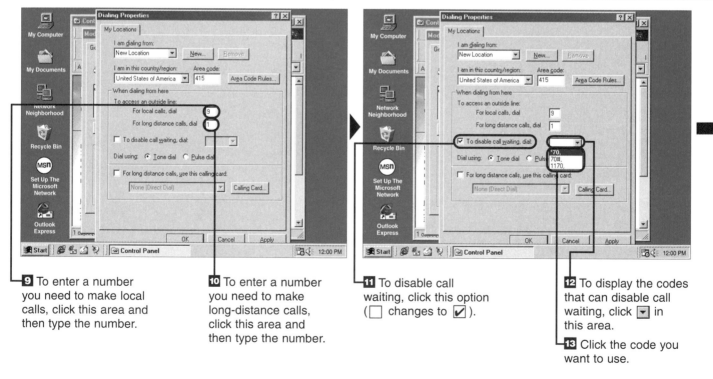

9 To enter a number you need to make local calls, click this area and then type the number.

10 To enter a number you need to make long-distance calls, click this area and then type the number.

11 To disable call waiting, click this option (☐ changes to ☑).

12 To display the codes that can disable call waiting, click ▼ in this area.

13 Click the code you want to use.

?

Why should I disable call waiting?

If your telephone and modem share the same line, make sure you turn off the call waiting feature when using your modem, since this feature could disrupt the modem connection. You should check with your local phone company to determine which code will disable call waiting.

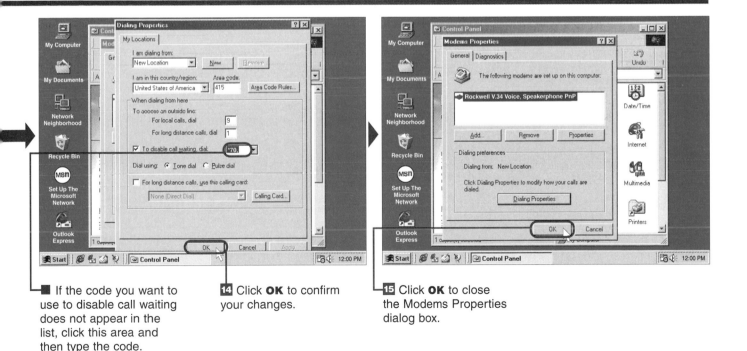

■ If the code you want to use to disable call waiting does not appear in the list, click this area and then type the code.

14 Click **OK** to confirm your changes.

15 Click **OK** to close the Modems Properties dialog box.

CHANGE MODEM PROPERTIES

You can change
the properties for
a modem installed
on your computer.

PROPERTIES

The properties you
can change depend
on the type of modem
you are using.

CHANGE MODEM PROPERTIES

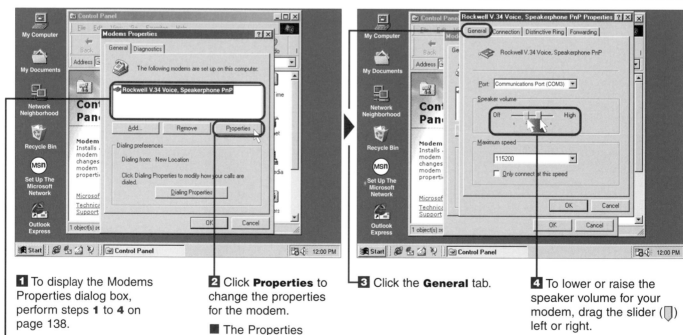

1 To display the Modems
Properties dialog box,
perform steps **1** to **4** on
page 138.

■ This area displays the
modem installed on your
computer.

2 Click **Properties** to
change the properties
for the modem.

■ The Properties
dialog box appears.

3 Click the **General** tab.

4 To lower or raise the
speaker volume for your
modem, drag the slider (▯)
left or right.

**What modem properties should
I consider changing?**

Speaker volume

You can increase the
speaker volume to
clearly hear the modem
dial and connect to
other modems. You may
want to decrease the
volume if you find the
sound distracting.

Disconnect calls if idle

You can have Windows
disconnect calls when
there is no activity for
a period of time. This can
prevent unnecessary
online charges.

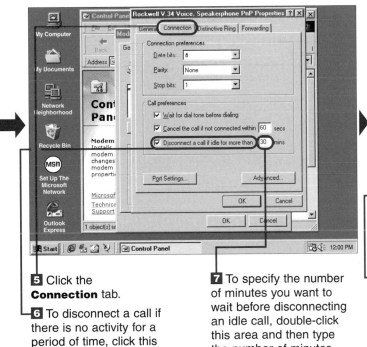

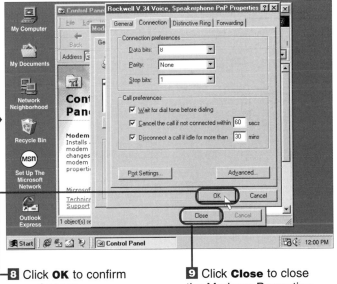

5 Click the
Connection tab.

6 To disconnect a call if
there is no activity for a
period of time, click this
option (☐ changes to ☑).

7 To specify the number
of minutes you want to
wait before disconnecting
an idle call, double-click
this area and then type
the number of minutes.

8 Click **OK** to confirm
your changes.

9 Click **Close** to close
the Modems Properties
dialog box.

USING MULTIPLE MONITORS

You can use more than one monitor to expand your working area.

To use a second monitor, you need to install a second video card. The video card sends information to the monitor.

USING MULTIPLE MONITORS

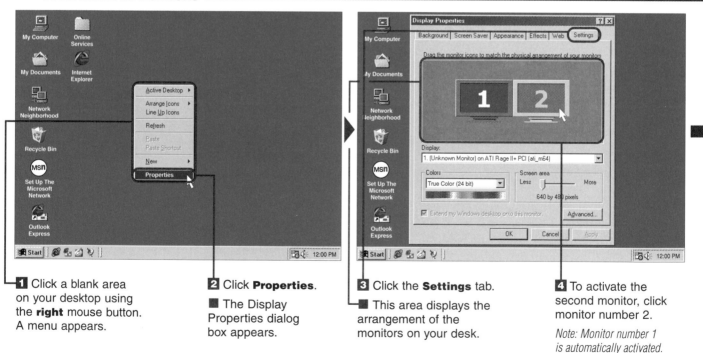

1 Click a blank area on your desktop using the **right** mouse button. A menu appears.

2 Click **Properties**.

■ The Display Properties dialog box appears.

3 Click the **Settings** tab.

■ This area displays the arrangement of the monitors on your desk.

4 To activate the second monitor, click monitor number 2.

Note: Monitor number 1 is automatically activated.

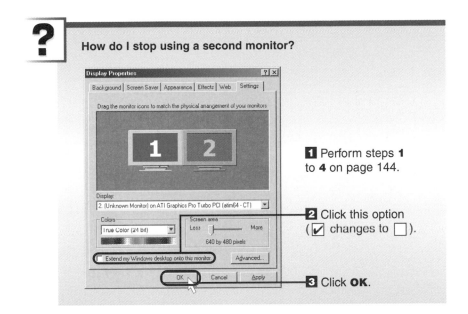

How do I stop using a second monitor?

1 Perform steps **1** to **4** on page 144.

2 Click this option (☑ changes to ☐).

3 Click **OK**.

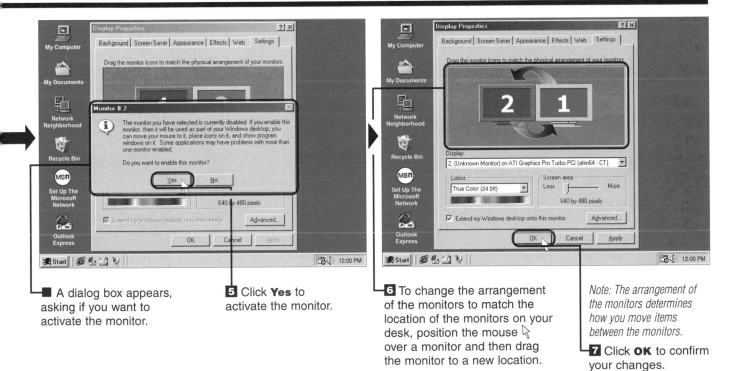

■ A dialog box appears, asking if you want to activate the monitor.

5 Click **Yes** to activate the monitor.

6 To change the arrangement of the monitors to match the location of the monitors on your desk, position the mouse ⌖ over a monitor and then drag the monitor to a new location.

Note: The arrangement of the monitors determines how you move items between the monitors.

7 Click **OK** to confirm your changes.

REMOVE HARDWARE

You may want to remove a hardware device you no longer use from your computer.

REMOVE HARDWARE

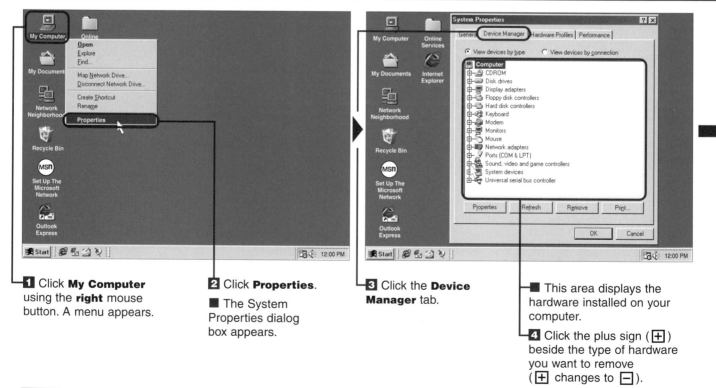

1 Click **My Computer** using the **right** mouse button. A menu appears.

2 Click **Properties**.

■ The System Properties dialog box appears.

3 Click the **Device Manager** tab.

■ This area displays the hardware installed on your computer.

4 Click the plus sign (⊞) beside the type of hardware you want to remove (⊞ changes to ⊟).

After using Windows to remove a hardware device, do I need to physically remove the device from my computer?

After using Windows to remove a hardware device, you should physically remove the device from your computer. If you do not physically remove a Plug and Play device, Windows will re-install the device the next time you start Windows. Physically removing a device will also free up computer resources for other devices.

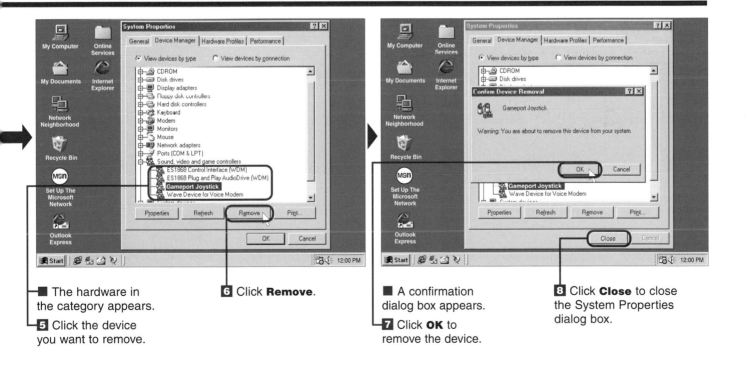

■ The hardware in the category appears.

5 Click the device you want to remove.

6 Click **Remove**.

■ A confirmation dialog box appears.

7 Click **OK** to remove the device.

8 Click **Close** to close the System Properties dialog box.

CHAPTER 7

Optimize and Troubleshoot Your Computer

This chapter teaches you how to use Windows 98 to enhance your computer's performance and troubleshoot problems.

View Hardware Information..............150

View System Information 152

Create a Startup Disk 154

Start Windows in Safe Mode............158

Using Windows Update 160

Convert Your Drive to FAT32 162

Programs You Can Use
    With Windows 98 166

EXTRA **Windows Components**

You can use the Device Manager to view a list of the hardware devices installed on your computer.

DEVICE MANAGER

HARDWARE

DISK DRIVES
IOMEGA JAZ-1GB
SYQUEST-SYJET

MONITOR
VIEWSONIC-PT813

SCANNER
UMAX-1200P

The Device Manager organizes hardware devices into categories, such as disk drives and monitors.

VIEW HARDWARE INFORMATION

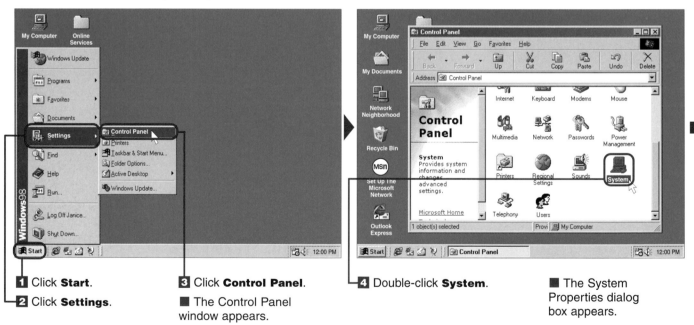

1 Click **Start**.

2 Click **Settings**.

3 Click **Control Panel**.

■ The Control Panel window appears.

4 Double-click **System**.

■ The System Properties dialog box appears.

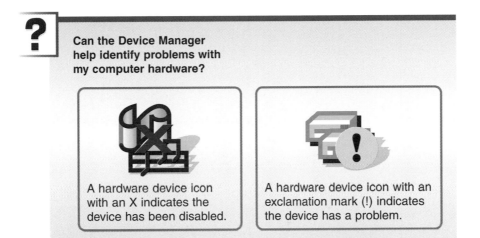

?

Can the Device Manager help identify problems with my computer hardware?

A hardware device icon with an X indicates the device has been disabled.

A hardware device icon with an exclamation mark (!) indicates the device has a problem.

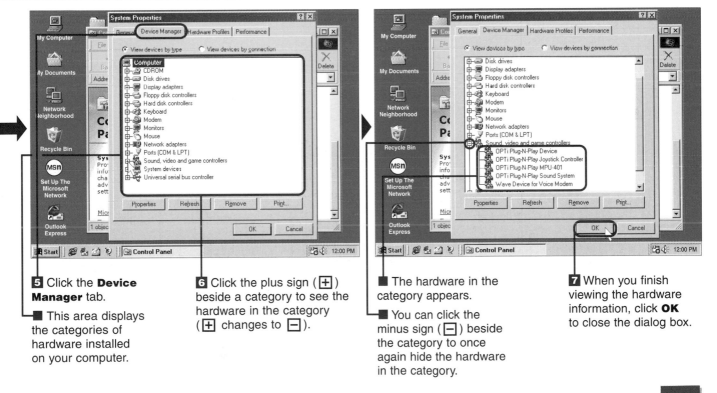

5 Click the **Device Manager** tab.

■ This area displays the categories of hardware installed on your computer.

6 Click the plus sign (⊞) beside a category to see the hardware in the category (⊞ changes to ⊟).

■ The hardware in the category appears.

■ You can click the minus sign (⊟) beside the category to once again hide the hardware in the category.

7 When you finish viewing the hardware information, click **OK** to close the dialog box.

VIEW SYSTEM INFORMATION

The System Properties dialog box offers information about Windows and your computer.

VIEW SYSTEM INFORMATION

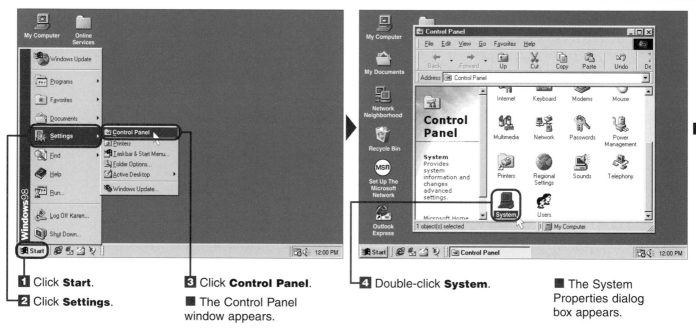

1 Click **Start**.

2 Click **Settings**.

3 Click **Control Panel**.

■ The Control Panel window appears.

4 Double-click **System**.

■ The System Properties dialog box appears.

What information does the System Properties dialog box provide?

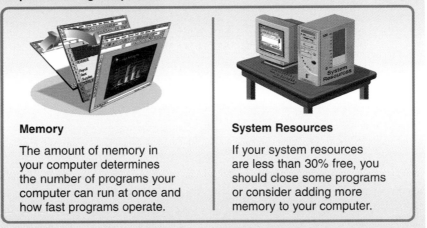

Memory

The amount of memory in your computer determines the number of programs your computer can run at once and how fast programs operate.

System Resources

If your system resources are less than 30% free, you should close some programs or consider adding more memory to your computer.

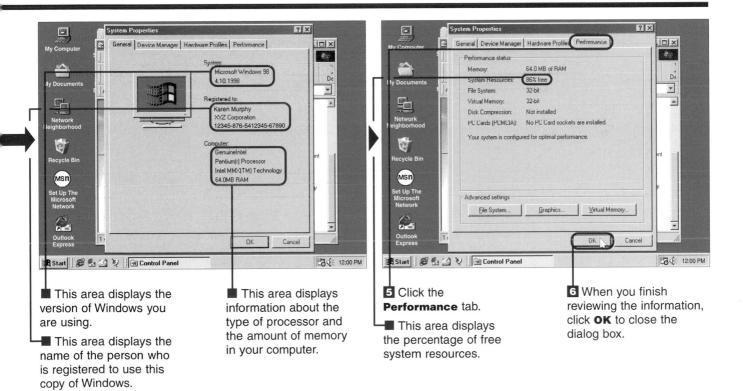

■ This area displays the version of Windows you are using.

■ This area displays the name of the person who is registered to use this copy of Windows.

■ This area displays information about the type of processor and the amount of memory in your computer.

5 Click the **Performance** tab.

■ This area displays the percentage of free system resources.

6 When you finish reviewing the information, click **OK** to close the dialog box.

CREATE A STARTUP DISK

You can create a
startup disk that you
can use to start your
computer when you
have trouble starting
Windows.

You will need a
floppy disk that can
store at least 1.2 MB
of information.

CREATE A STARTUP DISK

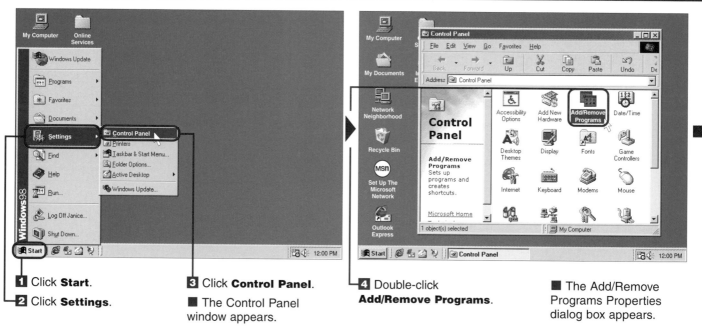

1 Click **Start**.

2 Click **Settings**.

3 Click **Control Panel**.

■ The Control Panel
window appears.

4 Double-click
Add/Remove Programs.

■ The Add/Remove
Programs Properties
dialog box appears.

What should I do if I'm having problems starting Windows and I haven't created a startup disk?

You can create a startup disk by using another Windows 98 computer.

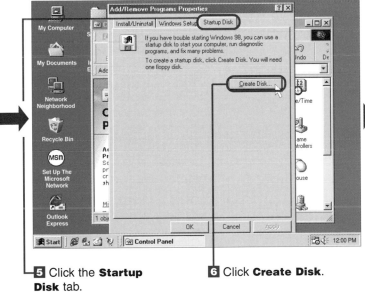

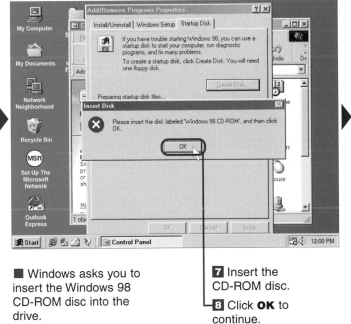

5 Click the **Startup Disk** tab.

6 Click **Create Disk**.

■ Windows asks you to insert the Windows 98 CD-ROM disc into the drive.

7 Insert the CD-ROM disc.

8 Click **OK** to continue.

CONTINUED

CREATE A STARTUP DISK

Make sure the floppy disk you use as your startup disk does not contain information you want to keep. Windows will remove all files currently stored on the disk.

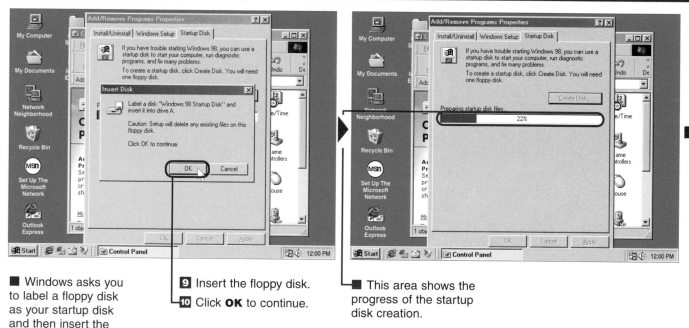

CREATE A STARTUP DISK (CONTINUED)

■ Windows asks you to label a floppy disk as your startup disk and then insert the disk into the drive.

9 Insert the floppy disk.

10 Click **OK** to continue.

■ This area shows the progress of the startup disk creation.

? **How can I protect my startup disk?**

After you create a startup disk, open the write-protect tab on the disk. When the tab is open, you cannot change or delete any information stored on the disk. Make sure you label your startup disk and keep the disk with your Windows 98 installation CD-ROM disc.

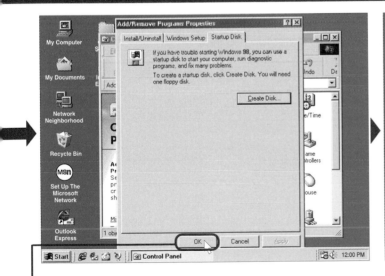

11 When the creation of the startup disk is complete, click **OK** to close the dialog box.

12 Remove the floppy disk from the drive and store the disk in a safe place.

START WINDOWS IN SAFE MODE

If Windows does not start properly, you can start Windows in safe mode to try to fix the problem.

Safe mode uses the minimum capabilities required to run Windows.

START WINDOWS IN SAFE MODE

Award Modular BIOS v4.51PC, An Energy Star Ally
Copyright (C) 1984-97, Award Software, Inc.

BT-1A2

PENTIUM-MMX CPU at 200MHz
Memory Test :   65536K   OK

Award Plug and Play BIOS Extension   v1.0A
Copyright (C) 1997, Award Software, Inc.

Press DEL to enter SETUP
07/14/97-i430IX-W977-2A59IS2BC-00

Microsoft Windows 98 Startup Menu

1. Normal
2. Logged (\BOOTLOG.TXT)
3. Safe mode
4. Step-by-step confirmation
5. Command prompt only
6. Safe mode command prompt only

Enter a choice: 3

F5=Safe mode   Shift+F5=Command prompt   Shift+F8=Step-by-step confirmation [N]

1 Turn on your computer and monitor.

2 Press and hold down the Ctrl key.

■ The Microsoft Windows 98 Startup Menu appears. The menu displays a list of choices for starting Windows in different modes.

3 Type **3** to start Windows in safe mode and then press the Enter key.

■ Windows starts in safe mode.

?

**When would I need to start
Windows in safe mode?**

You may need to start Windows in
safe mode when you have made
an inappropriate change to your
computer that prevents Windows
from starting properly. You may
have incorrectly installed a new
device or accidentally changed
an important Windows setting.

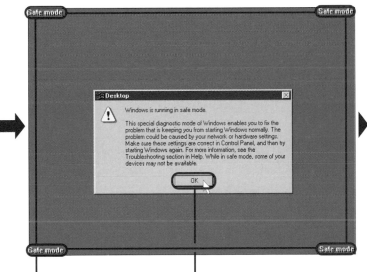

■ Windows displays the
words "Safe mode" in
each corner of your
screen.

■ A message appears,
telling you that Windows
is running in safe mode
and that some of your
devices may not be
available.

◀4 Click **OK** to continue.

■ You can now try
to fix the problem that
prevents Windows from
starting normally.

■ When you finish fixing
the problem, restart your
computer to once again
start Windows in the
normal mode.

USING WINDOWS UPDATE

You can use Windows Update to find software that can enhance and optimize the performance of your computer.

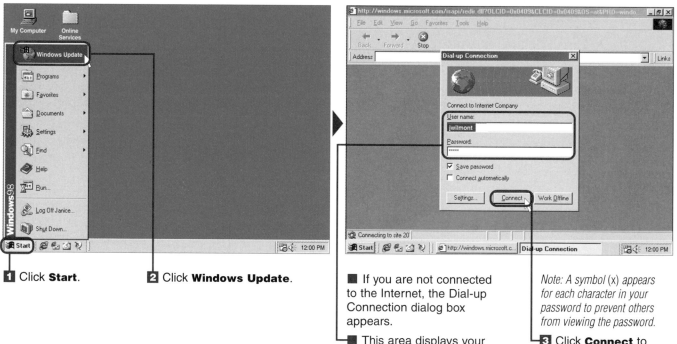

1 Click **Start**.

2 Click **Windows Update**.

■ If you are not connected to the Internet, the Dial-up Connection dialog box appears.

■ This area displays your user name and password.

Note: A symbol (x) appears for each character in your password to prevent others from viewing the password.

3 Click **Connect** to connect to your Internet service provider.

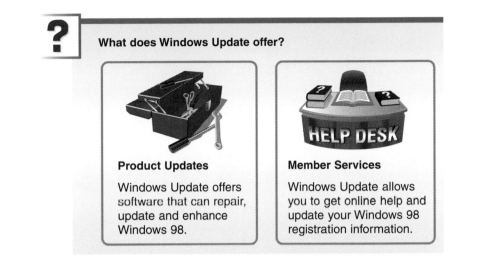

? **What does Windows Update offer?**

Product Updates

Windows Update offers software that can repair, update and enhance Windows 98.

Member Services

Windows Update allows you to get online help and update your Windows 98 registration information.

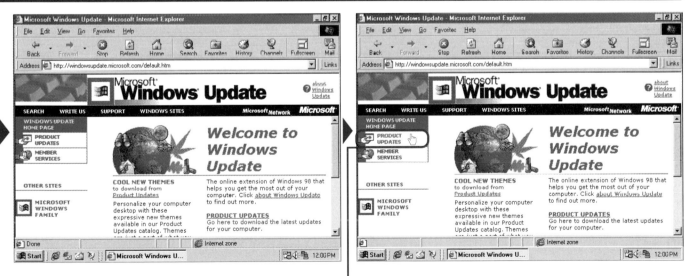

■ The Microsoft Windows Update Web page appears. You can use the Web page to update Windows.

Note: The Web page shown on your screen may look different than the Web page shown above. Companies often change their Web pages to update information and enhance the Web pages.

4 To view software that can optimize and enhance your computer, click **Product Updates**. Then follow the instructions on your screen.

CONVERT YOUR DRIVE TO FAT32

You can optimize your computer by converting your hard drive to the FAT32 file system.

Converting your hard drive to FAT32 will give you additional hard drive space and your programs will start faster.

CONVERT YOUR DRIVE TO FAT32

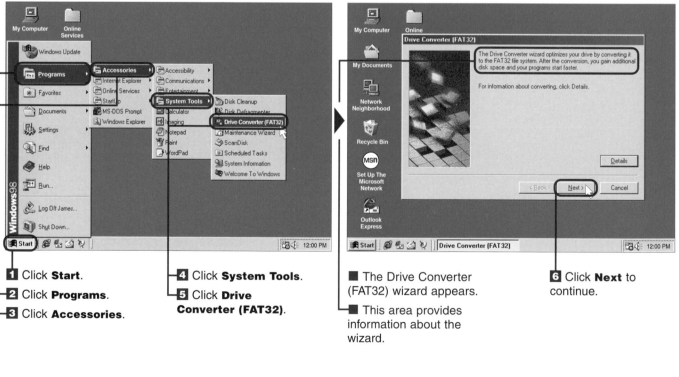

1 Click **Start**.

2 Click **Programs**.

3 Click **Accessories**.

4 Click **System Tools**.

5 Click **Drive Converter (FAT32)**.

■ The Drive Converter (FAT32) wizard appears.

■ This area provides information about the wizard.

6 Click **Next** to continue.

How does converting to FAT32 give me additional hard drive space?

Your hard drive stores data in groups called clusters. Windows uses the File Allocation Table (FAT) to keep track of which clusters store the files on your hard drive. The FAT32 file system stores data in smaller clusters than the older FAT system. This reduces wasted space on your hard drive, which provides additional storage space.

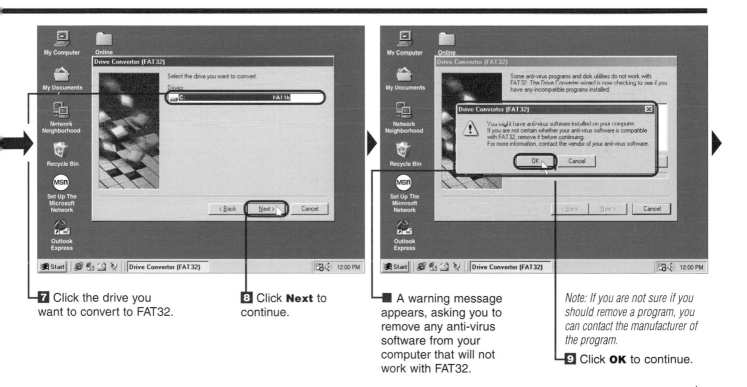

7 Click the drive you want to convert to FAT32.

8 Click **Next** to continue.

■ A warning message appears, asking you to remove any anti-virus software from your computer that will not work with FAT32.

Note: If you are not sure if you should remove a program, you can contact the manufacturer of the program.

9 Click **OK** to continue.

CONTINUED

CONVERT YOUR DRIVE TO FAT32

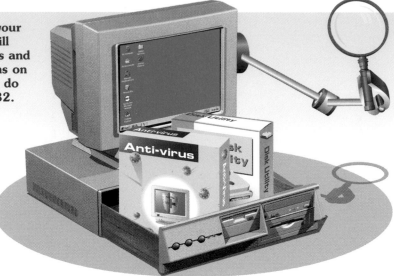

Before converting your drive, the wizard will search for anti-virus and disk utility programs on your computer that do not work with FAT32.

Anti-virus program

Detects and removes viruses to prevent computer problems.

Disk utility program

Optimizes your computer for better performance.

CONVERT YOUR DRIVE TO FAT32 (CONTINUED)

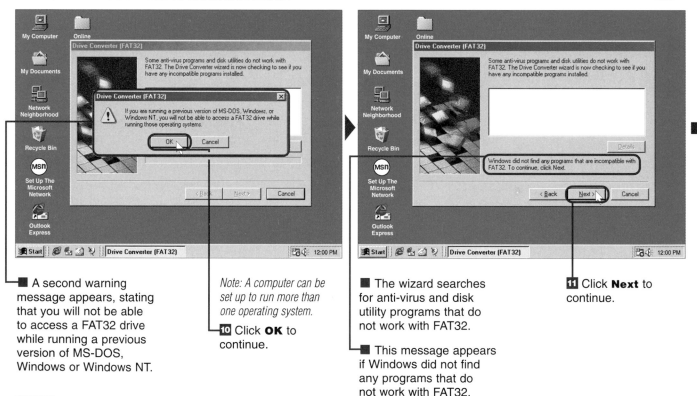

■ A second warning message appears, stating that you will not be able to access a FAT32 drive while running a previous version of MS-DOS, Windows or Windows NT.

Note: A computer can be set up to run more than one operating system.

10 Click **OK** to continue.

■ The wizard searches for anti-virus and disk utility programs that do not work with FAT32.

■ This message appears if Windows did not find any programs that do not work with FAT32.

11 Click **Next** to continue.

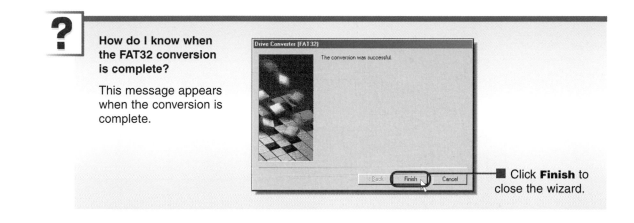

How do I know when the FAT32 conversion is complete?

This message appears when the conversion is complete.

■ Click **Finish** to close the wizard.

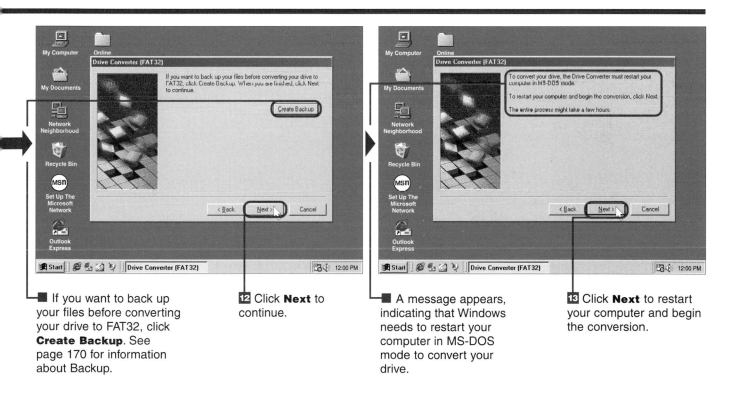

■ If you want to back up your files before converting your drive to FAT32, click **Create Backup**. See page 170 for information about Backup.

12 Click **Next** to continue.

■ A message appears, indicating that Windows needs to restart your computer in MS-DOS mode to convert your drive.

13 Click **Next** to restart your computer and begin the conversion.

There are many
programs available
that you can use
with Windows 98.

Adobe Acrobat Reader

You can use Adobe Acrobat Reader
to view and print Portable Document
Format (PDF) files that are often found
on the Web. PDF files allow you to
display documents, such as books and
magazines, on your screen exactly as
they appear in printed form. Acrobat
Reader is available free of charge at
www.adobe.com

Microsoft Office

Microsoft Office is a collection of
programs sold together in one package.
The package includes a word processor to
create documents (Word), a spreadsheet
program to manage financial information
(Excel), a presentation program to design
presentations (PowerPoint) and may
include a database program to manage
large collections of information (Access).
For information about Microsoft products,
you can visit the Web site at
www.microsoft.com

VirusScan Security Suite

You can reduce the risk of a virus infecting your computer by using an anti-virus program. A virus is a program that can cause problems such as displaying annoying messages on your screen or erasing all the information on your hard drive.

McAfee offers the VirusScan Security Suite which provides anti-virus programs that check for and remove viruses on your computer. You can get McAfee products at www.mcafeemall.com

WinFax PRO

With WinFax PRO, you can use your computer's fax modem to send and receive faxes. WinFax PRO includes Optical Character Recognition (OCR) software to convert faxes you receive into documents that you can edit using a word processor. You can get WinFax PRO at www.symantec.com

WinZip

WinZip can compress, or squeeze, files to speed the transfer of information from one computer to another. Many of the files you transfer from the Internet to your computer are compressed. Before you can use a compressed file, you can use WinZip to decompress the file. You can get WinZip at www.winzip.com

CHAPTER 8

Back Up Files

*Backing up files helps you minimize the
risk of losing important information.
This chapter shows you how to back
up and restore your files.*

Back Up Files.................................170

Open an Existing Backup Job 178

Restore Files..................................180

You can make backup copies of important information stored on your computer. This will protect the data from theft, fire, viruses and computer failure.

If the Backup feature is not available, you need to add the Backup component from the System Tools category. To add Windows components, see page 118.

BACK UP FILES

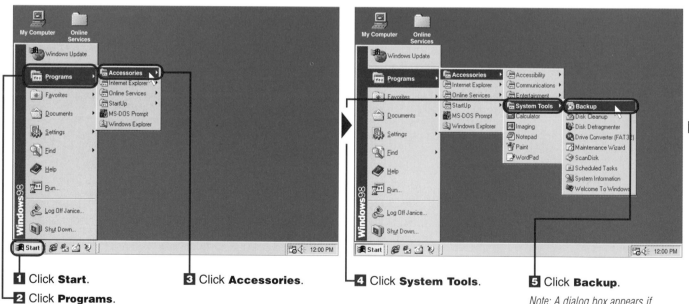

1 Click **Start**.

2 Click **Programs**.

3 Click **Accessories**.

4 Click **System Tools**.

5 Click **Backup**.

*Note: A dialog box appears if Windows does not find any backup devices on your computer. If you are using a tape drive, click **Yes** to install the device. If you are not using a tape drive as your backup device, click **No**.*

What devices can I use to back up my information?

You can use many types of devices to back up your information, including a floppy drive, second hard drive, removable drive, network drive or tape drive. Most people perform backups using a tape drive since this type of device is inexpensive and can back up a large amount of information.

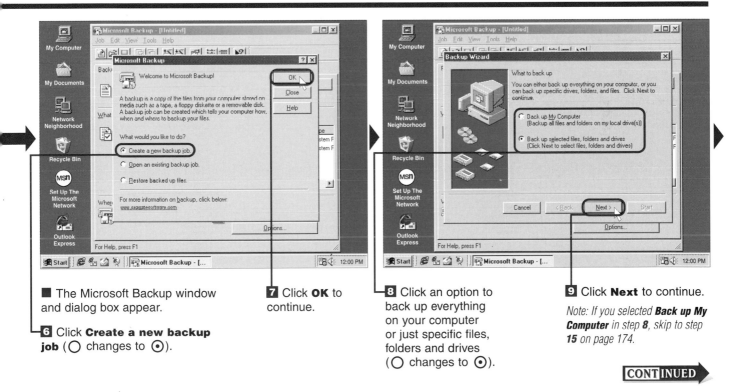

■ The Microsoft Backup window and dialog box appear.

6 Click **Create a new backup job** (○ changes to ⊙).

7 Click **OK** to continue.

8 Click an option to back up everything on your computer or just specific files, folders and drives (○ changes to ⊙).

9 Click **Next** to continue.

*Note: If you selected **Back up My Computer** in step **8**, skip to step **15** on page 174.*

CONTINUED

BACK UP FILES

You must select which files and folders you want to back up on your computer.

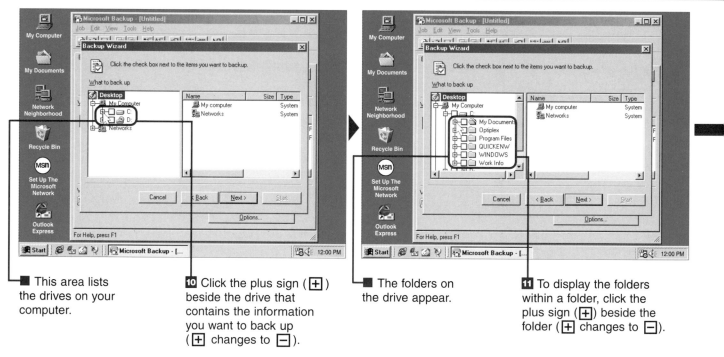

■ This area lists the drives on your computer.

10 Click the plus sign (⊞) beside the drive that contains the information you want to back up (⊞ changes to ⊟).

■ The folders on the drive appear.

11 To display the folders within a folder, click the plus sign (⊞) beside the folder (⊞ changes to ⊟).

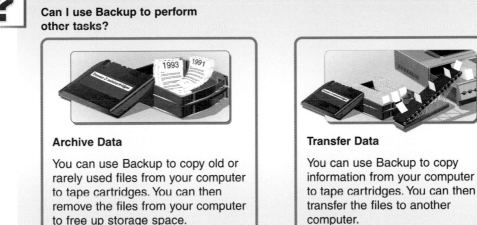

Can I use Backup to perform other tasks?

Archive Data

You can use Backup to copy old or rarely used files from your computer to tape cartridges. You can then remove the files from your computer to free up storage space.

Transfer Data

You can use Backup to copy information from your computer to tape cartridges. You can then transfer the files to another computer.

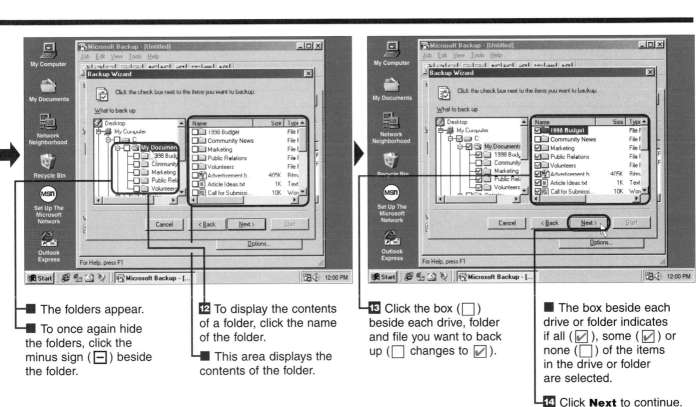

■ The folders appear.

■ To once again hide the folders, click the minus sign (☐) beside the folder.

12 To display the contents of a folder, click the name of the folder.

■ This area displays the contents of the folder.

13 Click the box (☐) beside each drive, folder and file you want to back up (☐ changes to ☑).

■ The box beside each drive or folder indicates if all (☑), some (☑) or none (☐) of the items in the drive or folder are selected.

14 Click **Next** to continue.

CONTINUED

You can back up all the
files you selected or only
the files that are new or
have changed since
a previous backup.

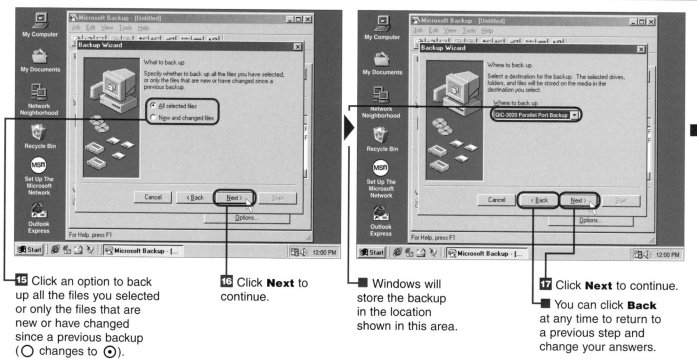

BACK UP FILES (CONTINUED)

15 Click an option to back
up all the files you selected
or only the files that are
new or have changed
since a previous backup
(○ changes to ◉).

16 Click **Next** to
continue.

■ Windows will
store the backup
in the location
shown in this area.

17 Click **Next** to continue.

■ You can click **Back**
at any time to return to
a previous step and
change your answers.

?

How often should I back up my information?

To determine how often you should back up your information, consider how much work you can afford to lose. If you cannot afford to lose the work accomplished in one day, back up your files once a day. If your work does not often change during the week, back up once a week.

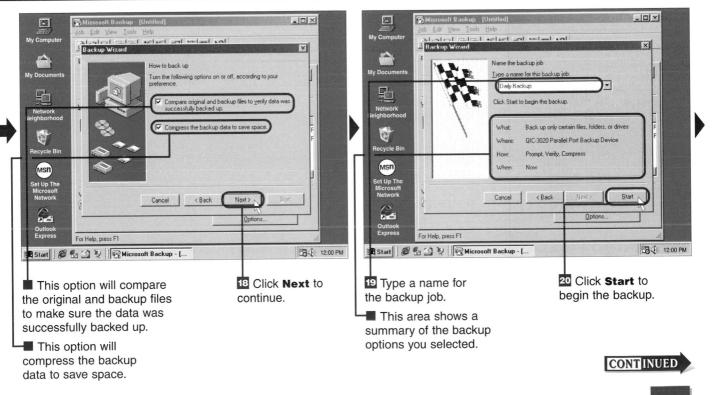

■ This option will compare the original and backup files to make sure the data was successfully backed up.

■ This option will compress the backup data to save space.

18 Click **Next** to continue.

19 Type a name for the backup job.

■ This area shows a summary of the backup options you selected.

20 Click **Start** to begin the backup.

CONTINUED

BACK UP FILES

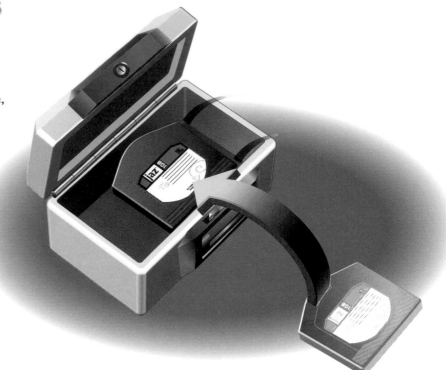

When the backup is complete, store the backup copies in a cool, dry place, away from electrical equipment and magnetic devices.

BACK UP FILES (CONTINUED)

■ The Backup Progress window appears, showing you the progress of the backup.

■ A dialog box may appear, asking you to enter a unique name for the tape.

21 Type a name for the tape.

22 Click **OK** to continue.

Why does this dialog box appear when I perform a backup?

This dialog box appears if the tape cartridge already contains a backup.

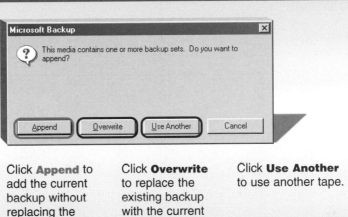

Click **Append** to add the current backup without replacing the existing backup.

Click **Overwrite** to replace the existing backup with the current backup.

Click **Use Another** to use another tape.

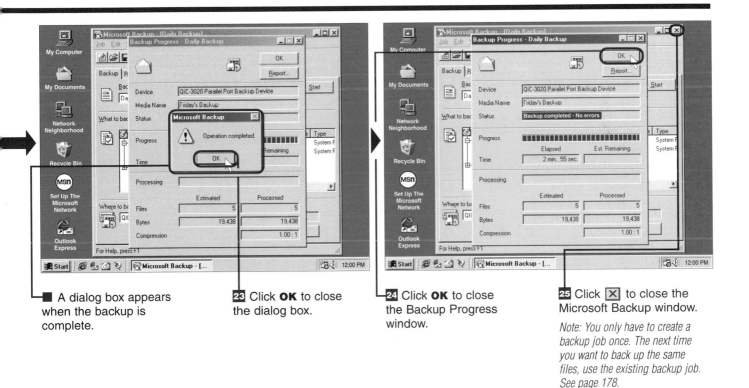

■ A dialog box appears when the backup is complete.

23 Click **OK** to close the dialog box.

24 Click **OK** to close the Backup Progress window.

25 Click ☒ to close the Microsoft Backup window.

Note: You only have to create a backup job once. The next time you want to back up the same files, use the existing backup job. See page 178.

OPEN AN EXISTING BACKUP JOB

You can open an existing
backup job to perform
another backup using
the same settings.

A backup job contains all
the settings for a backup,
such as the information to
be backed up and where
to store the information.
To create a backup job,
perform the steps starting
on page 170.

OPEN AN EXISTING BACKUP JOB

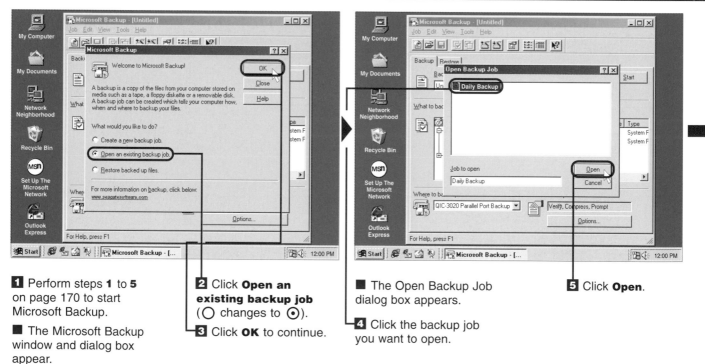

1 Perform steps **1** to **5**
on page 170 to start
Microsoft Backup.

■ The Microsoft Backup
window and dialog box
appear.

2 Click **Open an
existing backup job**
(○ changes to ⊙).

3 Click **OK** to continue.

■ The Open Backup Job
dialog box appears.

4 Click the backup job
you want to open.

5 Click **Open**.

? Can I have more than one backup job?

You can have many backup jobs. For example, you may have one backup job to back up all of your documents at the end of each week. You may have another backup job to back up all of your program files once a month.

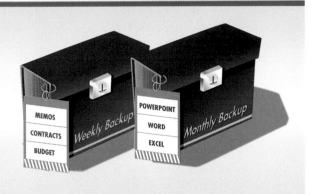

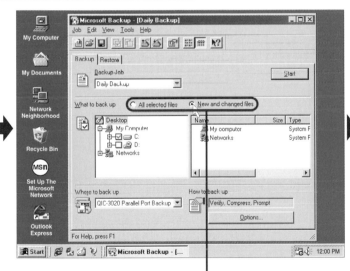

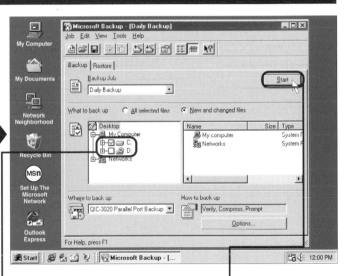

■ Information for the backup job appears in the Microsoft Backup window.

6 Click an option to back up all the files in the backup job or only the files that are new or have changed since a previous backup (○ changes to ⊙).

─■ This area lists the drives on your computer. Windows will back up information on each drive that displays a check mark (☑).

*Note: To change which folders and files you want to back up, perform steps **10** to **13** starting on page 172. Windows will ask you to save the changes before starting the backup.*

7 Click **Start** to start the backup.

■ To complete the backup, perform steps **21** to **25** starting on page 176.

If files on your computer are lost or damaged, you can use Backup to restore the files.

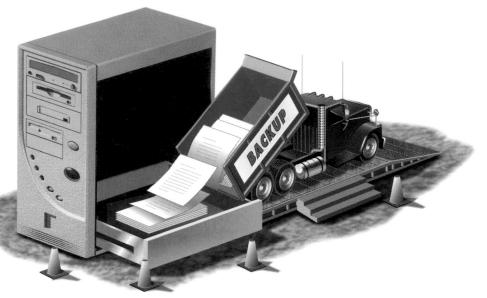

RESTORE FILES

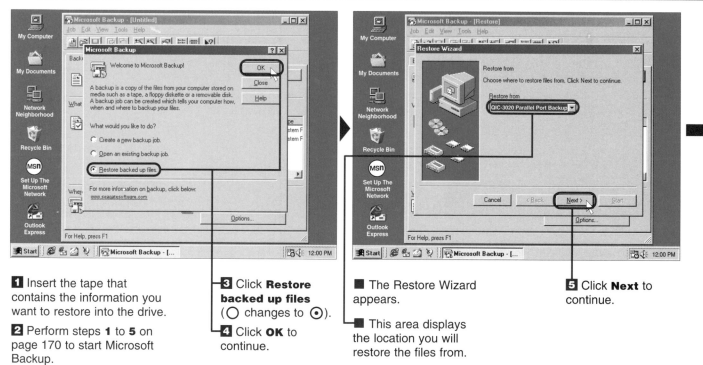

1 Insert the tape that contains the information you want to restore into the drive.

2 Perform steps **1** to **5** on page 170 to start Microsoft Backup.

■ The Microsoft Backup window and dialog box appear.

3 Click **Restore backed up files** (○ changes to ◉).

4 Click **OK** to continue.

■ The Restore Wizard appears.

■ This area displays the location you will restore the files from.

5 Click **Next** to continue.

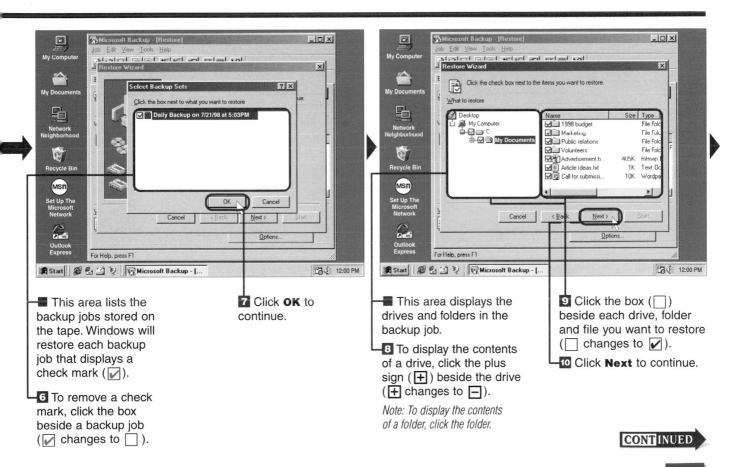

? Can I restore just one file?

Yes. You do not have to restore all the files you backed up. You can select only the files you want to restore. This is ideal if you accidentally deleted or made changes to an important file on your computer.

■ This area lists the backup jobs stored on the tape. Windows will restore each backup job that displays a check mark (☑).

6 To remove a check mark, click the box beside a backup job (☑ changes to ☐).

7 Click **OK** to continue.

■ This area displays the drives and folders in the backup job.

8 To display the contents of a drive, click the plus sign (⊞) beside the drive (⊞ changes to ⊟).

Note: To display the contents of a folder, click the folder.

9 Click the box (☐) beside each drive, folder and file you want to restore (☐ changes to ☑).

10 Click **Next** to continue.

CONTINUED ▶

The Restore wizard will take you through the process of restoring your files.

RESTORE FILES (CONTINUED)

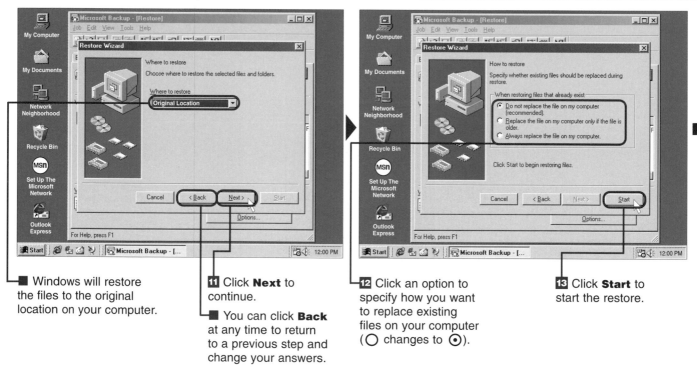

■ Windows will restore the files to the original location on your computer.

11 Click **Next** to continue.

■ You can click **Back** at any time to return to a previous step and change your answers.

12 Click an option to specify how you want to replace existing files on your computer (○ changes to ⊙).

13 Click **Start** to start the restore.

? When restoring files, will Backup replace existing files on my computer?

Backup offers you three choices when restoring files.

Do not replace files on your computer.

Replace files on your computer only if the files are older.

Always replace files on your computer.

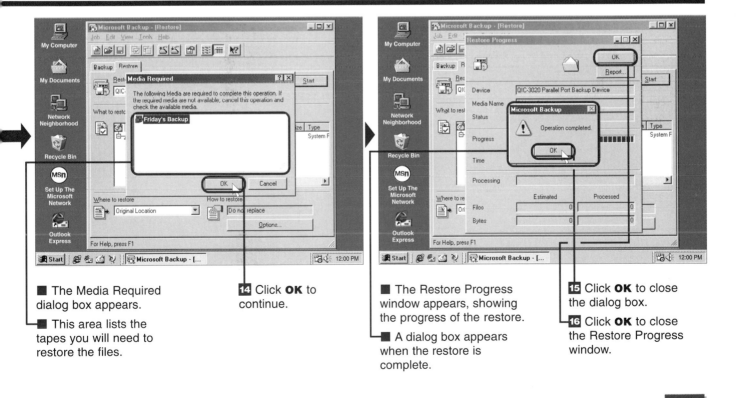

■ The Media Required dialog box appears.

■ This area lists the tapes you will need to restore the files.

14 Click **OK** to continue.

■ The Restore Progress window appears, showing the progress of the restore.

■ A dialog box appears when the restore is complete.

15 Click **OK** to close the dialog box.

16 Click **OK** to close the Restore Progress window.

CHAPTER 9

Exchange E-mail

Outlook Express allows you to exchange e-mail messages with people around the world. In this chapter you will learn how to work with e-mail messages and find e-mail addresses on the Internet.

Read Messages 186

Sort Messages 188

Print Messages................................189

Mark a Message as Unread 190

Check for New Messages
    Automatically 191

Compose a Message 192

Format Messages 194

Save a Draft 198

Find People on the Internet 200

Find Messages................................202

Create a New Folder 206

Filter Messages 208

You can use Outlook
Express to exchange
e-mail messages with
people around the
world.

READ MESSAGES

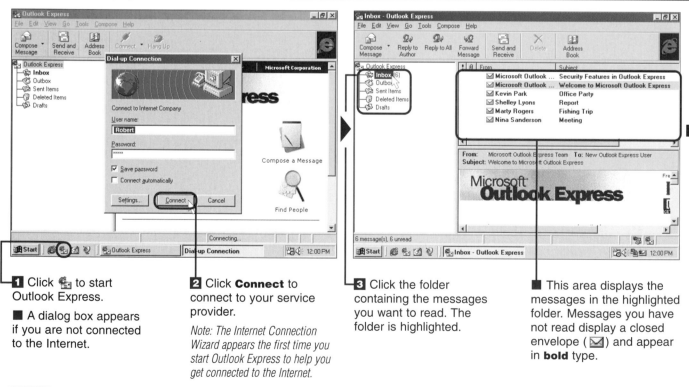

1 Click 🗐 to start
Outlook Express.

■ A dialog box appears
if you are not connected
to the Internet.

2 Click **Connect** to
connect to your service
provider.

*Note: The Internet Connection
Wizard appears the first time you
start Outlook Express to help you
get connected to the Internet.*

3 Click the folder
containing the messages
you want to read. The
folder is highlighted.

■ This area displays the
messages in the highlighted
folder. Messages you have
not read display a closed
envelope (🖂) and appear
in **bold** type.

? **What folders does Outlook Express use to store my messages?**

Inbox	Outbox	Sent Items	Deleted Items	Drafts
Stores messages sent to you.	Temporarily stores messages that have not yet been sent.	Stores copies of messages you have sent.	Stores messages you have deleted.	Stores messages you have not yet completed.

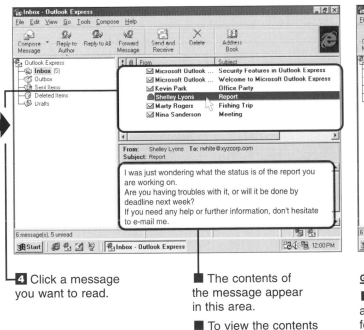

4 Click a message you want to read.

■ The contents of the message appear in this area.

■ To view the contents of another message, click the message.

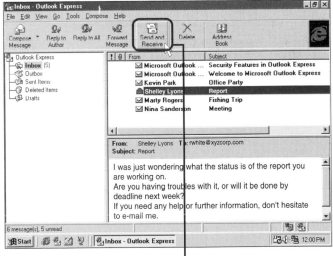

GET NEW MESSAGES

■ Outlook Express automatically checks for new messages every 30 minutes.

1 To immediately check for new messages, click **Send and Receive**.

SORT MESSAGES

You can sort your messages to quickly find the messages you want to view.

1 Click the heading for the column you want to use to sort the messages.

■ If you cannot see the heading you want to use to sort the messages, use this scroll bar to display the heading.

■ The messages appear in the new order.

■ You can click the heading again to sort the messages in the opposite order.

188

You can produce
a paper copy of a
message displayed
on your screen.

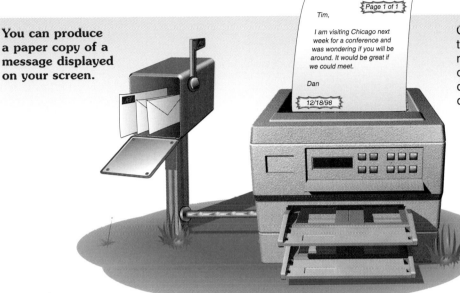

Tim,

I am visiting Chicago next
week for a conference and
was wondering if you will be
around. It would be great if
we could meet.

Dan

Page 1 of 1

12/18/98

Outlook Express prints
the page number and total
number of pages at the top
of each page. The current
date prints at the bottom
of each page.

PRINT MESSAGES

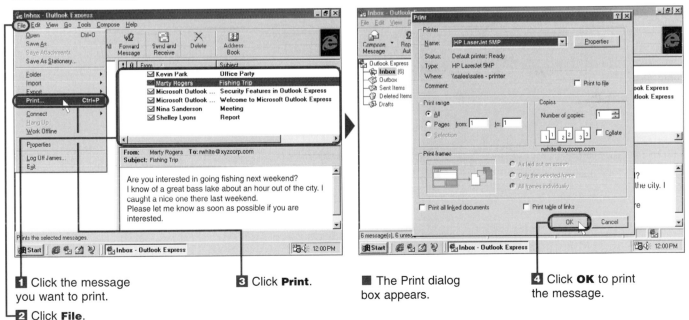

1 Click the message
you want to print.

2 Click **File**.

3 Click **Print**.

■ The Print dialog
box appears.

4 Click **OK** to print
the message.

MARK A MESSAGE AS UNREAD

You can make a message appear as if you have not read the message. Marking a message as unread can remind you to later review the message.

MARK A MESSAGE AS UNREAD

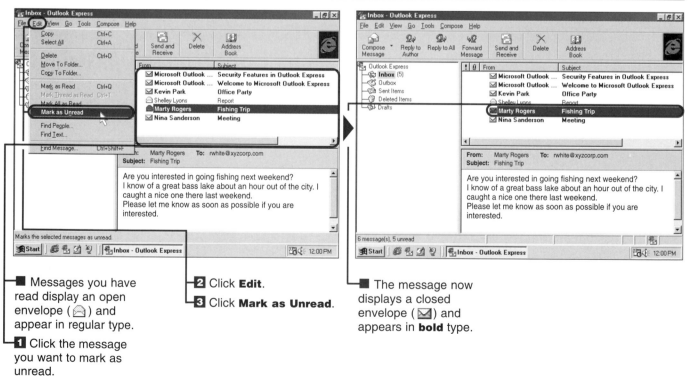

■ Messages you have read display an open envelope (📩) and appear in regular type.

1 Click the message you want to mark as unread.

2 Click **Edit**.

3 Click **Mark as Unread**.

■ The message now displays a closed envelope (✉) and appears in **bold** type.

CHECK FOR NEW MESSAGES AUTOMATICALLY

You can have Outlook Express check for new messages automatically.

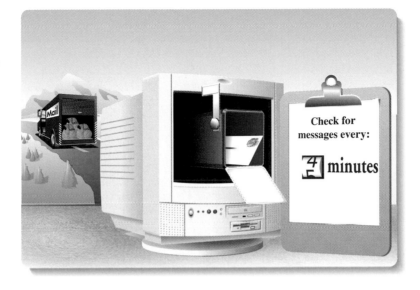

Check for messages every:

4 minutes

CHECK FOR NEW MESSAGES AUTOMATICALLY

1 Click **Tools**.

2 Click **Options**.

■ The Options dialog box appears.

3 This option indicates whether Outlook Express will automatically check for new messages. Click this option to turn the option on (☑) or off (☐).

4 Double-click this area and then type how often you want Outlook Express to check for new messages.

5 Click **OK** to confirm your changes.

COMPOSE A MESSAGE

You can compose and send
a message to exchange
ideas or request
information.

COMPOSE A MESSAGE

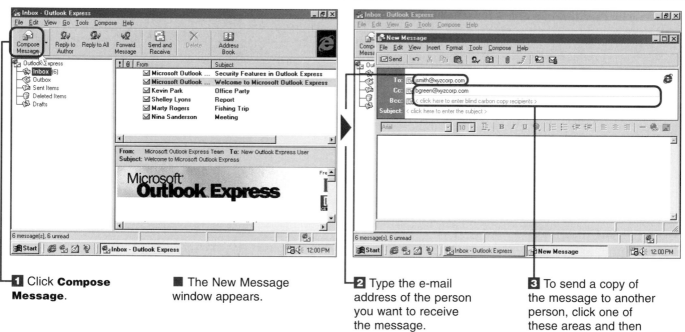

1 Click **Compose Message**.

■ The New Message window appears.

2 Type the e-mail address of the person you want to receive the message.

3 To send a copy of the message to another person, click one of these areas and then type the e-mail address.

How can I send a message to more than one person?

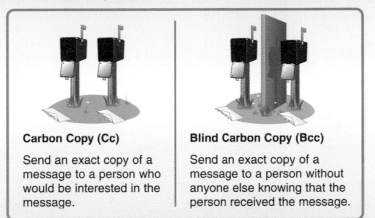

Carbon Copy (Cc)

Send an exact copy of a message to a person who would be interested in the message.

Blind Carbon Copy (Bcc)

Send an exact copy of a message to a person without anyone else knowing that the person received the message.

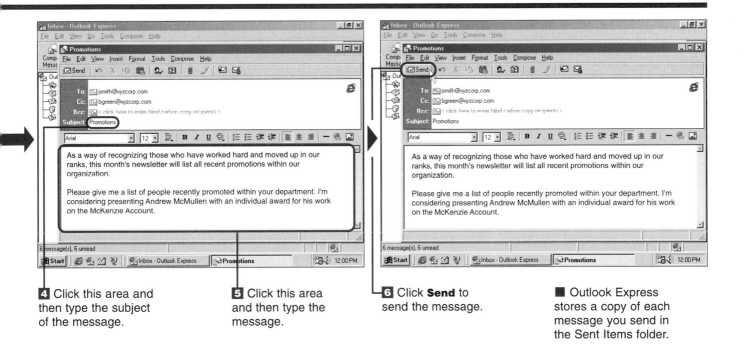

■ **4** Click this area and then type the subject of the message.

■ **5** Click this area and then type the message.

■ **6** Click **Send** to send the message.

■ Outlook Express stores a copy of each message you send in the Sent Items folder.

FORMAT MESSAGES

You can change the design and size of text in a message to make the message more interesting and attractive.

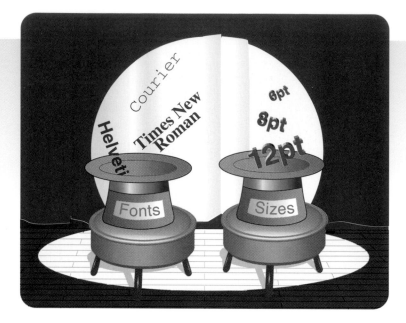

CHANGE THE FONT

■ To compose a message, perform steps **1** to **5** starting on page 192.

1 To select the text you want to change to a new font, drag the mouse I over the text.

2 Click ▾ in this area to display a list of the available fonts.

3 Click the font you want to use.

■ The text changes to the new font.

■ To deselect text, click outside the selected area.

Will the person receiving my message see the formatting I add to the message?

If the person you send the message to does not use Outlook Express or another e-mail program that can view formatting in messages, the message will appear without the formatting.

CHANGE THE FONT SIZE

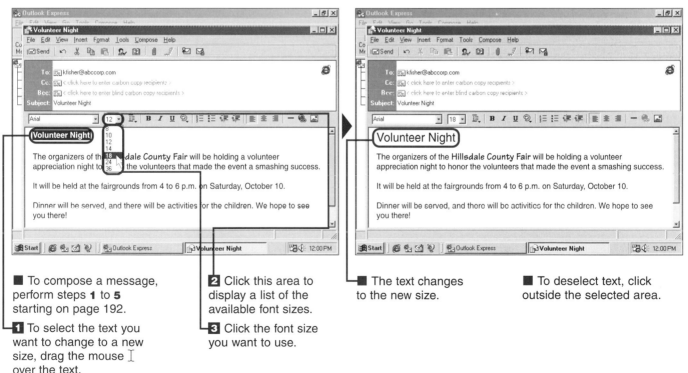

■ To compose a message, perform steps **1** to **5** starting on page 192.

1 To select the text you want to change to a new size, drag the mouse I over the text.

2 Click this area to display a list of the available font sizes.

3 Click the font size you want to use.

■ The text changes to the new size.

■ To deselect text, click outside the selected area.

FORMAT MESSAGES

You can use the bold, italic and underline styles to emphasize information in a message.

BOLD, ITALICIZE OR UNDERLINE TEXT

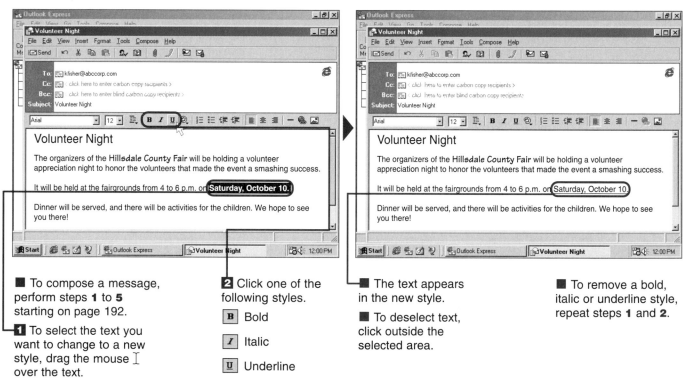

■ To compose a message, perform steps **1** to **5** starting on page 192.

1 To select the text you want to change to a new style, drag the mouse I over the text.

2 Click one of the following styles.

B Bold

I Italic

U Underline

■ The text appears in the new style.

■ To deselect text, click outside the selected area.

■ To remove a bold, italic or underline style, repeat steps **1** and **2**.

You can change
the color of text
in a message to
draw attention
to important
information.

■ ADD COLOR ■

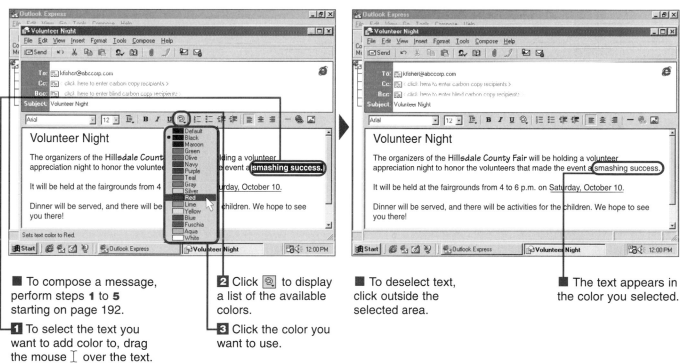

■ To compose a message, perform steps **1** to **5** starting on page 192.

1 To select the text you want to add color to, drag the mouse I over the text.

2 Click 🖾 to display a list of the available colors.

3 Click the color you want to use.

■ To deselect text, click outside the selected area.

■ The text appears in the color you selected.

SAVE A DRAFT

If you are unable to finish composing a message, you can save a draft of the message. You can then finish and send the message at a later time.

SEND LATER

SAVE A DRAFT

1 To compose a message, perform steps **1** to **5** starting on page 192.

2 Click **File**.

3 Click **Save**.

■ A dialog box appears, telling you the message was saved in your Drafts folder.

4 Click **OK** to close the dialog box.

5 Click ☒ to close the message.

Can I delete a draft message I no longer want to send?

Outlook Express stores draft messages in the Drafts folder until you complete and send the messages. If you no longer want to send a draft message, you can delete the message as you would delete any message. To delete a message, click the message and then press the Delete key.

COMPLETE A DRAFT

◼1 Click the **Drafts** folder to display the messages you have not completed.

■ This area displays the messages in the Drafts folder.

◼2 Double-click the message you want to complete.

■ A window appears, displaying the contents of the message.

◼3 Finish composing the message.

◼4 Click **Send** to send the message. Outlook Express sends the message and removes the message from the Drafts folder.

FIND PEOPLE ON THE INTERNET

You can search for the e-mail address of a friend or colleague. This is helpful if you lost an address or you want to surprise someone with a message.

E-MAIL ADDRESSES

FIND PEOPLE ON THE INTERNET

1 Click **Start**.

2 Click **Find**.

3 Click **People**.

■ The Find People dialog box appears.

4 Click this area to list the directory services you can search.

5 Click the directory service you want to search.

200

?

Why can't I find an e-mail address?

There is no central listing of e-mail addresses. Directories such as Bigfoot and SwitchBoard obtain addresses from newsgroups and from addresses people submit. Directories cannot possibly list every e-mail address on the Internet. The best way to find the e-mail address of a friend or colleague is to phone the person and ask.

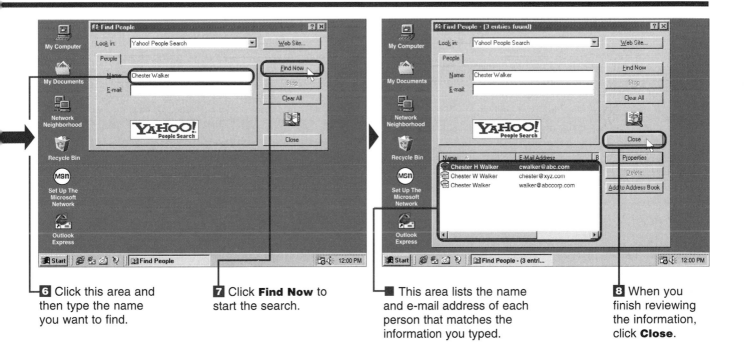

6 Click this area and then type the name you want to find.

7 Click **Find Now** to start the search.

■ This area lists the name and e-mail address of each person that matches the information you typed.

8 When you finish reviewing the information, click **Close**.

FIND MESSAGES

If you cannot find a
message you want to
review, you can have
Outlook Express search
for the message.

FIND MESSAGES

1 Click **Edit**.

2 Click **Find Message**.

■ The Find Message
window appears.

3 To find messages you
received from a specific
person, click this area
and then type the name
of the person.

4 To find messages
you sent to a specific
person, click this area
and then type the
name of the person.

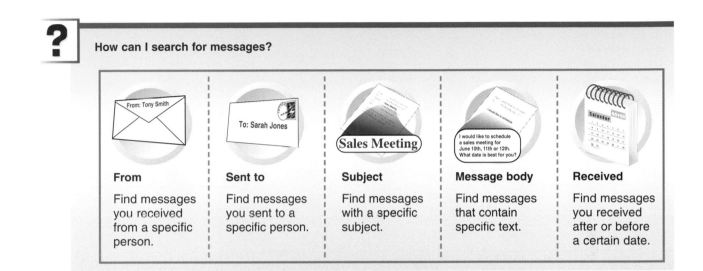

How can I search for messages?

From

Find messages you received from a specific person.

Sent to

Find messages you sent to a specific person.

Subject

Find messages with a specific subject.

Message body

Find messages that contain specific text.

Received

Find messages you received after or before a certain date.

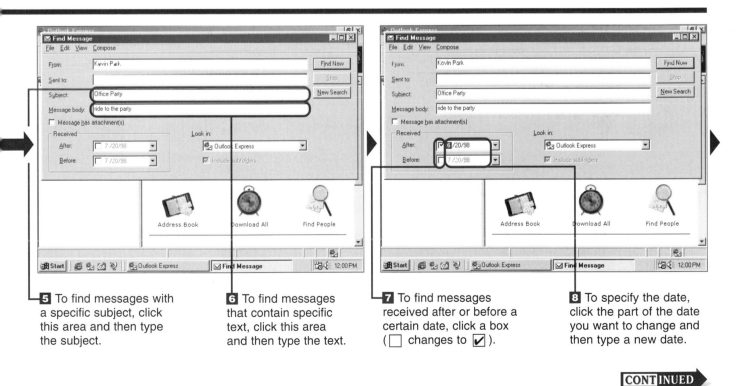

5 To find messages with a specific subject, click this area and then type the subject.

6 To find messages that contain specific text, click this area and then type the text.

7 To find messages received after or before a certain date, click a box (☐ changes to ☑).

8 To specify the date, click the part of the date you want to change and then type a new date.

CONTINUED

When the search is complete, Outlook Express displays a list of messages that match the information you specified. You can open and review any of these messages.

SEARCH FOR: YOGA

Messages Found:

- Yoga
- Yoga class
- Yoga classes

Hi Tim:

I am considering signing up for a yoga class. But I've heard mixed reviews.

Some people say it will just teach me to twist my body into a pretzel and other people say it really has proven health benefits. Can you tell me what yoga's all about and what benefits it provides?

Thanks,
Mike

FIND MESSAGES (CONTINUED)

9 Click this area to select which folder you want to search.

10 Click the folder you want to search.

*Note: To search all folders, choose **Outlook Express**.*

11 Click **Find Now** to start the search.

■ This area lists the messages that match the information you specified.

12 To display the contents of a message, double-click the message.

How can I make my messages easy to find?

If you spend a lot of time searching for messages, you can create folders to keep related messages together. For example, you can create a folder to store messages discussing a particular subject. To create your own personalized folders, see page 206.

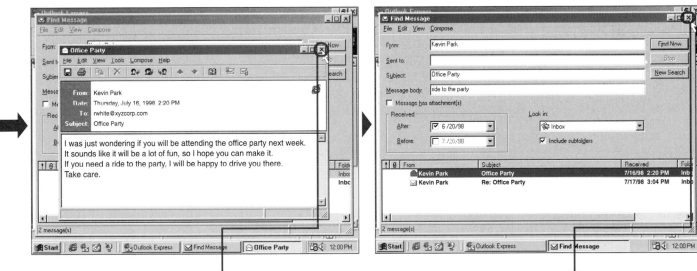

■ A window appears, displaying the contents of the message.

13 When you finish reviewing the message, click ⊠ to close the message window.

■ You can repeat steps **12** and **13** to view the contents of other messages.

14 When you finish reviewing the messages, click ⊠ to close the Find Message window.

CREATE A NEW FOLDER

You can create a new folder to help organize your messages. A folder allows you to keep related messages in one location.

CREATE A NEW FOLDER

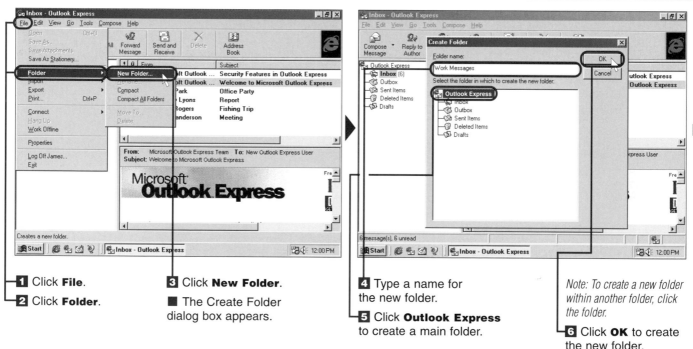

1 Click **File**.

2 Click **Folder**.

3 Click **New Folder**.

■ The Create Folder dialog box appears.

4 Type a name for the new folder.

5 Click **Outlook Express** to create a main folder.

Note: To create a new folder within another folder, click the folder.

6 Click **OK** to create the new folder.

? How do I delete a folder I no longer need?

To delete a folder, click the folder you want to remove and then press the Delete key. When a confirmation dialog box appears, click **Yes** to confirm the deletion. Outlook Express will permanently remove the folder and all the messages in the folder. You can only delete folders that you have created.

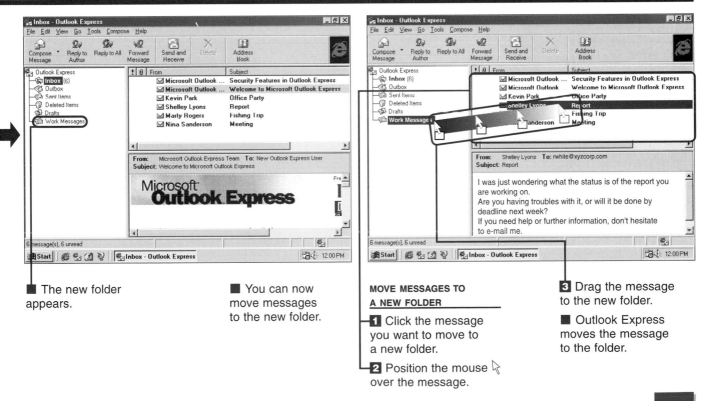

■ The new folder appears.

■ You can now move messages to the new folder.

MOVE MESSAGES TO A NEW FOLDER

1 Click the message you want to move to a new folder.

2 Position the mouse over the message.

3 Drag the message to the new folder.

■ Outlook Express moves the message to the folder.

FILTER MESSAGES

You can have Outlook Express
act as your personal assistant
by filtering messages you
receive.

You can use a filter to
place specific messages
you receive directly into
a personalized folder.
To create a personalized
folder that can store
messages, see page 206.

FILTER MESSAGES

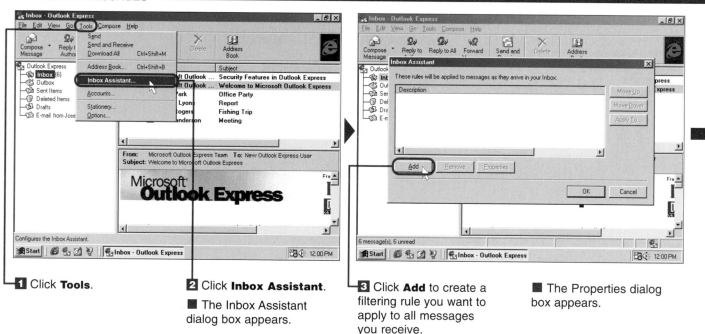

1 Click **Tools**.

2 Click **Inbox Assistant**.

■ The Inbox Assistant
dialog box appears.

3 Click **Add** to create a
filtering rule you want to
apply to all messages
you receive.

■ The Properties dialog
box appears.

How can I filter messages I receive?

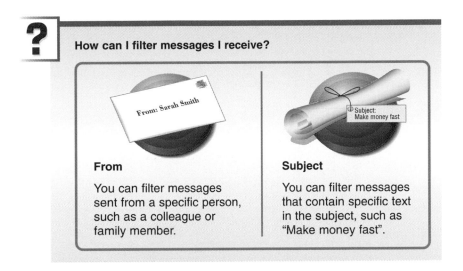

From

You can filter messages sent from a specific person, such as a colleague or family member.

Subject

You can filter messages that contain specific text in the subject, such as "Make money fast".

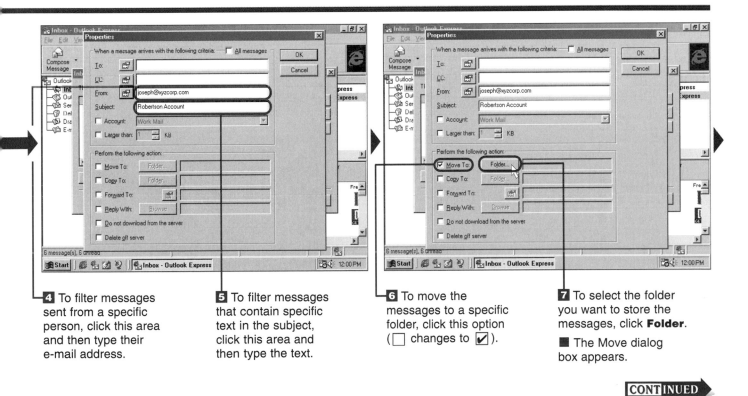

4 To filter messages sent from a specific person, click this area and then type their e-mail address.

5 To filter messages that contain specific text in the subject, click this area and then type the text.

6 To move the messages to a specific folder, click this option (☐ changes to ☑).

7 To select the folder you want to store the messages, click **Folder**.

■ The Move dialog box appears.

CONTINUED ▶

Filters are ideal for automatically moving messages of no interest to the Deleted Items folder. This can save you time when reading your messages.

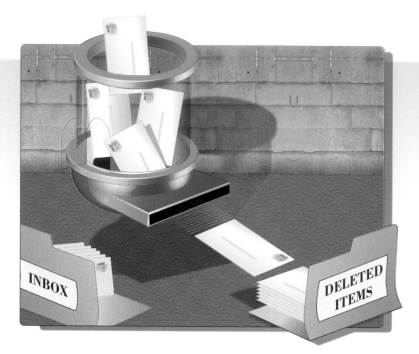

INBOX

DELETED ITEMS

FILTER MESSAGES (CONTINUED)

8 Click the folder you want to store the messages.

9 Click **OK** to confirm your selection.

■ This area displays the name of the folder you selected.

10 Click **OK** to confirm all of your selections.

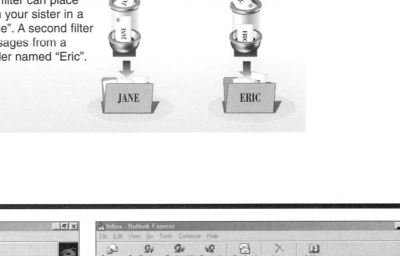

Can I use more than one filter?

Yes. You can create a filter for each person or subject of interest. For example, one filter can place all messages from your sister in a folder named "Jane". A second filter can place all messages from a colleague in a folder named "Eric".

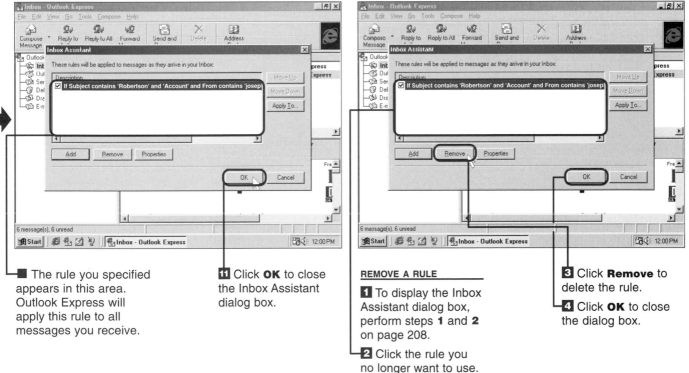

■ The rule you specified appears in this area. Outlook Express will apply this rule to all messages you receive.

11 Click **OK** to close the Inbox Assistant dialog box.

REMOVE A RULE

1 To display the Inbox Assistant dialog box, perform steps **1** and **2** on page 208.

2 Click the rule you no longer want to use.

3 Click **Remove** to delete the rule.

4 Click **OK** to close the dialog box.

CHAPTER 10

Using NetMeeting

You can use NetMeeting to communicate and work with other people on the Internet. This chapter shows you how to contact others, exchange information and share a program.

Start and Set Up NetMeeting............214

Place a Call....................................220

Exchange Messages 222

Using the Whiteboard 224

Share a Program 226

START AND SET UP NETMEETING

NetMeeting allows you to communicate with other people on the Internet.

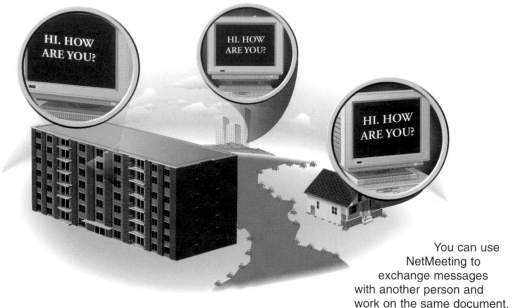

You can use NetMeeting to exchange messages with another person and work on the same document.

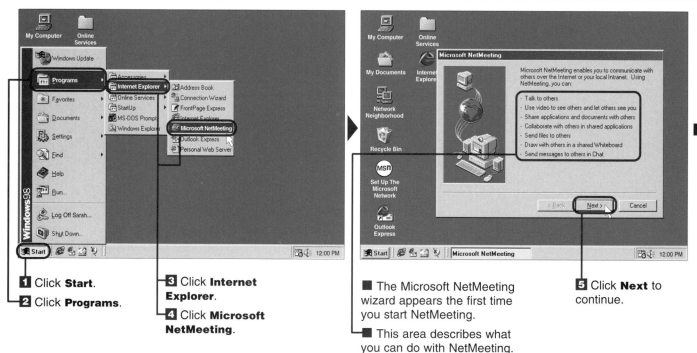

1 Click **Start**.

2 Click **Programs**.

3 Click **Internet Explorer**.

4 Click **Microsoft NetMeeting**.

■ The Microsoft NetMeeting wizard appears the first time you start NetMeeting.

■ This area describes what you can do with NetMeeting.

5 Click **Next** to continue.

214

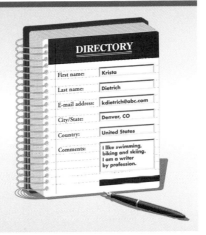

How can other NetMeeting users contact me?

Windows can include your name in a directory that everyone using NetMeeting can view. The directory shows your e-mail address, first name, last name, city/state, country and comments. The information that appears in the directory depends on the information you enter in the Microsoft NetMeeting wizard.

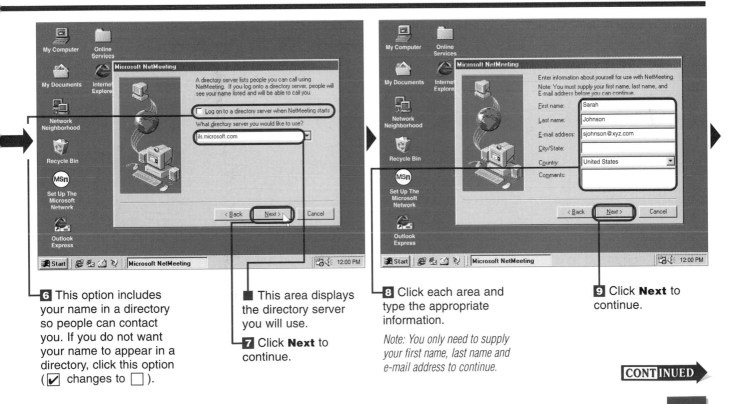

6 This option includes your name in a directory so people can contact you. If you do not want your name to appear in a directory, click this option (☑ changes to ☐).

■ This area displays the directory server you will use.

7 Click **Next** to continue.

8 Click each area and type the appropriate information.

Note: You only need to supply your first name, last name and e-mail address to continue.

9 Click **Next** to continue.

CONTINUED

START AND SET UP NETMEETING

You can choose to categorize your information as personal, business or adults-only.

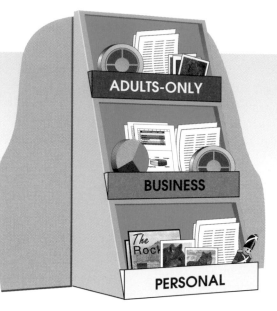

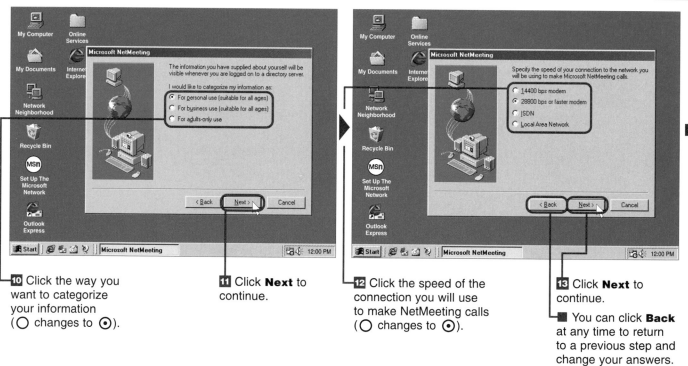

10 Click the way you want to categorize your information (○ changes to ⊙).

11 Click **Next** to continue.

12 Click the speed of the connection you will use to make NetMeeting calls (○ changes to ⊙).

13 Click **Next** to continue.

■ You can click **Back** at any time to return to a previous step and change your answers.

What equipment do I need to hear sound when using NetMeeting?

You need a sound card and speakers to hear sound when using NetMeeting. You need a microphone to talk to another person. Only two people in a meeting can use microphones to communicate.

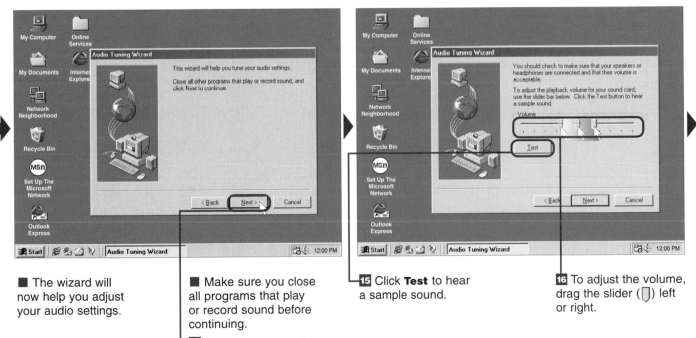

■ The wizard will now help you adjust your audio settings.

■ Make sure you close all programs that play or record sound before continuing.

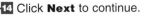 Click **Next** to continue.

15 Click **Test** to hear a sample sound.

16 To adjust the volume, drag the slider ( ) left or right.

CONTINUED ▶

START AND SET UP NETMEETING

The wizard will make
sure your microphone is
working and the volume
is at an acceptable level.

START AND SET UP NETMEETING (CONTINUED)

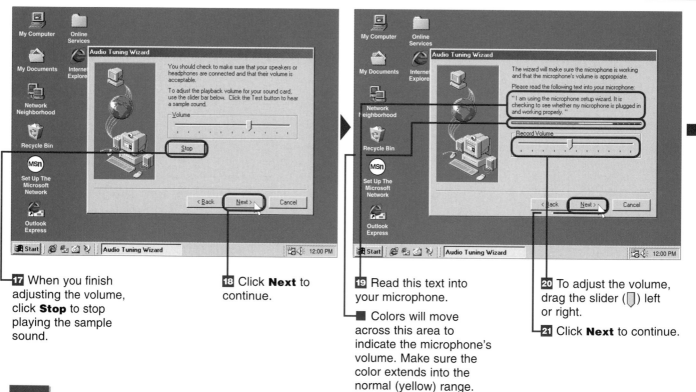

17 When you finish
adjusting the volume,
click **Stop** to stop
playing the sample
sound.

18 Click **Next** to
continue.

19 Read this text into
your microphone.

■ Colors will move
across this area to
indicate the microphone's
volume. Make sure the
color extends into the
normal (yellow) range.

20 To adjust the volume,
drag the slider (▯) left
or right.

21 Click **Next** to continue.

? Can I use NetMeeting to send video images?

You can use NetMeeting to send a video image of yourself to the person you contact. You need a video-capture card and camera or a camera that supports Video for Windows. If you do not have any video equipment, you can still receive a video image from the other person.

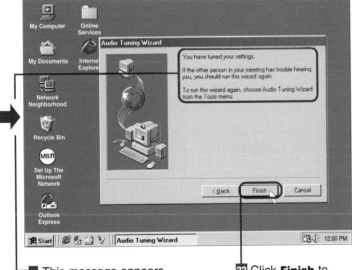

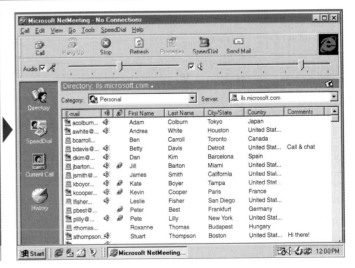

■ This message appears when the setup of NetMeeting is complete.

22 Click **Finish** to start NetMeeting.

■ The Microsoft NetMeeting window appears.

PLACE A CALL

You can place a call to contact another person on the Internet.

Dan Duncan

Call

The person you want to call must have NetMeeting open on their computer.

■ **PLACE A CALL** ■

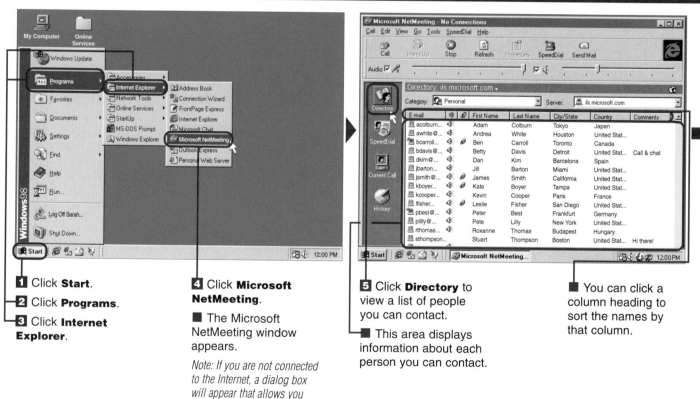

1 Click **Start**.

2 Click **Programs**.

3 Click **Internet Explorer**.

4 Click **Microsoft NetMeeting**.

■ The Microsoft NetMeeting window appears.

Note: If you are not connected to the Internet, a dialog box will appear that allows you to connect.

5 Click **Directory** to view a list of people you can contact.

■ This area displays information about each person you can contact.

■ You can click a column heading to sort the names by that column.

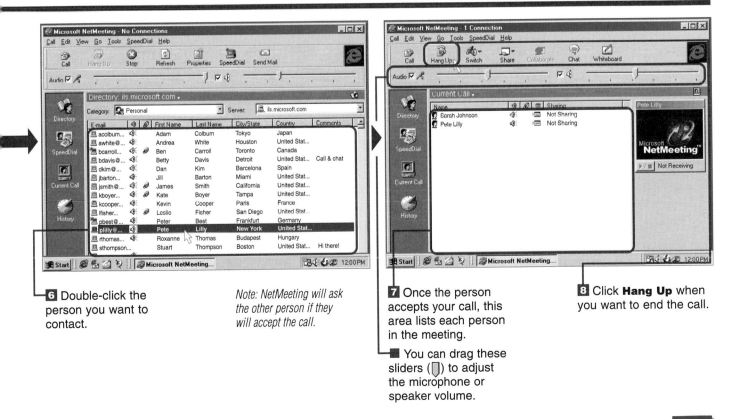

What do the symbols beside the names in the directory mean?

米旦	Person is in a call
旦	Person is not in a call
◁×	Person has a microphone and speakers
🎥	Person has a video camera

6 Double-click the person you want to contact.

Note: NetMeeting will ask the other person if they will accept the call.

7 Once the person accepts your call, this area lists each person in the meeting.

■ You can drag these sliders (▯) to adjust the microphone or speaker volume.

8 Click **Hang Up** when you want to end the call.

EXCHANGE MESSAGES

You can exchange messages with other people using NetMeeting. This is known as chatting. A message you send will instantly appear on the computer of each person in the meeting.

EXCHANGE MESSAGES

1 Call the person you want to chat with. See page 220 to place a call.

2 Click **Chat** to chat with the person.

■ The Chat window appears.

3 Click this area and then type the message you want to send.

4 Click 🔲 to send the message.

Note: The other person will not see the text you type until you send the message.

? **Is there a faster way to communicate when using NetMeeting?**

If you and the other person both have a microphone, sound card and speakers, you can talk to each other without paying any long-distance charges.

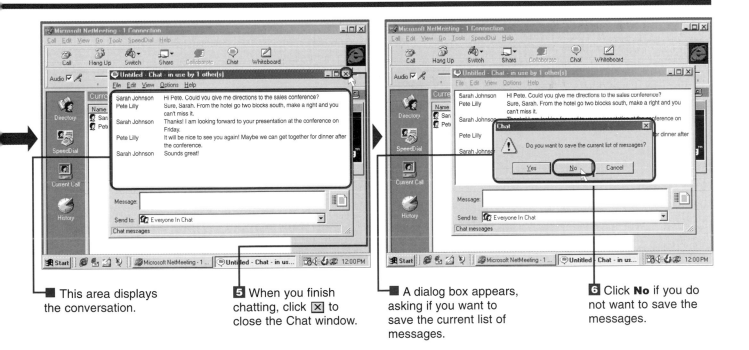

■ This area displays the conversation.

5 When you finish chatting, click ☒ to close the Chat window.

■ A dialog box appears, asking if you want to save the current list of messages.

6 Click **No** if you do not want to save the messages.

USING THE WHITEBOARD

You can use NetMeeting to work on a Whiteboard with other people. You can draw images on the Whiteboard that will instantly appear on the other computer screens.

USING THE WHITEBOARD

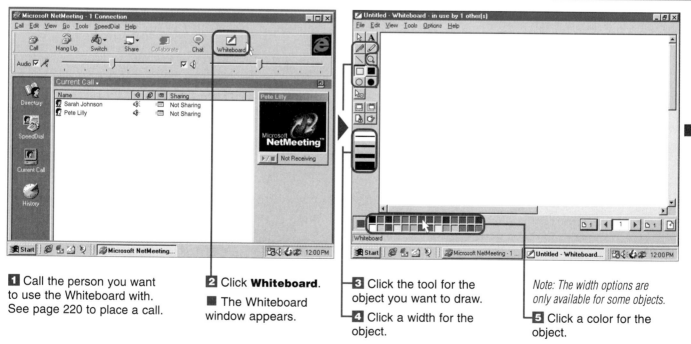

1 Call the person you want to use the Whiteboard with. See page 220 to place a call.

2 Click **Whiteboard**.

■ The Whiteboard window appears.

3 Click the tool for the object you want to draw.

4 Click a width for the object.

Note: The width options are only available for some objects.

5 Click a color for the object.

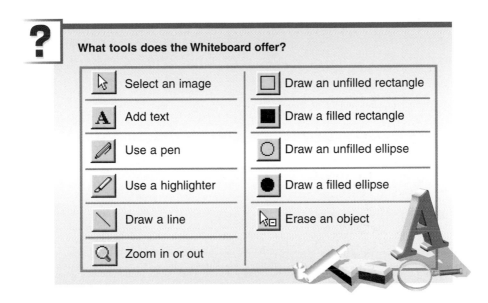

What tools does the Whiteboard offer?

▶	Select an image	□	Draw an unfilled rectangle
A	Add text	■	Draw a filled rectangle
✏	Use a pen	○	Draw an unfilled ellipse
✏	Use a highlighter	●	Draw a filled ellipse
╲	Draw a line	▶	Erase an object
🔍	Zoom in or out		

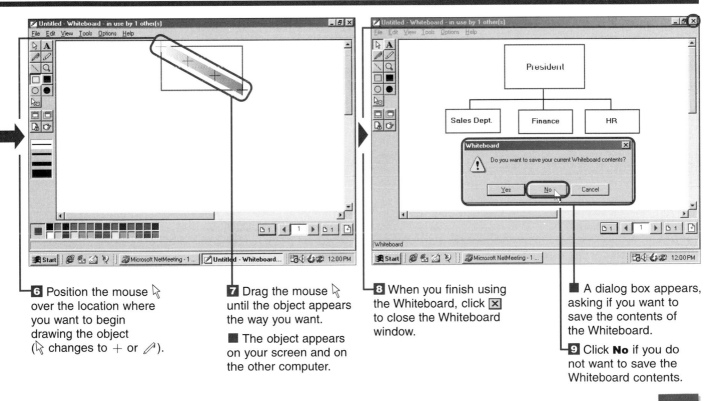

6 Position the mouse ▶ over the location where you want to begin drawing the object (▶ changes to + or ✏).

7 Drag the mouse ▶ until the object appears the way you want.

■ The object appears on your screen and on the other computer.

8 When you finish using the Whiteboard, click ☒ to close the Whiteboard window.

■ A dialog box appears, asking if you want to save the contents of the Whiteboard.

9 Click **No** if you do not want to save the Whiteboard contents.

SHARE A PROGRAM

You can use NetMeeting to work on a document with another person at the same time.

When you share a program, the other person does not need the program installed on their computer.

■ SHARE A PROGRAM ■

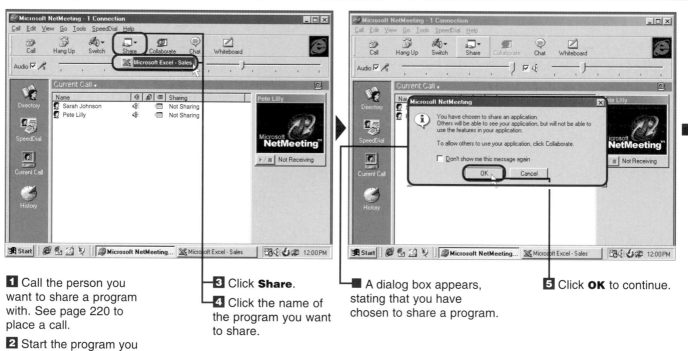

1 Call the person you want to share a program with. See page 220 to place a call.

2 Start the program you want to share. To start a program, see page 8.

3 Click **Share**.

4 Click the name of the program you want to share.

■ A dialog box appears, stating that you have chosen to share a program.

5 Click **OK** to continue.

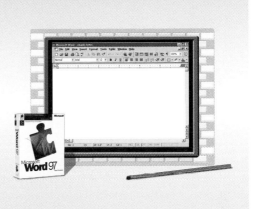

Why would I share a program with other people?

You can share a program to teach another person how to use the program. Sharing a program is also useful when two or more people are working on the same project. Each person can view and make changes to a document at the same time. This is known as collaborating.

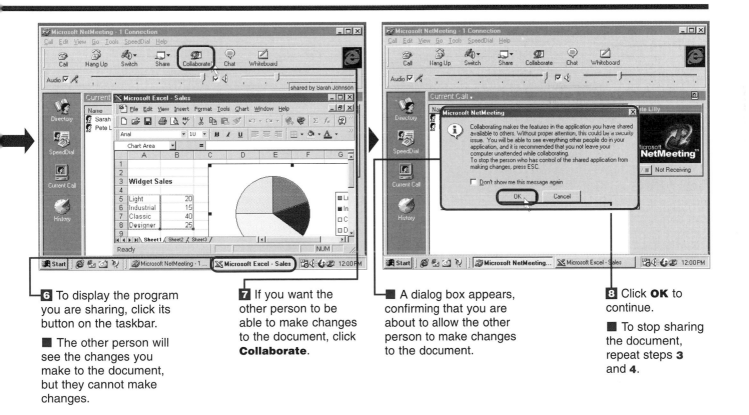

6 To display the program you are sharing, click its button on the taskbar.

■ The other person will see the changes you make to the document, but they cannot make changes.

7 If you want the other person to be able to make changes to the document, click **Collaborate**.

■ A dialog box appears, confirming that you are about to allow the other person to make changes to the document.

8 Click **OK** to continue.

■ To stop sharing the document, repeat steps **3** and **4**.

Using Chat

Chat is a fun way to communicate with other people on the Internet. Read this chapter and find out how to enter a chat room and join a conversation.

Enter a Chat Room 230

Join the Conversation 234

HAT

ENTER A CHAT ROOM

You can chat with others on the Internet by using Microsoft Chat. Each person in a chat room appears as a cartoon character in a comic strip.

If the Microsoft Chat feature is not available, you need to add the Microsoft Chat component from the Communications category. To add Windows components, see page 118.

■ ENTER A CHAT ROOM ■

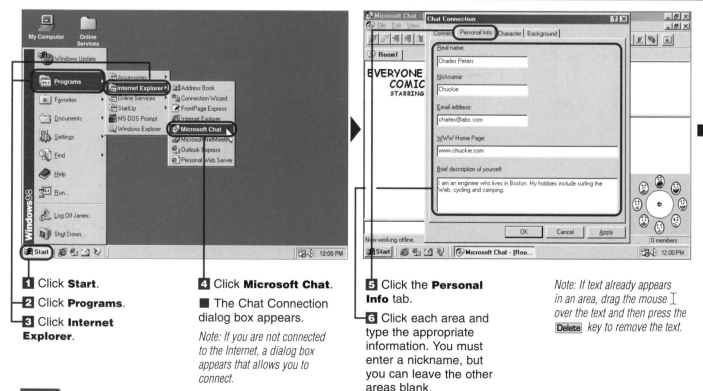

1 Click **Start**.

2 Click **Programs**.

3 Click **Internet Explorer**.

4 Click **Microsoft Chat**.

■ The Chat Connection dialog box appears.

Note: If you are not connected to the Internet, a dialog box appears that allows you to connect.

5 Click the **Personal Info** tab.

6 Click each area and type the appropriate information. You must enter a nickname, but you can leave the other areas blank.

Note: If text already appears in an area, drag the mouse I over the text and then press the Delete *key to remove the text.*

Do I need to enter personal information and select a character each time I start Microsoft Chat?

You only need to enter personal information and select a character the first time you use Microsoft Chat. Windows will remember the information you enter. The next time you start Microsoft Chat, you can skip steps **5** to **10** shown below.

Real name:
John Smith

Nickname:
Bashful

Email address:
jsmith@abc.com

Brief description of yourself:
I enjoy biking, running and softball

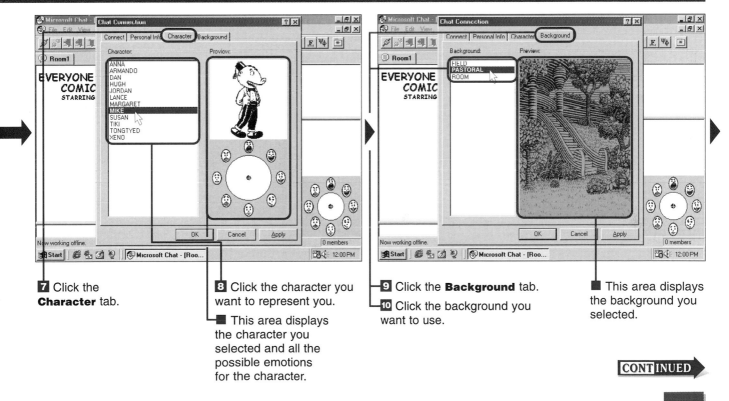

7 Click the **Character** tab.

8 Click the character you want to represent you.

■ This area displays the character you selected and all the possible emotions for the character.

9 Click the **Background** tab.

10 Click the background you want to use.

■ This area displays the background you selected.

CONTINUED

ENTER A CHAT ROOM

Microsoft Chat offers thousands of chat rooms that you can enter. Each chat room discusses a specific topic.

Entertainment   **Romance**   **Travel**

■ **ENTER A CHAT ROOM** (CONTINUED) ■

[Screenshot 1 - Chat Connection dialog]

Chat Connection

Connect | Personal Info | Character | Background |

Welcome to Microsoft Chat. You can specify chat server connection information here, and optionally adjust your Personal Information from the next tab.

Users of comics mode can choose a character and background from two additional tabs.

Favorites:

Server:
mschat.msn.com

○ Go to chat room: #Comic_Chat
⦿ Show all available chat rooms.

OK   Cancel   Apply

Now working offline.

[Screenshot 2 - Chat Room List / Message of the Day]

Chat Room List

Display chat rooms that contain: [   ]   ☐ Also search in room topics

☐ Show only registered rooms   Members: Min: 0   Max: 9999

Room
Accountan
Acting_Ge
Action_Mo
Al's_Room
Alaska_Ch
All_Career
Animal_Ca
Antiquaria
Antique_C
Antique_F
Aquatic_S
Archaeolo
Army_Cha
Art_Painti
Artists_Ge
Arts
Authors
Autos

Message of the Day

There are 3515 users and 1004 invisible on 1 servers
4 operator(s) online
70 unknown connection(s)
1212 channels formed
I have 3515 clients and 0 servers

Welcome to IRC.MSN.COM

The chats available in this area are not under the control of Microsoft.
Microsoft does not control or endorse the content, message,

☑ Show this whenever connecting   OK

Update List   Go To   Create Room...   Cancel

1271 rooms shown   Time of last search: 12:00:00 PM

11 Click the **Connect** tab.

12 Click this option to view a list of the available chat rooms (○ changes to ⦿).

13 Click **OK**.

■ The Chat Room List dialog box appears, listing the available chat rooms.

■ The Message of the Day dialog box also appears, showing today's message.

14 Click **OK** to close the dialog box.

How can I enter another chat room?

You can visit another chat room at any time. Click the Chat Room List button (🖼) at the top of your screen to redisplay the list of available chat rooms. This allows you to select another room.

■ This area lists the name, number of members and topic for each chat room.

15 To display chat room names containing a specific word, click this area and then type the word.

16 Double-click the chat room you want to join.

■ This area shows the conversation.

■ This area lists the people in the chat room.

■ This area shows the character that represents you and all the possible emotions for your character.

JOIN THE CONVERSATION

When you enter a chat room, you can immediately start chatting with other people in the room.

JOIN THE CONVERSATION

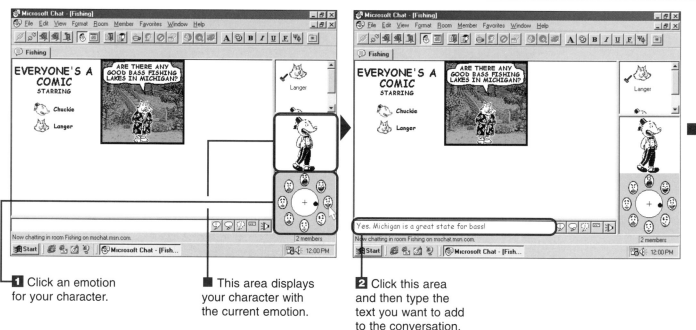

1 Click an emotion for your character.

■ This area displays your character with the current emotion.

2 Click this area and then type the text you want to add to the conversation.

How can I communicate with others in a chat room?

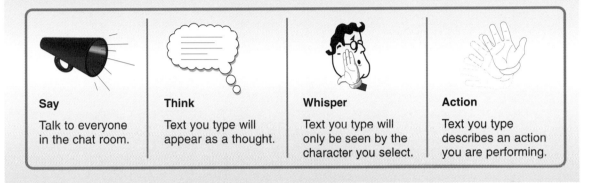

Say

Talk to everyone in the chat room.

Think

Text you type will appear as a thought.

Whisper

Text you type will only be seen by the character you select.

Action

Text you type describes an action you are performing.

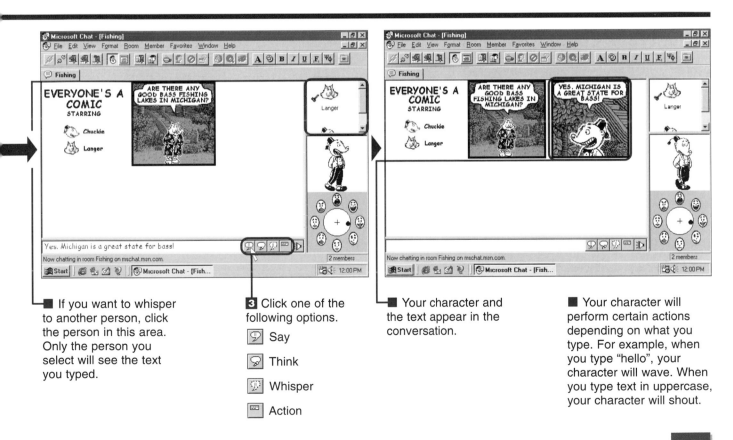

■ If you want to whisper to another person, click the person in this area. Only the person you select will see the text you typed.

3 Click one of the following options.

Say

Think

Whisper

Action

■ Your character and the text appear in the conversation.

■ Your character will perform certain actions depending on what you type. For example, when you type "hello", your character will wave. When you type text in uppercase, your character will shout.

CHAPTER 12

Exchange Information Between Computers

Windows 98 offers several ways for you to connect to other computers and exchange information. In this chapter you will learn how to exchange information between computers at the office or while traveling.

Using Briefcase 238

Using Direct Cable Connection 246

Using Dial-Up Networking................254

Using WinPopup to
    Exchange Messages......................264

USING BRIEFCASE

Briefcase lets you work with files while you are away from the office. When you return, Briefcase will update all the files you have changed.

TRANSFER FILES TO BRIEFCASE

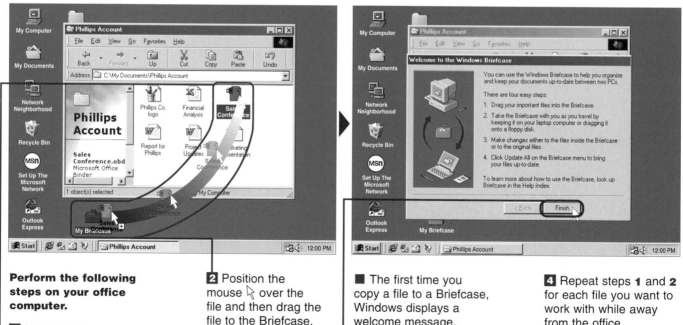

Perform the following steps on your office computer.

1 Locate a file you want to work with while away from the office.

2 Position the mouse ⬚ over the file and then drag the file to the Briefcase.

■ The first time you copy a file to a Briefcase, Windows displays a welcome message.

3 Click **Finish** to close the message.

4 Repeat steps **1** and **2** for each file you want to work with while away from the office.

? **Why doesn't a Briefcase icon appear on my desktop?**

If a Briefcase icon does not appear on your desktop, you may need to add the Briefcase component from the Accessories category. To add Windows components, see page 118. If Briefcase is not displayed in the Windows components list, Briefcase is already installed on your computer and you must create a new Briefcase icon on your desktop. See page 245 for more information.

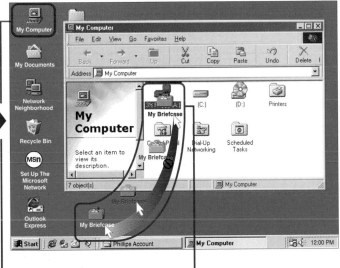

■ **5** Insert a floppy disk into the floppy drive.

■ **6** Double-click **My Computer**.

■ The My Computer window appears.

■ **7** Drag the Briefcase to the drive that contains the floppy disk.

■ Windows moves the Briefcase to the floppy disk. The Briefcase disappears from your screen.

■ You can now remove the floppy disk from the drive so you can transfer the Briefcase to your home or portable computer.

USING BRIEFCASE

When traveling or at home, you can work with Briefcase files as you would work with any files on your computer.

WORK WITH BRIEFCASE FILES

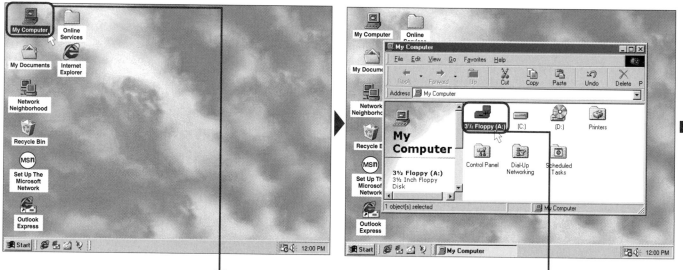

Perform the following steps on your home or portable computer.

1 Insert the floppy disk containing the Briefcase into the floppy drive.

2 Double-click **My Computer**.

■ The My Computer window appears.

3 Double-click the drive that contains the floppy disk.

12

EXCHANGE INFORMATION BETWEEN COMPUTERS

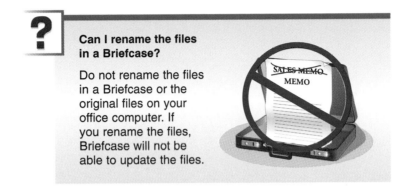

? Can I rename the files in a Briefcase?

Do not rename the files in a Briefcase or the original files on your office computer. If you rename the files, Briefcase will not be able to update the files.

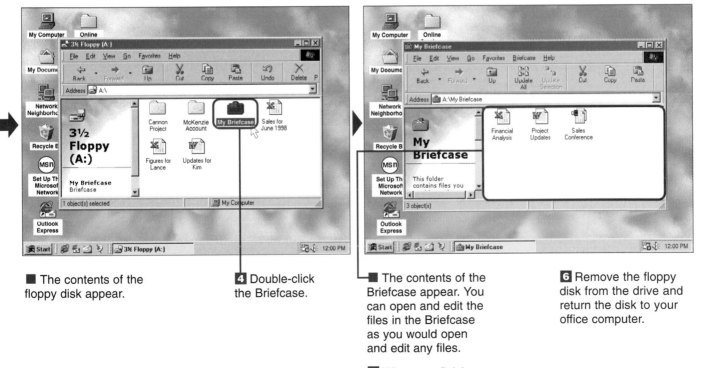

■ The contents of the floppy disk appear.

4 Double-click the Briefcase.

■ The contents of the Briefcase appear. You can open and edit the files in the Briefcase as you would open and edit any files.

5 When you finish working with the files, save and close the files.

6 Remove the floppy disk from the drive and return the disk to your office computer.

241

When you return to the office, you can update the files you have changed.

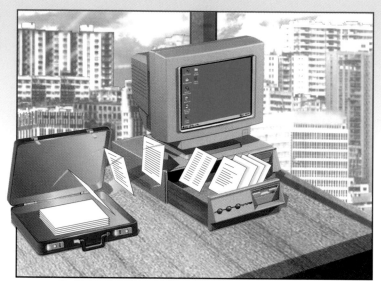

Windows compares the files in the Briefcase to the files on your office computer to decide which files need to be updated.

UPDATE BRIEFCASE FILES

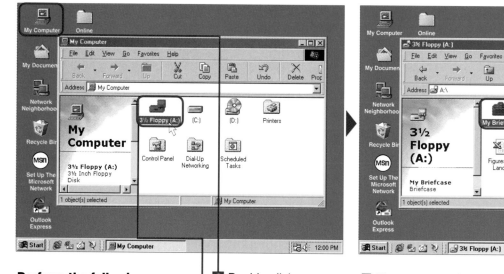

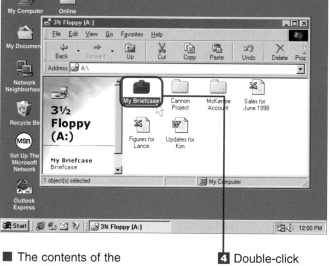

Perform the following steps on your office computer.

1 Insert the floppy disk containing the Briefcase into the floppy drive.

2 Double-click **My Computer**.

■ The My Computer window appears.

3 Double-click the drive containing the floppy disk.

■ The contents of the floppy disk appear.

4 Double-click the Briefcase.

? Is there a better way to transfer files between computers than using a floppy disk?

You can use Direct Cable Connection to exchange files between your office and portable computer. This is faster than using a floppy disk to transfer files and is ideal for transferring a large number of files. See page 246 for information on Direct Cable Connection.

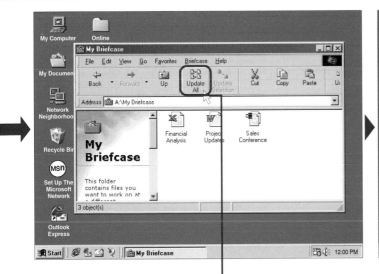

■ The contents of the Briefcase appear.

5 To update the files on your office computer, click **Update All**.

■ The Update dialog box appears.

■ This area displays the name of each file that needs to be updated and the way Windows will update each file.

CONTINUED

When using Briefcase, you can change the way Windows updates a file.

Do not update the file (↷).

Replace office file with Briefcase file (⟹).

Replace Briefcase file with office file (⟸).

UPDATE BRIEFCASE FILES (CONTINUED)

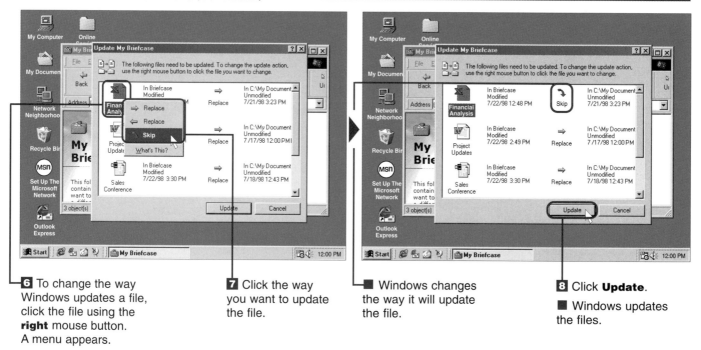

6 To change the way Windows updates a file, click the file using the **right** mouse button. A menu appears.

7 Click the way you want to update the file.

■ Windows changes the way it will update the file.

8 Click **Update**.

■ Windows updates the files.

Can I delete a Briefcase I no longer need?

You can delete an old Briefcase as you would delete any file. Click the Briefcase and then press the Delete key. When the confirmation dialog box appears, click **Yes**. Deleting a Briefcase does not remove the original files from your computer.

CREATE A NEW BRIEFCASE

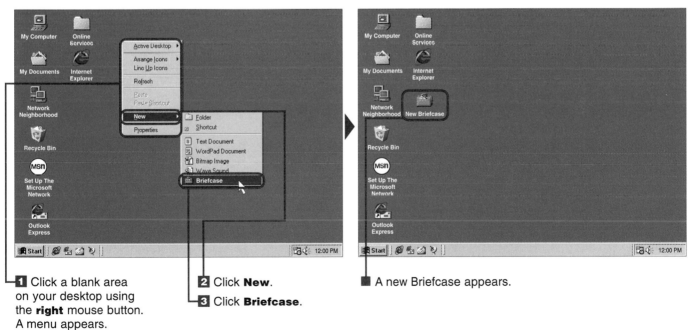

1 Click a blank area on your desktop using the **right** mouse button. A menu appears.

2 Click **New**.

3 Click **Briefcase**.

■ A new Briefcase appears.

USING DIRECT CABLE CONNECTION

You can use a
cable to connect
two computers to
share information.

Direct Cable Connection

Make sure you plug
the cable into both
computers before
setting up a connection.

SET UP DIRECT CABLE CONNECTION

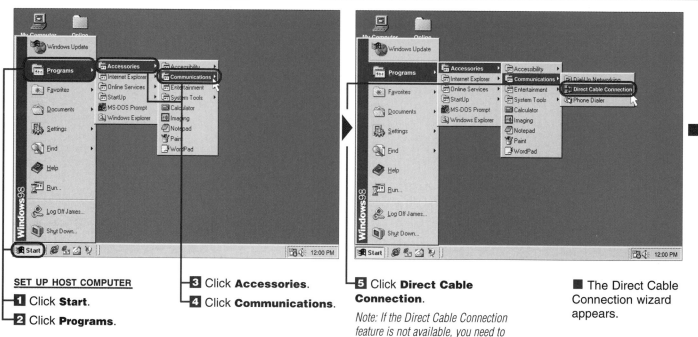

SET UP HOST COMPUTER

■ Click **Start**.

■ Click **Programs**.

■ Click **Accessories**.

■ Click **Communications**.

■ Click **Direct Cable Connection**.

*Note: If the Direct Cable Connection
feature is not available, you need to
add the Direct Cable Connection
component from the Communications
category. To add Windows components,
see page 118.*

■ The Direct Cable
Connection wizard
appears.

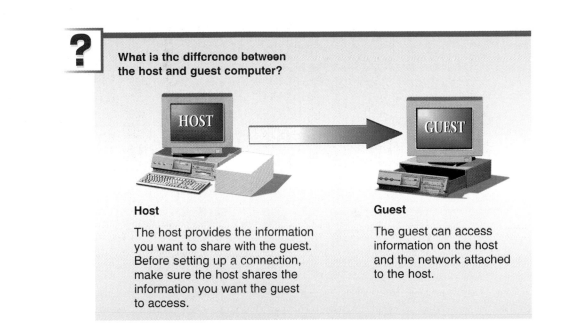

What is the difference between the host and guest computer?

Host

The host provides the information you want to share with the guest. Before setting up a connection, make sure the host shares the information you want the guest to access.

Guest

The guest can access information on the host and the network attached to the host.

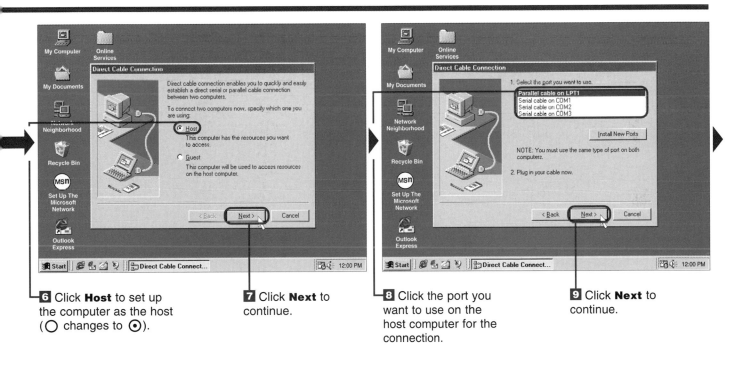

6 Click **Host** to set up the computer as the host (○ changes to ⊙).

7 Click **Next** to continue.

8 Click the port you want to use on the host computer for the connection.

9 Click **Next** to continue.

CONTINUED

USING DIRECT CABLE CONNECTION

You only need to set up a direct cable connection between two computers once. After you set up a connection, you can reconnect the computers at any time.

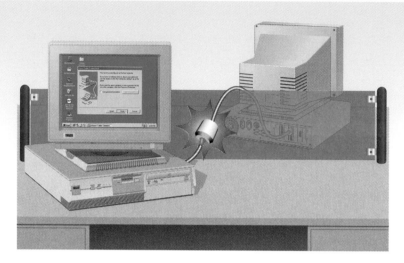

To re-establish a direct cable connection, see page 252.

SET UP DIRECT CABLE CONNECTION

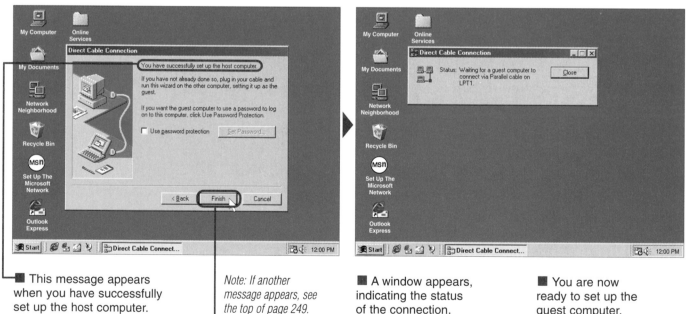

■ This message appears when you have successfully set up the host computer.

Note: If another message appears, see the top of page 249.

10 Click **Finish**.

■ A window appears, indicating the status of the connection.

■ You are now ready to set up the guest computer.

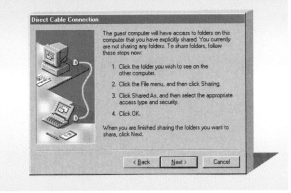

?

Why does this message appear when setting up a connection?

Before setting up a direct cable connection, you must share the information on the host that you want the guest to be able to access.

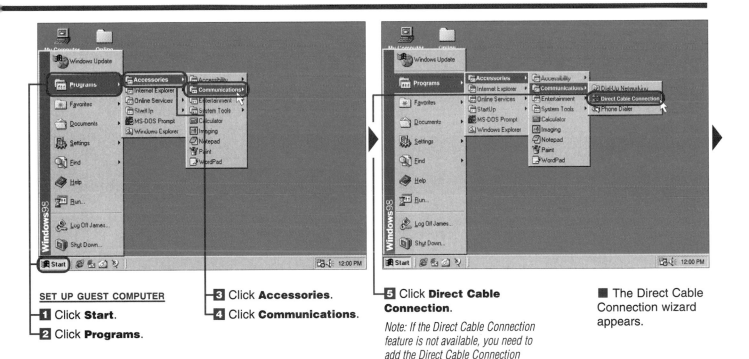

SET UP GUEST COMPUTER

1 Click **Start**.

2 Click **Programs**.

3 Click **Accessories**.

4 Click **Communications**.

5 Click **Direct Cable Connection**.

Note: If the Direct Cable Connection feature is not available, you need to add the Direct Cable Connection component from the Communications category. To add Windows components, see page 118.

■ The Direct Cable Connection wizard appears.

CONTINUED

USING DIRECT CABLE CONNECTION

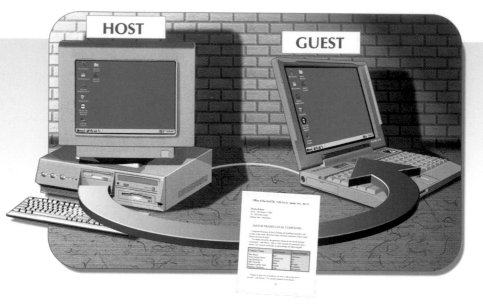

Once you set up a direct cable connection, the guest can access the information on the host and the network attached to the host.

■ SET UP DIRECT CABLE CONNECTION ■

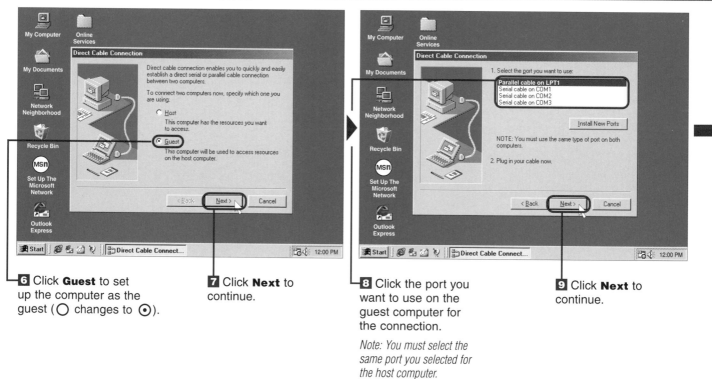

6 Click **Guest** to set up the computer as the guest (○ changes to ⊙).

7 Click **Next** to continue.

8 Click the port you want to use on the guest computer for the connection.

Note: You must select the same port you selected for the host computer.

9 Click **Next** to continue.

What type of cable can I use for a direct cable connection?

You need a parallel cable or a serial cable designed for transferring data. A parallel cable transfers information faster and is more commonly used for direct cable connections.

PARALLEL

SERIAL

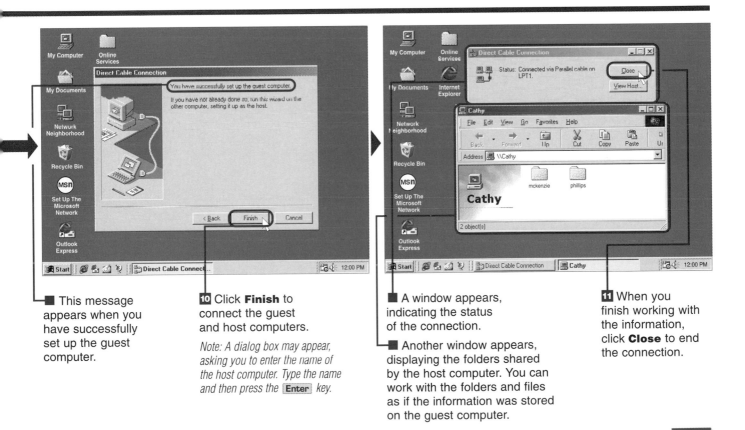

■ This message appears when you have successfully set up the guest computer.

10 Click **Finish** to connect the guest and host computers.

Note: A dialog box may appear, asking you to enter the name of the host computer. Type the name and then press the **Enter** *key.*

■ A window appears, indicating the status of the connection.

■ Another window appears, displaying the folders shared by the host computer. You can work with the folders and files as if the information was stored on the guest computer.

11 When you finish working with the information, click **Close** to end the connection.

USING DIRECT CABLE CONNECTION

After you set up a direct cable connection, you can re-establish a connection at any time.

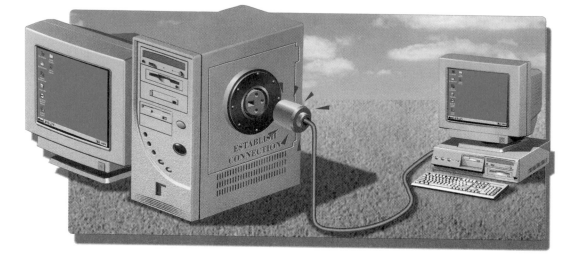

RE-ESTABLISH DIRECT CABLE CONNECTION

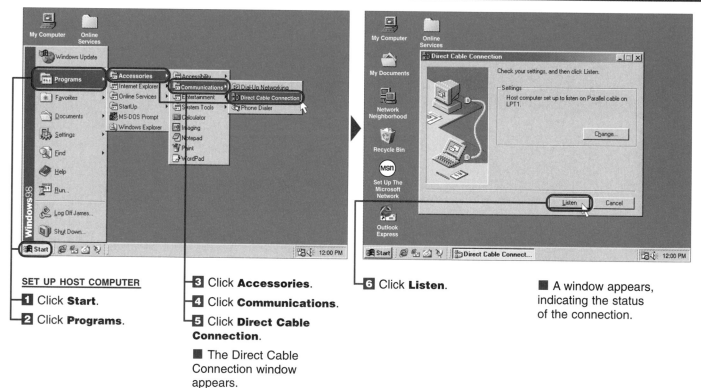

SET UP HOST COMPUTER

1 Click **Start**.

2 Click **Programs**.

3 Click **Accessories**.

4 Click **Communications**.

5 Click **Direct Cable Connection**.

■ The Direct Cable Connection window appears.

6 Click **Listen**.

■ A window appears, indicating the status of the connection.

?

When would I use a direct cable connection to connect two computers?

You can use a direct cable connection instead of floppy disks to transfer information from your office computer to a portable computer. You can then work with the files on your portable computer at home or when traveling. If you want the files to update automatically when you return to the office, use the Briefcase feature. For information on the Briefcase feature, see page 238.

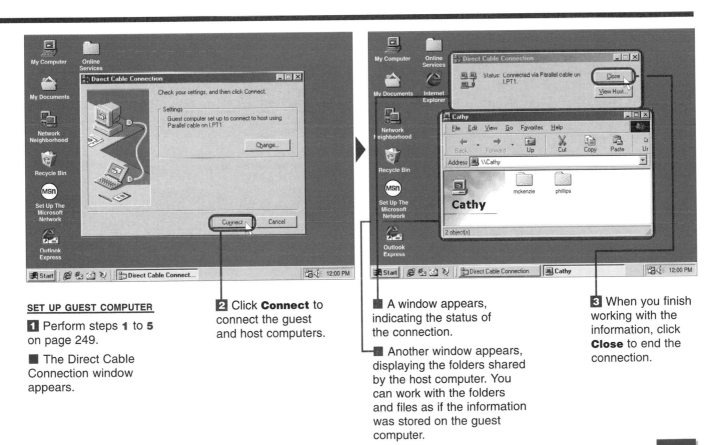

SET UP GUEST COMPUTER

1 Perform steps **1** to **5** on page 249.

■ The Direct Cable Connection window appears.

2 Click **Connect** to connect the guest and host computers.

■ A window appears, indicating the status of the connection.

■ Another window appears, displaying the folders shared by the host computer. You can work with the folders and files as if the information was stored on the guest computer.

3 When you finish working with the information, click **Close** to end the connection.

USING DIAL-UP NETWORKING

When at home or traveling, you can use Dial-Up Networking to access information on a computer at work.

You need a modem to connect to a computer at work.

SET UP A CONNECTION TO ANOTHER COMPUTER

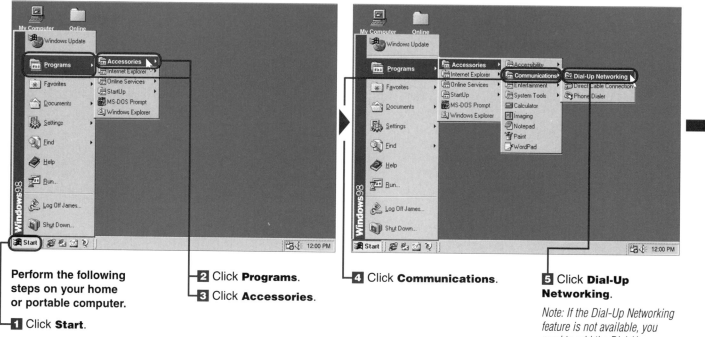

Perform the following steps on your home or portable computer.

1 Click **Start**.

2 Click **Programs**.

3 Click **Accessories**.

4 Click **Communications**.

5 Click **Dial-Up Networking**.

Note: If the Dial-Up Networking feature is not available, you need to add the Dial-Up Networking component from the Communications category. To add Windows components, see page 118.

? How do I prepare my office computer to be accessed?

The computer you want to contact at work must have a modem, be turned on and be set up as a dial-up server. You also need to share the information you want to access on the computer. See page 262 to set up an office computer as a dial-up server.

Dial-Up Server

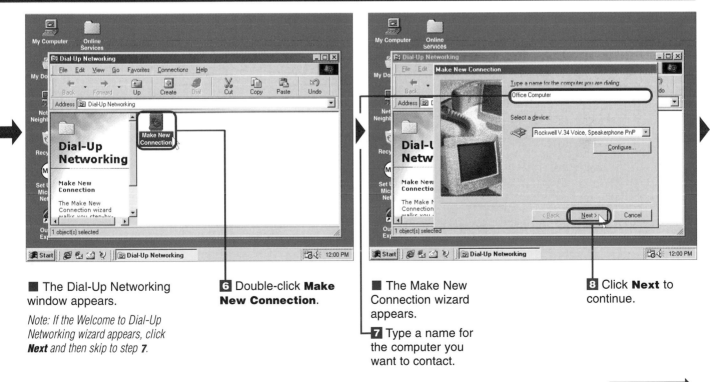

■ The Dial-Up Networking window appears.

Note: If the Welcome to Dial-Up Networking wizard appears, click ***Next*** *and then skip to step* ***7***.

6 Double-click **Make New Connection**.

■ The Make New Connection wizard appears.

7 Type a name for the computer you want to contact.

8 Click **Next** to continue.

CONTINUED

USING DIAL-UP NETWORKING

Before connecting to another computer, you must provide Windows with information about the computer you want to contact.

SET UP A CONNECTION TO ANOTHER COMPUTER (CONTINUED)

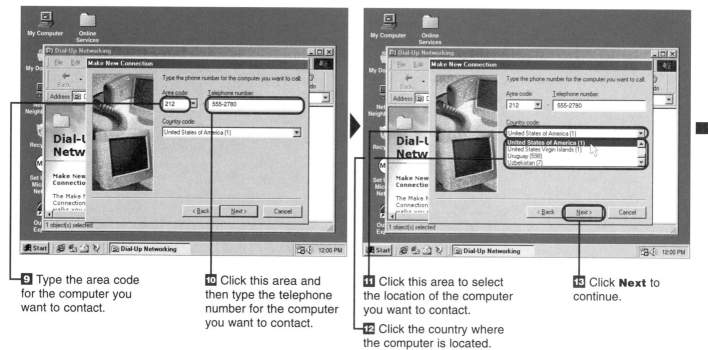

9 Type the area code for the computer you want to contact.

10 Click this area and then type the telephone number for the computer you want to contact.

11 Click this area to select the location of the computer you want to contact.

12 Click the country where the computer is located.

13 Click **Next** to continue.

?

Do I need to set up a connection every time I want to contact a computer at work?

You only need to set up a connection to a computer once. After you set up the connection, you can dial in to the computer at any time. To dial in to another computer, see page 258.

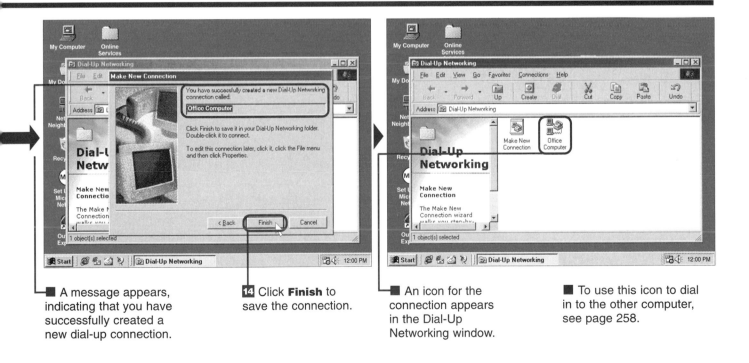

■ A message appears, indicating that you have successfully created a new dial-up connection.

14 Click **Finish** to save the connection.

■ An icon for the connection appears in the Dial-Up Networking window.

■ To use this icon to dial in to the other computer, see page 258.

USING DIAL-UP NETWORKING

After you set up a connection to the office computer, you can dial in to the computer to access information.

DIAL IN TO ANOTHER COMPUTER

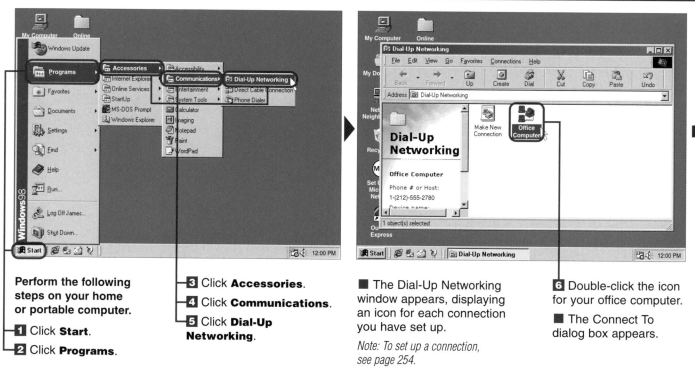

Perform the following steps on your home or portable computer.

1 Click **Start**.

2 Click **Programs**.

3 Click **Accessories**.

4 Click **Communications**.

5 Click **Dial-Up Networking**.

■ The Dial-Up Networking window appears, displaying an icon for each connection you have set up.

Note: To set up a connection, see page 254.

6 Double-click the icon for your office computer.

■ The Connect To dialog box appears.

? **Why did my modem disconnect from the office computer?**

Your modem may disconnect if there is interference on the phone line. Try connecting again to get a better connection. Your modem may also disconnect if you do not use your computer for a long period of time.

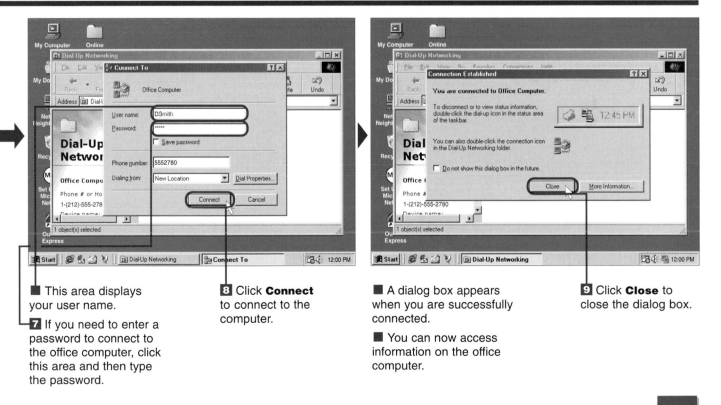

■ This area displays your user name.

7 If you need to enter a password to connect to the office computer, click this area and then type the password.

8 Click **Connect** to connect to the computer.

■ A dialog box appears when you are successfully connected.

■ You can now access information on the office computer.

9 Click **Close** to close the dialog box.

USING DIAL-UP NETWORKING

Once you connect to the office computer, you can work with the files as if the files were stored on your own computer.

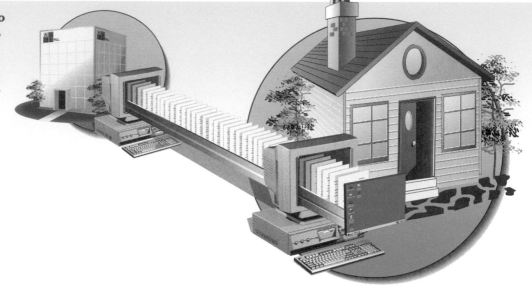

DIAL IN TO ANOTHER COMPUTER (CONTINUED)

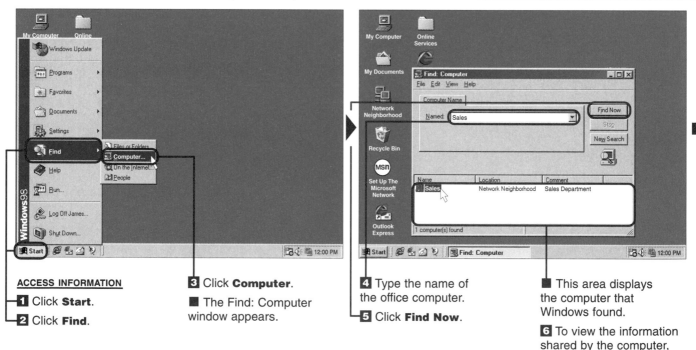

ACCESS INFORMATION

1 Click **Start**.

2 Click **Find**.

3 Click **Computer**.

■ The Find: Computer window appears.

4 Type the name of the office computer.

5 Click **Find Now**.

■ This area displays the computer that Windows found.

6 To view the information shared by the computer, double-click the computer.

?

How do I access information on the network?

Once you connect to the office computer, you will be able to access files stored on the computer and the network attached to the computer. You can use Network Neighborhood to browse through the information stored on the network.

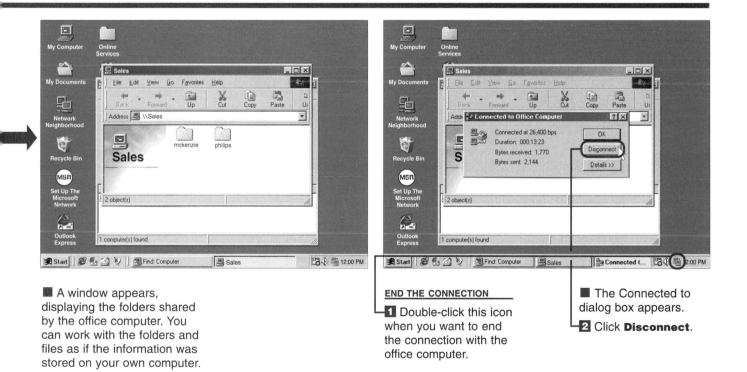

■ A window appears, displaying the folders shared by the office computer. You can work with the folders and files as if the information was stored on your own computer.

END THE CONNECTION

1 Double-click this icon when you want to end the connection with the office computer.

■ The Connected to dialog box appears.

2 Click **Disconnect**.

USING DIAL-UP NETWORKING

You can set up a computer at work as a dial-up server. This allows you to access information on the computer from another location.

The dial-up server needs a modem to receive calls.

If the Dial-Up Networking or Dial-Up Server feature is not available, you need to add the components from the Communications category. To add Windows components, see page 118.

SET UP A DIAL-UP SERVER

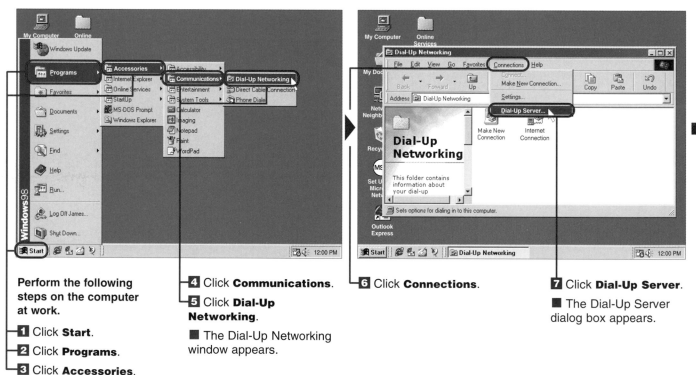

Perform the following steps on the computer at work.

1 Click **Start**.

2 Click **Programs**.

3 Click **Accessories**.

4 Click **Communications**.

5 Click **Dial-Up Networking**.

■ The Dial-Up Networking window appears.

6 Click **Connections**.

7 Click **Dial-Up Server**.

■ The Dial-Up Server dialog box appears.

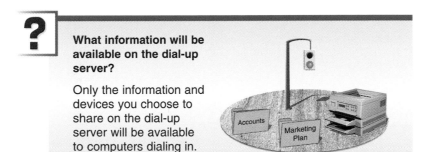

What information will be available on the dial-up server?

Only the information and devices you choose to share on the dial-up server will be available to computers dialing in.

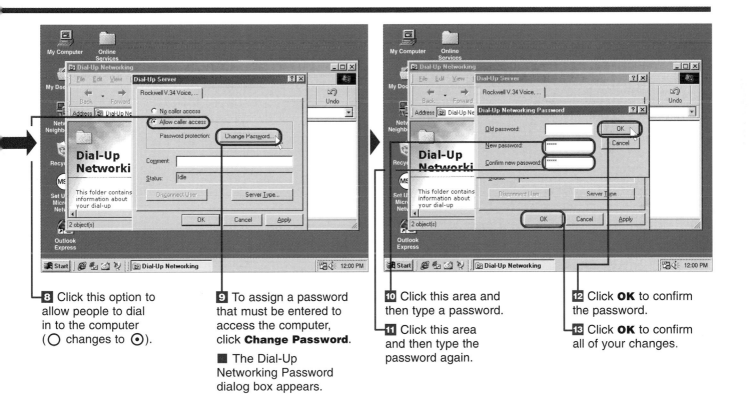

8 Click this option to allow people to dial in to the computer (○ changes to ⊙).

9 To assign a password that must be entered to access the computer, click **Change Password**.

■ The Dial-Up Networking Password dialog box appears.

10 Click this area and then type a password.

11 Click this area and then type the password again.

12 Click **OK** to confirm the password.

13 Click **OK** to confirm all of your changes.

USING WINPOPUP TO EXCHANGE MESSAGES

You can use WinPopup to send and receive quick messages with people on a network.

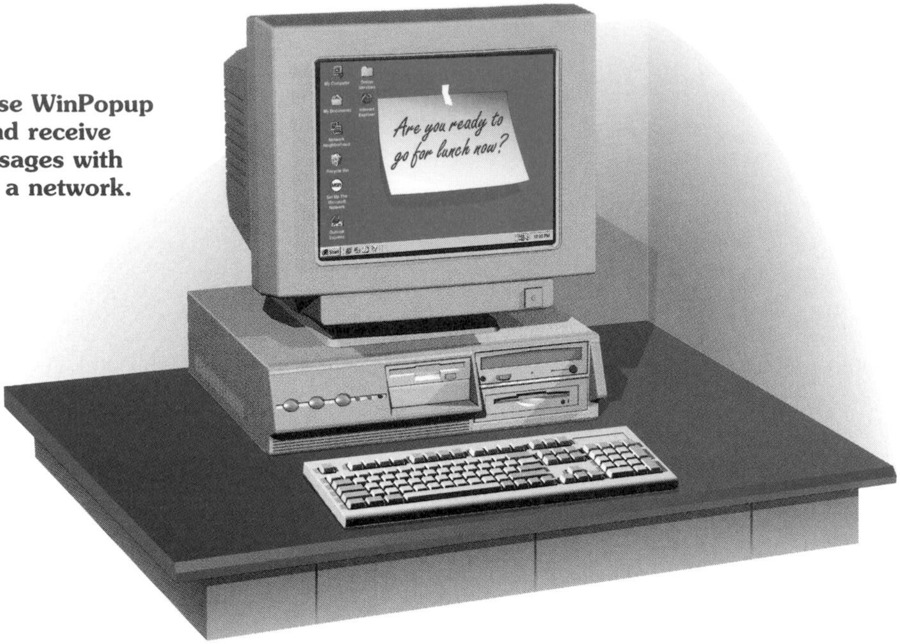

WinPopup is useful for asking questions, expressing ideas and making short announcements.

USING WINPOPUP TO EXCHANGE MESSAGES

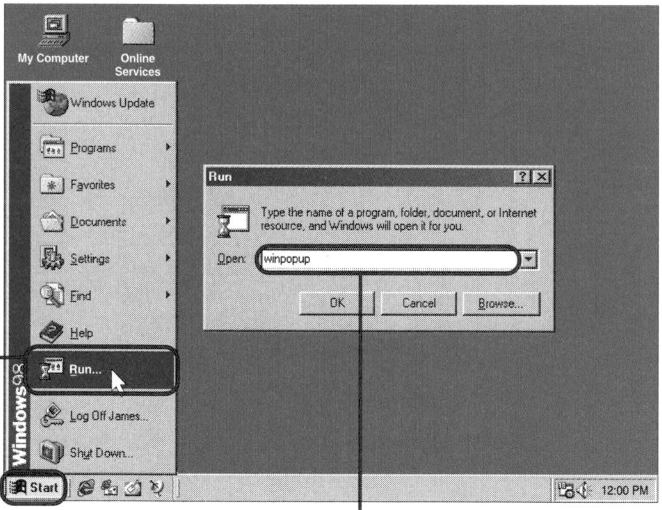

START WINPOPUP

1 Click **Start**.

2 Click **Run**.

■ The Run dialog box appears.

3 Type **winpopup** and then press the **Enter** key.

■ The WinPopup window appears.

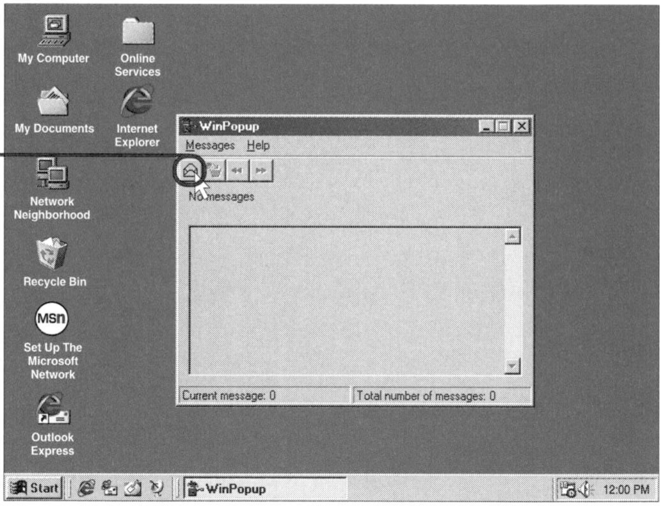

SEND A MESSAGE

1 Click 🏠 to send a new message.

■ The Send Message dialog box appears.

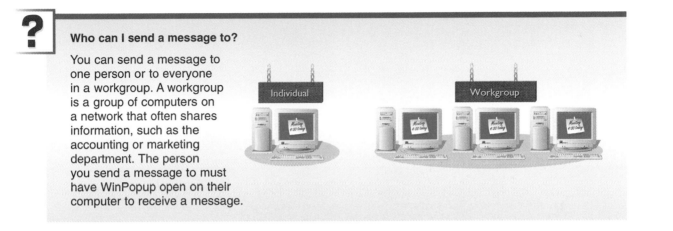

?

Who can I send a message to?

You can send a message to one person or to everyone in a workgroup. A workgroup is a group of computers on a network that often shares information, such as the accounting or marketing department. The person you send a message to must have WinPopup open on their computer to receive a message.

Individual

Workgroup

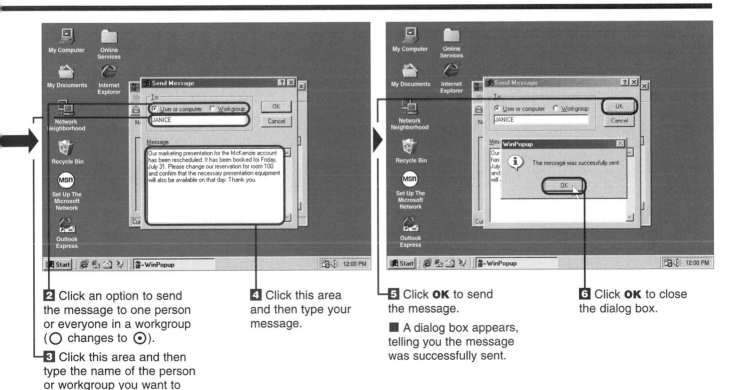

2 Click an option to send the message to one person or everyone in a workgroup (○ changes to ⊙).

3 Click this area and then type the name of the person or workgroup you want to receive the message.

4 Click this area and then type your message.

5 Click **OK** to send the message.

■ A dialog box appears, telling you the message was successfully sent.

6 Click **OK** to close the dialog box.

You can browse through
the messages you receive
and delete the messages
you do not want to keep.

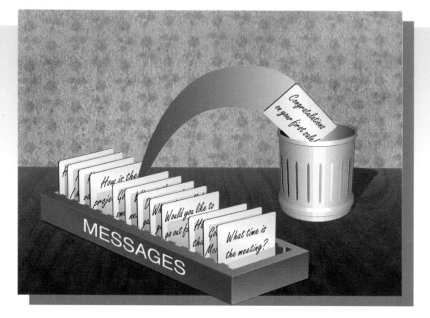

USING WINPOPUP TO EXCHANGE MESSAGES (CONTINUED)

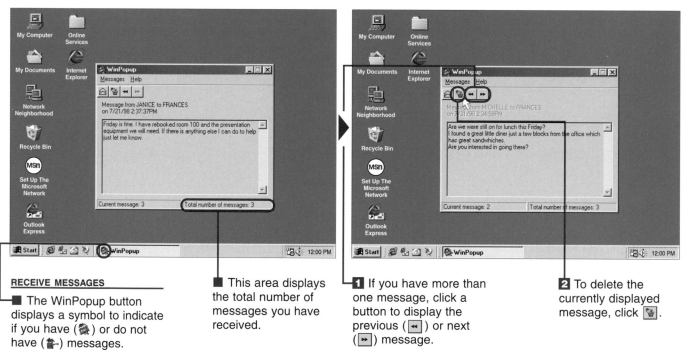

RECEIVE MESSAGES

■ The WinPopup button
displays a symbol to indicate
if you have (🖳) or do not
have (🖳) messages.

■ This area displays
the total number of
messages you have
received.

1 If you have more than
one message, click a
button to display the
previous (◄◄) or next
(►►) message.

2 To delete the
currently displayed
message, click 🖳.

? How can I customize WinPopup?

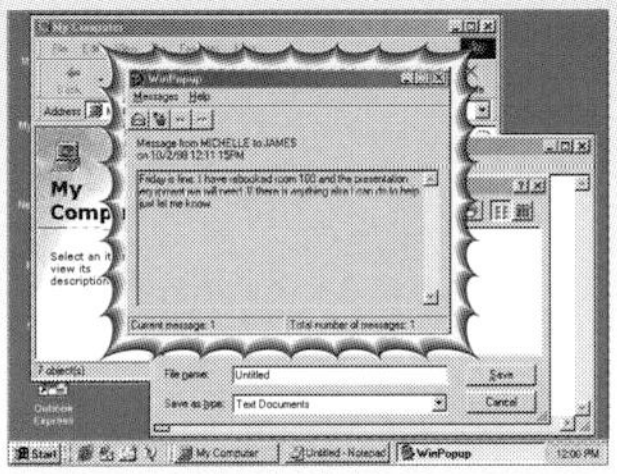

Always on top

You can have the WinPopup window always appear in front of other windows. This allows you to clearly view the window at all times.

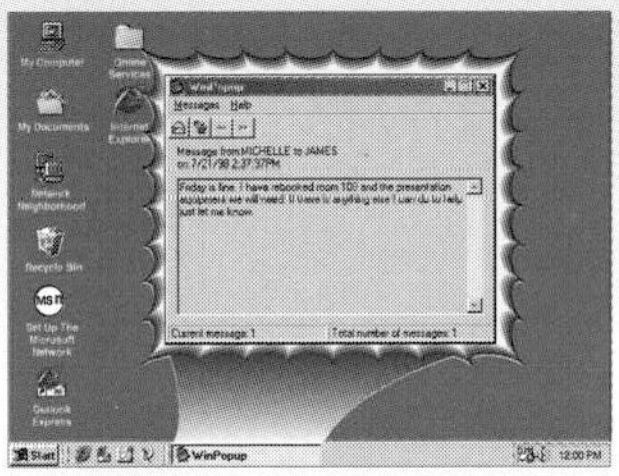

Pop up dialog on message receipt

You can have the WinPopup window open automatically when you receive a message. This allows you to instantly view a message you receive.

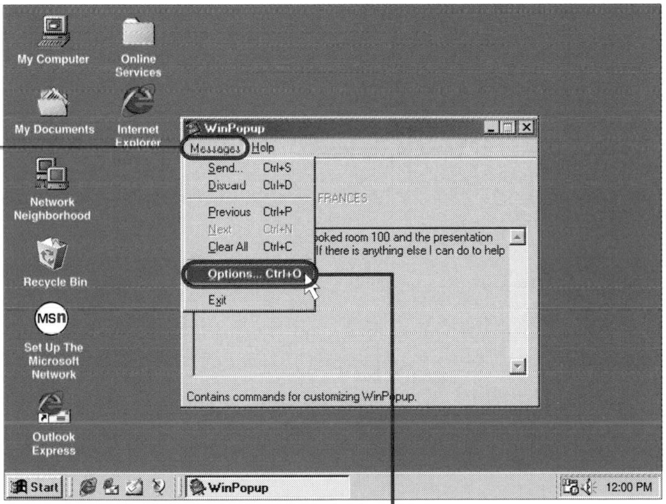

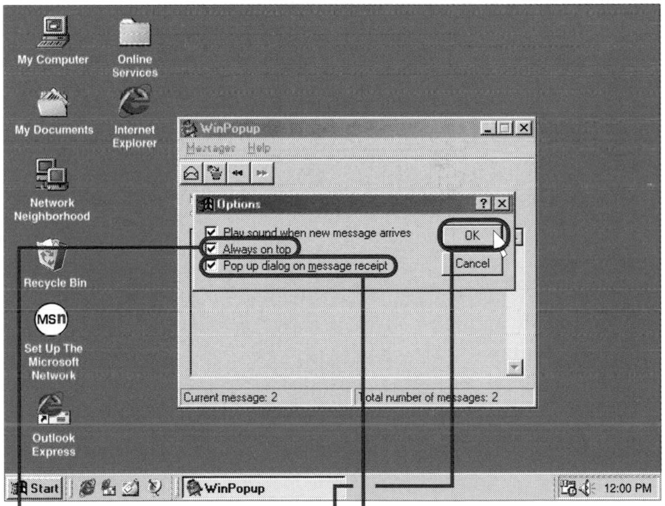

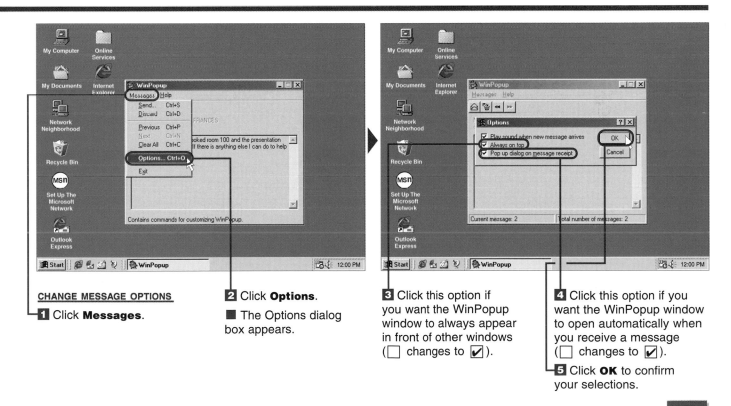

CHANGE MESSAGE OPTIONS

1 Click **Messages**.

2 Click **Options**.

■ The Options dialog box appears.

3 Click this option if you want the WinPopup window to always appear in front of other windows (☐ changes to ☑).

4 Click this option if you want the WinPopup window to open automatically when you receive a message (☐ changes to ☑).

5 Click **OK** to confirm your selections.

CHAPTER 13

Watch TV on Your Computer

WebTV can help make your computer more entertaining. In this chapter you will learn how to set up WebTV and search for programs you want to watch.

Start and Set Up WebTV 270

Using the Program Guide 274

Search for Programs 276

START AND SET UP WEBTV

You can use WebTV to watch television programs on your computer.

START AND SET UP WEBTV

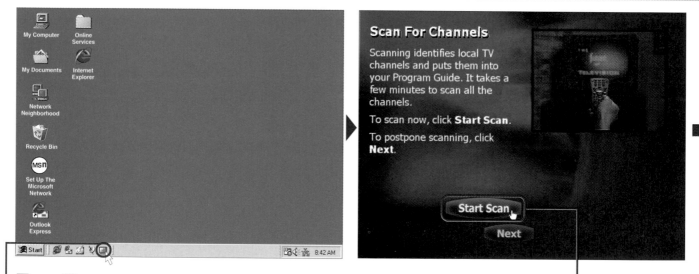

1 Click to start WebTV.

Note: If you have added the Web TV for Windows component to your computer but the icon is not displayed, see page 112 to change the size of the toolbar.

Scan For Channels

Scanning identifies local TV channels and puts them into your Program Guide. It takes a few minutes to scan all the channels.

To scan now, click **Start Scan**.

To postpone scanning, click **Next**.

■ A message appears, stating that you can scan for local TV channels.

2 Click **Start Scan** to begin the scan.

?

What software and hardware do I need to watch television programs on my computer?

You need to add the Web TV for Windows component. To add Windows components, see page 118.

You need a TV tuner card. If you do not have a TV tuner card installed on your computer, you can use WebTV to view TV listings, but you cannot watch programs.

You need a sound card and speakers to hear sound when watching programs.

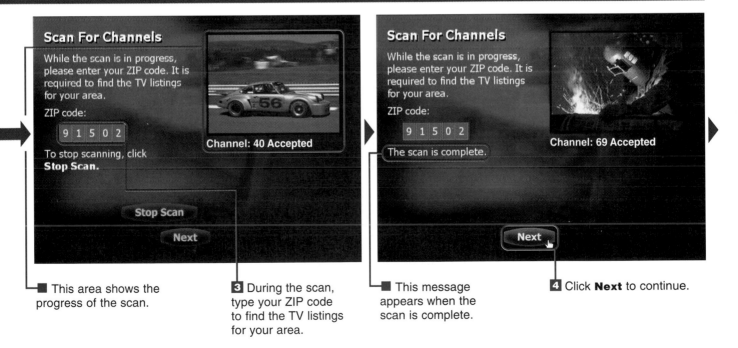

Scan For Channels

While the scan is in progress, please enter your ZIP code. It is required to find the TV listings for your area.

ZIP code:

9 1 5 0 2

To stop scanning, click **Stop Scan.**

Channel: 40 Accepted

Stop Scan

Next

Scan For Channels

While the scan is in progress, please enter your ZIP code. It is required to find the TV listings for your area.

ZIP code:

9 1 5 0 2

The scan is complete.

Channel: 69 Accepted

Next

■ This area shows the progress of the scan.

3 During the scan, type your ZIP code to find the TV listings for your area.

■ This message appears when the scan is complete.

4 Click **Next** to continue.

CONTINUED ▶

START AND SET UP WEBTV

While setting up WebTV, you can get free local TV listings on the Internet.

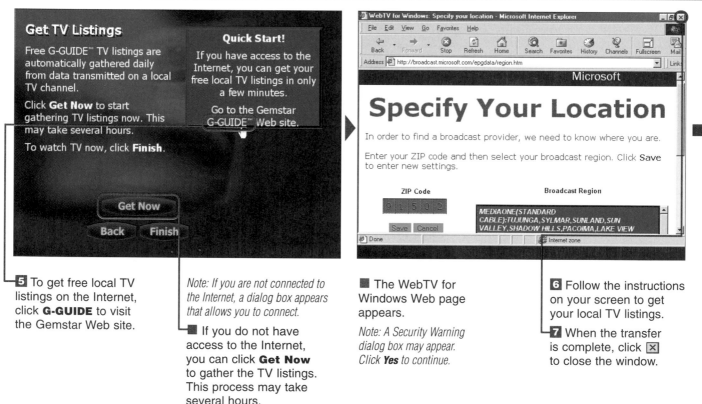

Get TV Listings

Free G-GUIDE™ TV listings are automatically gathered daily from data transmitted on a local TV channel.

Click **Get Now** to start gathering TV listings now. This may take several hours.

To watch TV now, click **Finish**.

Quick Start!

If you have access to the Internet, you can get your free local TV listings in only a few minutes.

Go to the Gemstar G-GUIDE™ Web site.

Get Now

Back   **Finish**

WebTV for Windows: Specify your location - Microsoft Internet Explorer

File   Edit   View   Go   Favorites   Help

Back   Forward   Stop   Refresh   Home   Search   Favorites   History   Channels   Fullscreen   Mail

Address http://broadcast.microsoft.com/epgdata/region.htm

Microsoft

Specify Your Location

In order to find a broadcast provider, we need to know where you are.

Enter your ZIP code and then select your broadcast region. Click **Save** to enter new settings.

ZIP Code   **Broadcast Region**

9 1 5 0 2   MEDIAONE(STANDARD CABLE):TUJUNGA,SYLMAR,SUNLAND,SUN VALLEY,SHADOW HILLS,PACOIMA,LAKE VIEW

Save   Cancel

Done   Internet zone

---

5 To get free local TV listings on the Internet, click **G-GUIDE** to visit the Gemstar Web site.

Note: If you are not connected to the Internet, a dialog box appears that allows you to connect.

■ If you do not have access to the Internet, you can click **Get Now** to gather the TV listings. This process may take several hours.

■ The WebTV for Windows Web page appears.

*Note: A Security Warning dialog box may appear. Click **Yes** to continue.*

6 Follow the instructions on your screen to get your local TV listings.

7 When the transfer is complete, click ☒ to close the window.

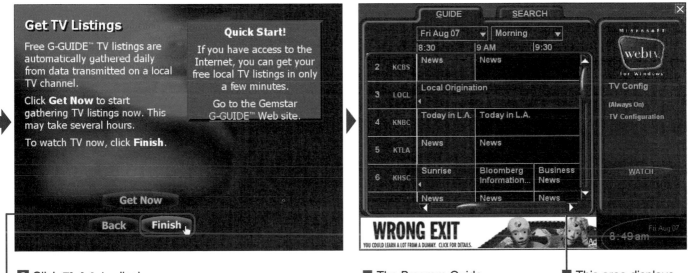

How can I tell which programs are currently playing?

Programs shown in green in the Program Guide are currently playing. Programs shown in blue are not currently playing.

You can instantly display the programs that are currently playing by double-clicking the time at the bottom right corner of your screen.

Get TV Listings

Free G-GUIDE™ TV listings are automatically gathered daily from data transmitted on a local TV channel.

Click **Get Now** to start gathering TV listings now. This may take several hours.

To watch TV now, click **Finish**.

Quick Start!

If you have access to the Internet, you can get your free local TV listings in only a few minutes.

Go to the Gemstar G-GUIDE™ Web site.

Get Now

Back   **Finish**

■8 Click **Finish** to display the Program Guide.

■ The Program Guide appears, showing your local TV listings.

■ This area displays the channels and the programs on each channel.

USING THE PROGRAM GUIDE

You can view the TV listings in the Program Guide to see when your favorite television programs are playing.

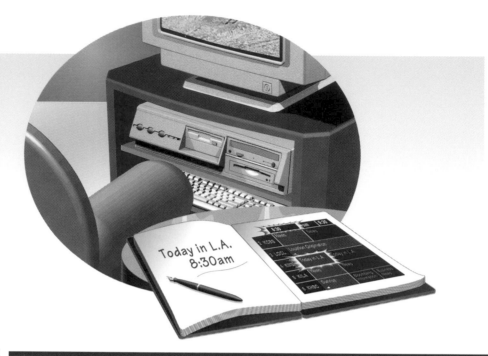

■ USING THE PROGRAM GUIDE ■

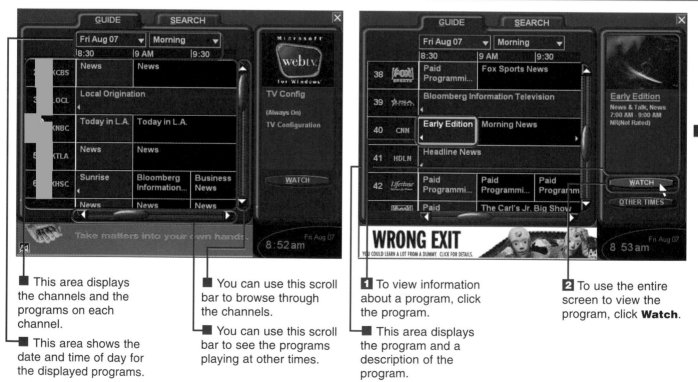

■ This area displays the channels and the programs on each channel.

■ This area shows the date and time of day for the displayed programs.

■ You can use this scroll bar to browse through the channels.

■ You can use this scroll bar to see the programs playing at other times.

1 To view information about a program, click the program.

■ This area displays the program and a description of the program.

2 To use the entire screen to view the program, click **Watch**.

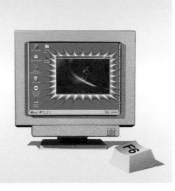

Can I watch a program in a window?

When you are watching a program using your entire screen, you can press the `F6` key to display the program in a window. This allows you to perform other tasks on your computer while you watch the program.

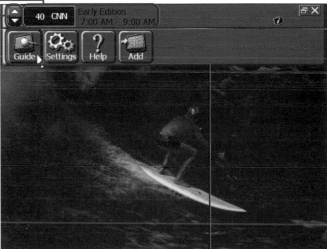

■ The program fills the screen.

3 To view the TV banner, move the mouse ▷ over the top of the screen or press the `F10` key.

■ The TV banner appears.

Note: To once again remove the TV banner, press the `F10` key.

■ This area displays the current channel number and the name of the program.

4 To display the previous or next channel, click ▲ or ▼ .

5 To return to the Program Guide, click **Guide**.

SEARCH FOR PROGRAMS

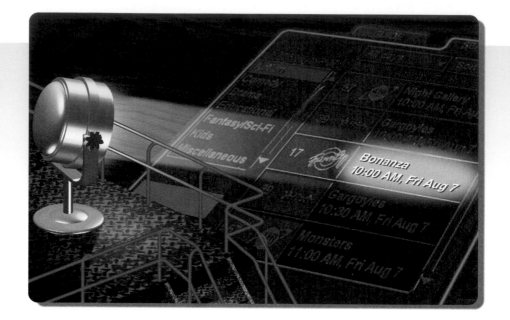

You can use the
Program Guide to
search for programs
of interest.

■ SEARCH FOR PROGRAMS ■

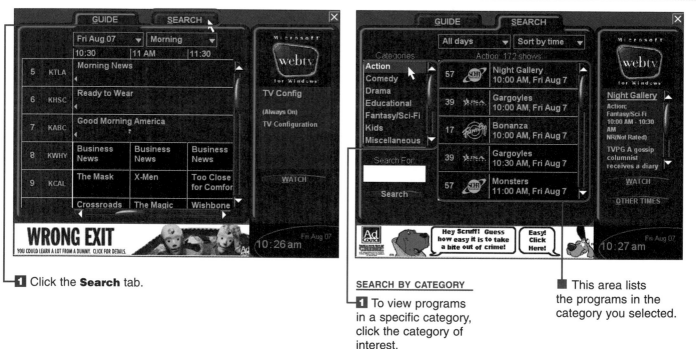

1 Click the **Search** tab.

SEARCH BY CATEGORY

1 To view programs
in a specific category,
click the category of
interest.

■ This area lists
the programs in the
category you selected.

How can I search for programs?

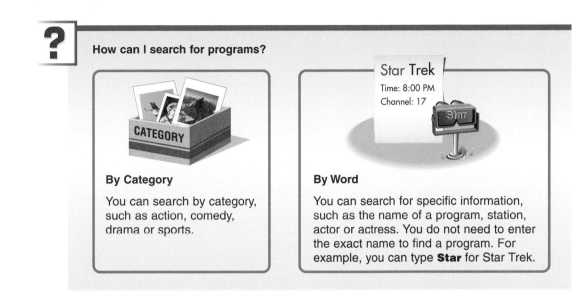

By Category

You can search by category, such as action, comedy, drama or sports.

By Word

You can search for specific information, such as the name of a program, station, actor or actress. You do not need to enter the exact name to find a program. For example, you can type **Star** for Star Trek.

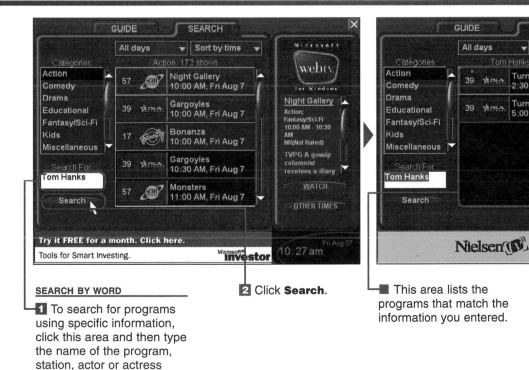

SEARCH BY WORD

1 To search for programs using specific information, click this area and then type the name of the program, station, actor or actress you want to search for.

2 Click **Search**.

■ This area lists the programs that match the information you entered.

INDEX

A

access information on networks,
  using Dial-Up Networking, 260-261
Accessibility Tools component, 119
Accessibility Wizard, using, 98-101
action, in chat rooms, 235
active windows, 18
    copy contents of, 41
add
    annotations to Imaging documents, 61
    color to text in e-mail messages, 197
    destinations to Send To menu, 84-87
    folders
        to Favorites, 36-37
        to Start menu, 108-111
    fonts, 90-93
    information to Clipboard, 70
    items
        to Quick Launch Toolbar, 112-113
        to Start menu, 104
    joysticks, 130-133
    notes to Imaging documents, 61
    part of document to desktop, 42-43
    programs, 122-124
    sound effects to recordings, 64
    special characters to documents, 54-57
    telephone numbers to speed-dial buttons, 68-69
    toolbars to taskbar, 114-115
    Windows components, 118-121
Address Bar toolbar, 26
Address toolbar, 115
Adobe Acrobat Reader, 166
annotations, add to Imaging documents, 61
anti-virus programs, 164, 167
appearance of desktop icons, change, 74-75
archive data, using Backup, 173
arrows on toolbars, 79

B

back strain, prevent when using computer, 129
back up files, 170-177
Backup, 119
    archive data, using, 173
    back up files, using 170-177
    restore files, using, 180-183
    transfer data, using, 173

backup
    devices, 171
    jobs
        create, 170-177
        open, 178-179
blind carbon copies (Bcc), 193
blink rate of cursor, change, 128
bold text in e-mail messages, 196
Briefcase
    create new, 245
    delete, 245
    files
        transfer to, 238-239
        update, 242-244
        work with, 240-241

C

cable, types used for direct cable connection, 251
calibrate joysticks, 132-133
call waiting, disable, 140-141
calls
    in NetMeeting
        hang up, 221
        place, 220-221
    in Phone Dialer
        hang up, 67, 69
        place, 66-69
carbon copies (Cc), 193
Channel Bar, 5, 7
    remove from desktop, 7
channels, view, using Program Guide, 274-275
Channels folder, on Favorites menu, 37
Character Map, using, 54-57
characters
    in Microsoft Chat
        choose, 230-231
        select emotions for, 234-235
    repeated, adjust keyboard settings for, 126-127
    special, insert in documents, 54-57
Chat. See Microsoft Chat
chat rooms
    change, 233
    enter, 230-233
    list, display, 233
chatting, in NetMeeting, 222-223
Clipboard Viewer, using, 70-71

close
    Clipboard Viewer, 71
    Magnifier, 97
    MS-DOS, 13
    Notepad, 53
    programs, 9
        misbehaving, 27
    Start menu, using keyboard, 9
    Whiteboard, 225
    windows, 19
    Windows 98, 21
collaborate, using NetMeeting, 227
color, add to text in e-mail messages, 197
commands
    Run, start programs using, 11
    use in MS-DOS, 12-13
components, Windows
    add, 118-121
    remove, 121
compose e-mail messages, 192-193
computers
    add fonts to, 90-93
    change power management settings, 94-95
    dial in to, 258-261
    find on networks, 260-261
    reestablish connection, using direct cable
      connection, 252-253
    set up
        connection, using Dial-Up Networking, 254-257
        as dial-up servers, 262-263
        as guests, 249-251
        as hosts, 246-248
    turn off, 21
    use modems to connect to, 139
    view
        contents of, 24-25
        fonts on, 88-89
    watch TV on, 270-277
connect
    to computer, using Dial-Up Networking, 258-261
    computers, using direct cable connection, 246-253
    to Internet, 160, 186
connection between computers
    end, using Dial-Up Networking, 261
    re-establish, using direct cable connection, 252-253
    set up
        using Dial-Up Networking, 254-257
        using direct cable connection, 246-251
convert drives to FAT32, 162-165

copy
    data between documents, 38-39
    floppy disks, 46-49
    information onto Clipboard, 70
    screen contents, 40-41
    vs. move, 39
create
    backup jobs, 170-177
    Briefcase, new, 245
    documents in Notepad, 52-53
    e-mail
        folders, 206-207
        messages, 192-193
    files, new, 28-29
    recordings, 62-65
    scraps, 42
    startup disks, 154-157
    toolbars, new, 78-79
cursor blink rate, change, 128
custom program installation, 124

D

data
    archive, using Backup, 173
    copy between documents, 38-39
    move between documents, 38-39
    transfer, using Backup, 173
date, current, enter in Notepad documents, 53
delete
    bold in e-mail messages, 196
    Briefcase, 245
    Channel Bar from desktop, 7
    e-mail
        folders, 207
        messages, drafts, 199
    fonts, 93
    hardware, 146-147
    italics in e-mail messages, 196
    items
        from Quick Launch Toolbar, 113
        from Start menu, 106-107
    notes, in Imaging documents, 61
    programs, 125
    rules for filtering e-mail messages, 211
    toolbars, 79
    underline in e-mail messages, 196
    Windows components, 121
Deleted Items folder, in Outlook Express, 187

INDEX

desktop, 5
> create new files on, 29
> display properties of files located on, 31
> icons
>> change appearance, 74-75
>> change to default, 75
> place part of document on, 42-43
> preview files located on, 33
> show, 20
Desktop toolbar, 115
destinations, add to Send To menu, 84-87
devices
> hardware, remove, 146-147
> use to back up files, 171
> use to record sounds, 63
dial in to another computer, 258-261
dialing properties for modems, change, 138-141
Dial-Up Networking
> access information on network, 260-261
> dial in to computer, 258-261
> dial-up server, set up, 262-263
> end connection, 261
> find computers on network, 260-261
> set up connection to computer, 254-257
dial-up servers, set up computers as, 262-263
direct cable connection
> cable used for, 251
> re-establish, 252-253
> set up, 246-251
disconnect from computer, 261
disk utility programs, 164
disks
> floppy
>> copy, 46-49
>> protect information on, 49
> startup
>> create, 154-157
>> protect, 157
display
> contents
>> of Clipboard, 70-71
>> of computer, 24-25
> desktop, 20
> file properties, 30-31
> files, using Quick View, 32-33
> folders
>> on computer, 24-25
>> in Favorites list, 37
>> on Start menu, 111

fonts, 88-89
hardware information, 150-151
hidden files, 34-35
list of chat rooms, 233
programs currently playing in WebTV, 273, 274-275
Start menu, using keyboard, 8
system
> files, 34-35
> information, 150-151
toolbars, 26
Web pages, using Run command, 11
documents. *See also* files
> copy data between, 38-39
> in Imaging
>> add notes to, 61
>> magnify, 60
>> reduce, 60
>> scan, 58-59
> move data between, 38-39
> Notepad
>> insert current time and date, 53
>> save, 53
> place part on desktop, 42-43
> share, using NetMeeting, 226-227
double-density floppy disks, 47
drafts, e-mail messages
> delete, 199
> save, 198-199
Drafts folder, in Outlook Express, 187
draw images, using Whiteboard, 224-225
drives
> convert to FAT32, 162-165
> view contents, 24-25

E

effects
> sound, add to recording, 64
> visual, change, for items on screen, 76-77
electronic mail. *See* e-mail
e-mail
> folders
>> create, 206-207
>> delete, 207
> messages
>> add text color, 197
>> bold text, 196

check for new, automatically, 191
compose, 192-193
drafts
    delete, 199
    save, 198-199
filter, 208-211
find, 202-205
font, change, 194
font size, change, 195
format, 194-197
italicize text, 196
mark as unread, 190
move to folders, 207
new, receive, 187
print, 189
read, 186-187
send, 192-193
sort, 188
underline text, 196
emotions, select, for characters in chat rooms, 234-235
enlarge. *See* magnify; maximize windows
enter chat rooms, 230-233
equipment needed to hear sound in NetMeeting, 217
exit. *See also* close
    Magnifier, 97
    MS-DOS, 13
    Notepad, 53
    Windows 98, 21
eye strain, prevent when using computer, 129

F

FAT32, convert hard drive to, 162-165
Favorites
    add folders to, 36-37
    display folders, 37
File Allocation Table. *See* FAT32
files. *See also* documents
    add to folders on Start menu, 111
    back up, 170-177
    Briefcase
        transfer to, 238-239
        update, 242-244
        work with, 240-241
    create, 28-29
    display on computer, 24-25
    hidden, show, 34-35

location on computer, 31
path, 31
preview, 32-33
print, offline, 44-45
properties, display, 30-31
rename, 29
restore, using Backup, 180-183
system, show, 34-35
filter e-mail messages, 208-211
find
    computers on network, using Dial-Up
      Networking, 260-261
    e-mail messages, 202-205
    files on computer, 31
    people on Internet, 200-201
    programs, using WebTV, 276-277
floppy disks
    copy, 46-49
    protect information on, 49
folders
    add
        to Favorites, 36-37
        to Start menu, 108-111
    create new toolbars from, 78-79
    display
        on computer, 24-25
        in Favorites list, 37
        on Start menu, 111
    e-mail
        create, 206-207
        delete, 207
        move messages to, 207
    Outlook Express, 187
    on Start menu, add items to, 111
fonts
    add to computer, 90-93
    delete, 93
    e-mail messages, change, 194
        size, 195
    types, 89
    view, on computer, 88-89
    where to get, 91
format e-mail messages, 194-197
full separator pages, 135

INDEX

G

graphics. *See* images
guests
    set up computers as, 249-251
    vs. host computers, 247

H

hang up calls
    in NetMeeting, 221
    in Phone Dialer, 67, 69
hard drives, convert to FAT32, 162-165
hardware
    information, view, 150-151
    needed to watch TV on computer, 271
    remove, 146-147
hearing, accessibility options, 99
hidden files, show, 34-35
hide toolbars, 26
high-density floppy disks, 47
hosts
    set up computers as, 246-248
    vs. guest computers, 247

I

icons, desktop
    change appearance, 74-75
    change to default, 75
images
    draw, using Whiteboard, 224-225
    video, send, using NetMeeting, 219
Imaging, using, 58-61
Inbox folder, in Outlook Express, 187
insert, characters in documents, 54-57
install
    fonts on computer, 90-93
    joysticks, 130-133
    programs, 122-124
Internet
    connect to, 160
    find people on, 200-201
    use modems to connect to, 139
italicize text in e-mail messages, 196
items
    add to Quick Launch Toolbar, 112-113
    add to Start menu, 104
    rearrange on Start menu, 105

    remove from Quick Launch Toolbar, 113
    remove from Start menu, 106-107
    on screen, change visual effects for, 76-77

J

join conversations in chat rooms, 234-235
joysticks, install, 130-133

K

keyboards
    display Start menu using, 8
    settings, change, 126-128
    tips for using, 129

L

language used in Windows, change, 81
Links
    folder, on Favorites menu, 37
    toolbar, 26
        display on taskbar, 115
location of files, determine, 31

M

Magnifier, using, 96-97
magnify
    documents in Imaging, 60
    screen contents, 96-97
mark e-mail messages as unread, 190
maximize windows, 14
memory, view, 152-153
messages
    e-mail
        add text color, 197
        bold text, 196
        check for new, automatically, 191
        compose, 192-193
        drafts
            delete, 199
            save, 198-199
        filter, 208-211
        find, 202-205
        font, change, 194
        font size, change, 195
        format, 194-197
        italicize text, 196
        mark as unread, 190
        move to folders, 207

new, receive, 187
print, 189
read, 186-187
send, 192-193
sort, 188
underline text, 196
NetMeeting, exchange, 222-223
WinPopup
options, change, 267
receive, 266
send, 264-265
Microsoft Chat
participate in, 234-235
start, 230-233
Microsoft Office, 166
minimize windows, 15
all, 20
minimum program installation, 124
mobility, accessibility options, 99
modems
connect telephones to, 67
dialing properties, change, 138-141
properties, change, 142-143
use to connect to computers, 139
use to connect to Internet, 139
monitors, multiple
stop using, 145
using, 144-145
move
data between documents, 38-39
e-mail messages to folders, 207
vs. copy, 39
windows, 16
MS-DOS Prompt window, start, 12-13
My Computer, 5
My Documents, 5

N

neck strain, prevent when using computer, 129
NetMeeting
calls
hang up, 221
place, 220-221
exchange messages, 222-223
send video images using, 219
set up, 214-219
share programs, 226-227
start, 214-219
use Whiteboard, 224-225

Network Neighborhood, 5
Notepad, using, 52-53
notes, add to Imaging documents, 61
numeric keypad, use to enter numbers for special
characters, 57

O

OCR (Optical Character Recognition) software, 167
offline, print, 44-45
open. See also start
backup jobs, 178-179
Character Map, 54
Imaging, 58
Magnifier, 96
Microsoft Chat, 230-233
MS-DOS Prompt window, 12-13
NetMeeting, 214-219
Notepad, 52
Phone Dialer, 66
programs, 8-9
using Run command, 10-11
Sound Recorder, 62
WebTV, 270-273
Windows 98, 6-7
in safe mode, 158-159
WinPopup, 264
Optical Character Recognition (OCR) software, 167
Outbox folder, in Outlook Express, 187
Outlook Express
folders, 187
start, 186

P

pages
orientation, change, 137
separator, 135
test, print, 136
Web, open, using Run command, 11
Paint, 9
paper options, change, 137
parallel cable, 251
passwords
assign to dial-up server, 262-263
use to connect to Internet, 160
use when starting Windows 98, 6
path, file, 31
PDF (Portable Document Format) files, 166

INDEX

Phone Dialer, using, 66-69
phone numbers, store on speed dial buttons, 68-69
place calls
    in NetMeeting, 220-221
    using Phone Dialer, 66-69
play recordings, saved, 65
Portable Document Format (PDF) files, 166
power management settings, change, 94-95
prevent injury when using computer, 129
preview files, 32-33
print
    e-mail messages, 189
    offline, 44-45
printer fonts, 89
printers
    options, change, 134-137
    use offline, 44-45
Program Guide, using, 274-275
programs
    add to folders on Start menu, 111
    anti-virus, 164, 167
    close, 9
        misbehaving, 27
    disk utility, 164
    included with Windows 98, 9
    install, 122-124
    remove, 125
    search for, using WebTV, 276-277
    share, using NetMeeting, 226-227
    start, 8-9
        using Run command, 10-11
    on TV
        display currently playing, 273, 274-275
        watch, using WebTV, 270-277
    for use with Windows 98, 166-167
properties
    dialing, of modems, change, 138-141
    of files, display, 30-31
    of modems, change, 142-143
    of Recycle Bin, change, 82-83
protect
    information on floppy disks, 49
    startup disks, 157

Q

Quick Launch Toolbar, 5
    add items to, 112-113
    display on taskbar, 115
    items on, 113
    remove items, 113
Quick View, use to preview files, 32-33

R

read e-mail messages, 186-187
rearrange items on Start menu, 105
receive messages
    e-mail, 187
    WinPopup, 266
record sounds, using Sound Recorder, 62-65
recordings
    add sound effects to, 64
    create, 62-63
    play, saved, 65
    save, 65
Recycle Bin, 5
    properties, change, 82-83
reduce documents in Imaging, 60
reestablish direct cable connection, 252-253
regional settings, change, 80-81
remove
    bold in e-mail messages, 196
    Briefcase, 245
    Channel Bar from desktop, 7
    e-mail
        folders, 207
        messages, 199
    fonts, 93
    hardware, 146-147
    italics in e-mail messages, 196
    items
        from Quick Launch Toolbar, 113
        from Start menu, 106-107
    notes in Imaging documents, 61
    programs, 125
    rules for filtering e-mail messages, 211
    toolbars, 79
    underline in e-mail messages, 196
    Windows components, 121
rename files, 29
repeated characters, adjust keyboard settings for, 126-127
resize. *See* size
resources, view system, 152-153

restore files using Backup, 180-183
Run command
  display Web pages using, 11
  start programs using, 10-11

S

safe mode, start Windows in, 158-159
save
  drafts of e-mail messages, 198-199
  Notepad documents, 53
  recordings, 65
say, in chat rooms, 235
scan documents, 58-59
ScanDisk, 9
scraps
  create, 42
  use, 43
screen
  contents, copy, 40-41
  items, change visual effects for, 76-77
  view enlarged, using Magnifier, 96-97
  Windows 98, parts of, 5
search
  for computers on network, using Dial-Up
    Networking, 260-261
  for e-mail messages, 202-205
  for files on computer, 31
  for people on Internet, 200-201
  for programs, using WebTV, 276-277
send
  messages
    e-mail, 192-193
      completed drafts, 199
    NetMeeting, 222-223
    WinPopup, 264-265
  video images using NetMeeting, 219
Send To menu, add destinations, 84-87
Sent Items folder, in Outlook Express, 187
separator pages, 135
serial cable, 251
set up
  computers
    connection, using Dial-Up Networking, 254-257
    as dial-up servers, 262-263
    as guests, 249-251
    as hosts, 246-248
  NetMeeting, 214-219
  WebTV, 270-273

settings
  keyboard, change, 126-128
  power management, change, 94-95
  regional, change, 80-81
share programs using NetMeeting, 226-227
show
  contents
    of Clipboard, 70-71
    of computer, 24-25
  desktop, 20
  file properties, 30-31
  files, using Quick View, 32-33
  folders
    on computer, 24-25
    in Favorites list, 37
    on Start menu, 111
  fonts, 88-89
  hardware information, 150-151
  hidden files, 34-35
  list of chat rooms, 233
  programs currently playing in WebTV, 273, 274-275
  Start menu, using keyboard, 8
  system
    files, 34-35
    information, 150-151
  toolbars, 26
  Web pages, using Run command, 11
shut down Windows, 21
simple separator pages, 135
size
  documents in Imaging, 60
  of font in e-mail messages, change, 195
  of Recycle Bin, change, 82-83
  toolbars on taskbar, 115
  windows, 17
software needed to watch TV on computer, 271
Software Updates folder, on Favorites menu, 37
sort e-mail messages, 188
sound effects, add to recordings, 64
Sound Recorder, using, 62-65
speed-dial buttons, use in Phone Dialer, 68-69
Standard Buttons toolbar, 26
standby, power management setting, 94-95
start. See also open
  backups, 170-175
  Character Map, 54
  Imaging, 58
  Magnifier, 96
  Microsoft Chat, 230-233

MS-DOS Prompt window, 12-13
NetMeeting, 214-219
Notepad, 52
Outlook Express, 186
Phone Dialer, 66
programs, 8-9
    using Run command, 10-11
Sound Recorder, 62
WebTV, 270-273
Windows 98, 6-7
    in safe mode, 158-159
WinPopup, 264
Start button, 5
Start menu
    add folders to, 108-111
    add items to, 104
    close, using keyboard, 9
    display, using keyboard, 8
    folders
        add items to, 111
        display on, 111
    rearrange items on, 105
    remove items from, 106-107
startup disks
    create, 154-157
    protect, 157
stop using, multiple monitors, 145
store phone numbers, in Phone Dialer, 68-69
switch between windows, 18
symbols
    in NetMeeting directory, 221
    in windows, 25
system
    files, show, 34-35
    fonts, 89
    information, view, 152-153
    resources, view information on, 152-153

T

taskbar, 5
    add toolbars to, 114-115
    size toolbars on, 115
telephones
    calls, make using Phone Dialer, 66-69
    connect to modems, 67
television, watch on computer, 270-277
test pages, print, 136

text
    in e-mail messages
        add color, 197
        bold, 196
        font, change, 194
        font size, change, 195
        format, 194-197
        italicize, 196
        underline, 196
    in Notepad, wrap, 52
think, in chat rooms, 235
time, current, enter in Notepad documents, 53
title bar, 5
toolbars
    add to taskbar, 114-115
    Address, 115
    Address Bar, 26
    create, new, 78-79
    Desktop, 115
    display, 26
    hide, 26
    Links, 26
    Quick Launch, 5
        add items to, 112-113
        display on taskbar, 115
        items on, 113
        remove items, 113
    remove, 79
    size on taskbar, change, 115
    Standard Buttons, 26
tools, Whiteboard, 225
transfer
    data, using Backup, 173
    files to Briefcase, 238-239
TrueType fonts, 89
turn off computer, 21
TV
    listings, view, using WebTV, 272-273
    watch on computer, 270-277
typical program installation, 124

U

underline text in e-mail messages, 196
update
    Briefcase files, 242-244
    Windows, 160-161

V

video images, send, using NetMeeting, 219
view
    contents
        of Clipboard, 70-71
        of computer, 24-25
    desktop, 20
    file properties, 30-31
    files, using Quick View, 32-33
    folders
        on computer, 24-25
        in Favorites list, 37
        on Start menu, 111
    fonts on computer, 88-89
    hardware information, 150-151
    hidden files, 34-35
    list of chat rooms, 233
    programs currently playing in WebTV, 273, 274-275
    Start menu, using keyboard, 8
    system
        files, 34-35
        information, 152-153
    toolbars, 26
    Web pages, using Run command, 11
virus, 167
VirusScan Security Suite, 167
vision, accessibility options, 99
visual effects, change for items on screen, 76-77

W

Web pages, display using Run command, 11
WebTV, 119
    start and set up, 270-273
whisper, in chat rooms, 235
Whiteboard
    tools, 225
    using, 224-225
windows, 5
    close, 19
    maximize, 14
    minimize, 15
        all, 20
    move, 16
    size, 17
    switch between, 18
    symbols in, 25
    watch TV programs in, 275

Windows 98
    change language used, 81
    components
        add, 118-121
        remove, 121
    introduction, 4
    parts of screen, 5
    programs for use with, 166-167
    shut down, 21
    start, 6-7
        in safe mode, 158-159
Windows Update, using, 160-161
WinFax PRO, 167
WinPopup
    customize, 267
    messages
        options, change, 267
        receive, 266
        send, 264-265
    start, 264
WinZip, 91, 167
wizards
    Accessibility, 98-101
    Backup, 170-175
    Direct Cable Connection, 246-251
    Drive Converter, 162-165
    Make New Connection, 254-257
    Microsoft NetMeeting, 214-219
    Restore, 180-183
WordPad, 9
work
    offline, 44-45
    with Briefcase files, 240-241
wrap text, in Notepad, 52
wrist strain, prevent when using computer, 129

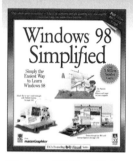
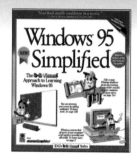

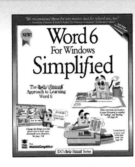

ORDER FORM

IDG BOOKS ®

TRADE & INDIVIDUAL ORDERS
Phone: **(800) 762-2974**
or **(317) 596-5200**
(8 a.m. – 6 p.m., CST, weekdays)
FAX : **(800) 550-2747**
or **(317) 596-5692**

EDUCATIONAL ORDERS & DISCOUNTS
Phone: **(800) 434-2086**
(8:30 a.m.–5:00 p.m., CST, weekdays)
FAX : **(317) 596-5499**

CORPORATE ORDERS FOR 3-D VISUAL™ SERIES
Phone: **(800) 469-6616**
(8 a.m.–5 p.m., EST, weekdays)
FAX : **(905) 890-9434**

Qty	ISBN	Title	Price	Total

Shipping & Handling Charges

	Description	First book	Each add'l. book	Total
Domestic	Normal	$4.50	$1.50	$
	Two Day Air	$8.50	$2.50	$
	Overnight	$18.00	$3.00	$
International	Surface	$8.00	$8.00	$
	Airmail	$16.00	$16.00	$
	DHL Air	$17.00	$17.00	$

Subtotal _____

*CA residents add
applicable sales tax* _____

*IN, MA and MD
residents add
5% sales tax* _____

*IL residents add
6.25% sales tax* _____

*RI residents add
7% sales tax* _____

*TX residents add
8.25% sales tax* _____

Shipping _____

Total _____

Ship to:

Name_____

Address_____

Company_____

City/State/Zip_____

Daytime Phone_____

Payment: ☐ Check to IDG Books (US Funds Only)
☐ Visa ☐ Mastercard ☐ American Express

Card # _____ Exp. _____ Signature_____

*maran*Graphics™